H. E. Kup...

Wayne U.   1951

DATE DUE			

CONTINUITIES IN SOCIAL RESEARCH

CONTINUITIES IN SOCIAL RESEARCH

Studies in the Scope and Method of
"The American Soldier"

EDITED BY ROBERT K. MERTON
AND PAUL F. LAZARSFELD

THE FREE PRESS, GLENCOE, ILLINOIS

1950

FOR

STEPHANIE AND LOTTE

EXPERIMENTS IN CONTINUITY

CONTENTS

INTRODUCTION

The American Soldier constitutes two of the four volumes, *Studies in Social Psychology in World War II,* reporting the substance of researches conducted by the Research Branch, Information and Education Division of the War Department.[1] Based upon data collected and partly analyzed by the Research Branch for the practical purposes of the Army command during the war, these volumes are largely the result of a new analysis of the data designed to indicate the scientific by-products of these applied researches. Together they represent a body of empirical findings that push forward on several frontiers of social psychology and sociology.

This symposium seeks to examine certain of these advancing frontiers and to explore the nature of the social science terrain that has been opened up.

The American Soldier has been described as drawing on a mine of empirical data on the attitudes, sentiments and behavior of large numbers of men. The term "empirical data" is deceptively simple, obscuring the important fact that it is used to designate quite distinct kinds of material. Often in social science, it refers to casual observation of scattered episodes of behavior—essentially, the anecdotal report—which is indeed empirical since it deals with actual experience. Moreover, the anecdotal observation may often be insightful and suggestive. But social scientists who confine themselves to such empirical materials have a way of treating them as "typical"

---

[1] The authors of the first of these volumes, "Adjustment during Army Life," are S. A. Stouffer, E. A. Suchman, L. C. DeVinney, S. A. Star, and R. M. Williams, Jr.; of the second, entitled "Combat and Its Aftermath," S. A. Stouffer, A. A. Lumsdaine, M. H. Lumsdaine, R. M. Williams, Jr., M. B. Smith, I. L. Janis, S. A. Star, and L. S. Cottrell, Jr. Both were published in 1949 by the Princeton University Press.

of individuals or groups before the fact of their typicality is established.

In contrast to the anecdotal kind of data are *systematic* empirical data of the kind found in *The American Soldier*. Here, a major effort is made to find out the distribution of behaviors or attitudes in various groups or social categories of men under varying conditions. The incidental observation or the revealing statement in an interview is utilized, to be sure, as a point of departure for interpreting an empirical finding, but these anecdotal materials are not confused with systematic materials. The systematic data allow one to establish the fact of differences and similarities among the attitudes and behavior prevailing in diverse groups: certainly one of the primary tasks of a soundly based social science. Often, these facts become visible only through such systematically collected material—for example, until now, how would one know whether soldiers from rural areas were more or less effectively adapted to life in the Army than those from urban areas, or whether Negro enlisted men were more or less likely to aspire to the status of non-commissioned officers than were their white counterparts? And these newly established social facts often become the basis for raising new questions of theoretical concern, questions which might otherwise not be raised at all or not for some time.

The substantive papers in this symposium set forth numerous cases in which the systematic data of *The American Soldier* help to clarify and extend social theory. Shils reviews the contributions of these volumes to current knowledge of primary groups. That the face-to-face interpersonal environment greatly affects beliefs, sentiments, and action is of course a well-established conception in sociology. But Shils goes on to show how data of the kind presented in these volumes point to new strategic questions about the workings of primary groups. As a first approximation, the behavior of members of a social organization is taken to be the resultant of formal authority, ideological conviction (values), and the balance of forces operating in the primary group units. How do changes in each of these affect behavior in specific situations? At present, only slight intimations are available, but the work reported in these volumes and its discussion by Shils will lead to more precise formulations, provided that research follows out this line of continuity.

A companion-piece by Merton and Kitt centers on the contributions of *The American Soldier* to the theory of reference group behavior. Here, too, previous studies have taken account of the fact that individuals variously orient their behavior to different groups. But the systematic evidence of *The American Soldier* allows the formulation of further, more specific problems: for example, how does behavior vary when the individual's reference groups are of his own or of superior status? when he is in direct social contact with these groups or not?

In his paper, Speier finds that the systematic evidence in these volumes also allows the clarification of a central problem in the sociology of knowledge. Once again, he begins with an established conception: the judgments and perspectives of individuals and groups are closely related to their position in a social system. And indeed, among the more striking empirical findings of *The American Soldier* are the vast differences between the judgments and attitudes of officers and enlisted men. But, as Speier goes on to show, these differences vary systematically according to the subject-matter on which a judgment is expressed: the more closely the subject relates to values involved in the organization and to status within the organization, the greater the differences in judgments among men of differing social position. These systematic data of social psychology thus enlarge upon the analytical framework of, say, Mannheim, by showing that group affiliation or social position have regularly varying relations with judgments, depending upon the subject-matter of the judgment.

Throughout, the aim is not to provide a précis of *The American Soldier*—indeed, large parts of these volumes have been barely touched upon—but to examine selected hypotheses, methods and findings with an eye to their specific implications for the further advancement of certain parts of social science. Through such re-analysis, it is hoped that these materials will be the more likely to enter into the main stream of future research and theory, rather than being left to find their own way. What is attempted here with regard to *The American Soldier* in an effort to stimulate continuity in social research can, of course, be done for other major works of social science. And if this pattern of systematic re-analysis and codification of what is implied by significant social research is more generally adopted, there will be, perhaps, less discontinuity in social science and a more rapid accumulation of social science knowledge.

The importance of *The American Soldier* extends beyond its empirical findings: it is actually the first major work which enables the reader, not specializing in social-psychological research, to learn the details of the more advanced methods in the relatively new field of attitude sampling surveys. For the most part, this new development in social psychology is known to the public in the form of routine opinion polls or election forecasts published in newspapers. Yet this growing branch of the social sciences deserves the instructed attention of a wider public. In their paper, Kendall and Lazarsfeld point out the major analytical operations involved in this type of research: they take this occasion to dispel some of the misunderstandings that have developed in various controversies regarding the nature of such analysis. It is not the public at large but social scientists themselves who have yet to work out the numerous relations of this newer kind of analysis to more traditional problems of research in the social sciences.

Several papers in this symposium deal with some of the relations between what is sometimes loosely called "attitude or opinion research" and sociological research on the structure and functions of groups. From these papers, it will soon be seen that there need not be, and in *The American Soldier* there is not, a wide gulf between the two. The reasons for this merit brief statement.

In the last analysis, the data of sociology and social psychology are of course provided by records of the behavior or the statements of individuals. Sometimes, this fact is lost to view. Whether it is the data recorded in governmental censuses, the observation of small groups in a laboratory, or the reports by informants in field work, the data originate in the behavior and verbalizations of individuals. But although in one form or another the data are obtained *from* individuals, they need not invariably be *about* individuals. The informant may report on what he takes to be practices prevailing in a group or social stratum or social status; he may, moreover, be reporting, not *qua* individual (in all his idiosyncratic uniqueness), but in his capacity as an officer, a married man, a veteran, or so through any one or more of his standardized roles. When these reports—data on sentiments, attitudes, practices, relationships—are obtained independently from a cross-section of the membership of a group or of a social stratum, as was the case with the researches reported in *The Amercian Soldier*, there is then the possibility of ascertaining the typical (modal, median or mean) sentiments, attitudes, practices or relationships obtaining among various social categories of men. The appropriate arrangement of such data stemming from individuals, then, can provide systematic evidence on the cultural norms and social organization of groups.

In other words, it need not be readily assumed that "opinion or attitude data" are remote from data on attributes of groups. Whether one likes to note this fact or not, behavior or sentiments held to be "characteristic" of a group invariably implies a central tendency in a distribution of behavior on the part of group members. Systematic data enable us to learn the characteristic patterns in a group and, further, to discover the degree to which individuals occupying diverse positions in the group exhibit that behavior or express a given sentiment. An earlier generation was often charitable in accepting, without further ado, the claims implicit in such summary terms as "typical," "characteristic," "usually," etc. Yet it takes only a moment's thought to recognize that terms such as these are only disguised summaries of statistical distributions of behavior, or of central tendencies in such distributions.

The type of research represented by *The American Soldier* is sufficiently new for its assimilation into the stream of contemporary thought to remain a matter of concern. In this connection, it is hoped that the present symposium will help college and university instructors incorporate salient parts of this work into their courses. Those not familiar at first hand with research of this kind might well find it difficult to select from the 1500 pages of these volumes the parts most pertinent to their special spheres of theoretical or empirical interest. They may be aided in their selection by the papers in this symposium, all of which make copious references to specific research findings, interpretations, or procedures. And from discussions of the same material by several symposiasts in different contexts, it becomes clear that any one empirical study has numerous and ramified implications for seemingly unconnected sectors of social science. Multiple implications—methodological, theoretical, and empirical—are drawn from the same research. Furthermore, since *The American Soldier* covers a wide variety of problems, its use as a single unit for instruction is not likely to be of maximum value. It is our hope that the symposium will help instructors to distinguish the diverse elements in *The American Soldier* and will thus contribute to its diffusion in educational programs of social science.

Like other intellectual products, *The American Soldier* will not have a uniform reception in all groups. Yet little is in general known of these differences in reception, or of the factors that determine them. This symposium therefore includes an exploratory study by Lerner of the patterns of response to the book in various social circles, academic, political and military, so far as these are indicated by published reviews.

It is probable that public recognition of a work of social science is affected by the extent of its practical applications. The relation between attitude surveys and policy formation therefore calls for some comment. Although this is treated only briefly in several of the following chapters, much can be learned from the experience of the Research Branch with respect to the application of social research to the formation of policy. Practically all of the studies under examination were in the first instance designed to provide sociological and social-psychological information needed (or thought to be needed) by those in staff and command positions in the Army. Numerous problems involved in the development of such applied research are opened to study—the restraints upon basic research imposed by the urgency of obtaining specific information, the points at which applied research generates problems which require re-thinking in terms of basic theory and methodology, the respects in which these research data constitute one factual basis for policy, the role of research in sensitizing policy-officials to otherwise unperceived problems, the methods of translating practical problems into researchable problems—these are but a few of the many aspects of the use of social research which might well be clarified by a more intensive review of the Research Branch experience. Speier, for example, has some pertinent observations on the place of attitude-survey research in the decision-making process. Further aspects of this problem are now being developed in case-studies of the utilization of social research.[2]

[2] This inquiry, now in progress, is being conducted by the Bureau of Applied Social Research, Columbia University, under a grant by the Carnegie Corporation. For a preliminary statement of the study, see R. K. Merton, "The role of applied social science in the formation of policy: a research memorandum," *Philosophy of Science*, July 1949, 16, 161-181, and the remainder of the issue devoted to a discussion of this memorandum.

As a contributor to *The American Soldier* reflecting on the longer-run implications of that work, Stouffer examines the dangers and potentialities of applied social research. He underscores the theme, running throughout the symposium, that in principle such research can advance the development of social theory. But he suggests, also, that exclusive concern with the problems defined as practical by superiors plays havoc with this development. And he lays stress upon the thesis central to the pages that follow: that continuity and cumulation of social science requires the unending interplay of theory and empirical research.

EDWARD A. SHILS

PRIMARY GROUPS
IN THE AMERICAN ARMY

*S*INCE the time of Charles Cooley, the primary group has been acknowledged in American social science as one of the most important modes of concerted human action—important both by virtue of its universality and by the wide ramifications of its influence on behavior. In recent years the primary group in various concrete manifestations has become the object of many concrete investigations and some theoretical analysis. Valuable techniques for the accurate observation and description of small groups have been developed and a considerable body of descriptive clinical material has accumulated. Much of the exact observation has however been done in experimental situations, often without a parallel in the concrete, real world. Many of the observations have been made on very narrow segments of primary group life and they have been reported so free of reference to the context of the events observed that the growth of general theoretical understanding has been but little enhanced. The clinical observation of primary groups in real situations has been extremely rich and suggestive but it has often been so impressionistic in nature and so undisciplined by hypotheses that the general propositions formulated from these observations have been and must necessarily be rather unreliable. Moreover, neither in the exact and experimental nor in the clinical observational work have there been many attempts to construct general propositions which will account for the observed concrete relationships.

The American Soldier brings a new combination into the field. It suffers neither from the refined emptiness of the experimental work nor the overpowering profusion of the clinical work. It deals precisely with many concrete attitudes and relationships which can be understood as elements in the problems of the primary group in the life of the Army. The data refer sufficiently often to contextual events to allow the construction of explanatory hypotheses on both concrete and general levels. The authors attempt to construct many of these hypotheses.

It is evident that the Research Branch did not originally set out in the course of their labors during the Second World War to study the inner workings of the primary group or its consequences in the American Army.[1] The data which illuminate primary groups in *The American Soldier* seem to have been gathered with other ends in view—they were usually immediate, practical ends rather than scientific or theoretical. But the practical ends and the variables which bore on their attainment often had, naturally, genuine though only belatedly perceived connections with the theoretical problems of primary group formation, operation and function. A result of these studies undertaken for the general and immediate purposes of Army officials, a large volume of scrupulously gathered and reported observations pertinent to the understanding of primary groups has now become available to scholars and should aid materially in the formulation of a systematic empirical theory of the primary group. The authors of *The American Soldier* and particularly Profs. M. Brewster Smith and Robin Williams[2] have not however simply delivered the raw materials to the builders of sociological theory. They too have seen very many of the numerous potentialities of their data and have in various sections of the first two volumes often confronted primary group problems with theoretical sensitivity and constructive art. The essay which follows aims only to reorganize the

---

[1] *The American Soldier* might well be made the object of a special case study of the interrelations between social science and social policy. Such a study would clarify the limitations and possibilities which the service of various types of practical ends creates for theoretical social science. It might reconsider some of the indices and variables which would be needed to test the hypotheses on primary groups or other problems and compare these with the data actually made available by the various surveys. It might inquire into the question as to whether the discrepancies could not have been eliminated to the advantage of social theory without damaging the practical ends which the surveys served. There are few works in social science, which by their combination of theoretical analysis and systematic empirical observation, would offer so many occasions to enter into the manifold relationships of science and practice, of theory and application.

[2] Especially Vol. II, Chapter 3, "Combat Motivations Among Ground Troops" (pp. 105-191), and Chapter 5, "The Combat Replacement" (pp. 242-289).

data and reformulate more specifically in terms of primary group theory some of the hypotheses already to be found in the first two volumes of *The American Soldier*.

For the most part, *The American Soldier* is based on studies of the attitudes of individuals. There is no direct observation of groups in action and only occasional, indirect observations of group performance.[3] The actual operation of primary group life is not described and indeed is seldom referred to. There are occasional glimpses which reveal both the wealth of the data which they have gathered and the almost ascetic discipline of the authors when they quote such passages as the following:

The men in my squad were my special friends. My best friend was the sergeant of the squad. We bunked together, slept together, fought together, told each other where our money was pinned in our shirts. We write to each other now. Expect to get together when the war is over. . . . If one man gets a letter from home the whole company reads it. Whatever belongs to me belongs to the whole outfit.[4]

But such concrete depictions are rare. Even when the authors present hypotheses for which they have no adequate quantitative data and which are probably based on their own feeling for reality and on the vivid comments which soldiers often added to the questionnaires, they always refrain from the use of rhetorically striking illustrations as evidence of their contentions. From the standpoint of scientific scrupulousness this is an advance over much current sociological practice. Nonetheless it is regrettable that more was not made of this kind of material—not only because it is interesting and evocative, but more important, because it would have enabled us to discern the large and important problems in the study of primary groups which have still to be approached with the rigor with which some of the problems have already been approached in this treatise.

The American Soldier's strength does not lie in the description of the working constitution of primary groups in the U. S. Army, either in combat situations or outside them. Its strength *does* lie in the analysis of (1) the influence of membership in such primary groups (whatever their constitution) on the behavior of the soldier

---

[3] The senior authors say: "The problem of measuring the cooperative effort of a unit was never solved satisfactorily, and it must be set down as one of the subjects which should call for the best efforts of sociologists and psychologists in the years ahead." Vol. I, p. 85.

[4] Vol. II, p. 99.

and of (2) the factors which promote or obstruct the formation of primary groups and the acceptance of membership in them.

The first problem of primary group analysis in relation to corporate bodies is: how does the influence of membership in the group affect the operation of the corporate body, and particularly, the attainment of the goals of the corporate body. This problem is forthrightly faced in *The American Soldier.*

The re-discovery of the primary group (or the informal group as it is usually called in *The American Soldier*) has not blinded them—as it has blinded some of its other re-discoverers—to the fundamental fact that a large corporate body like an Army is more than an assembly of primary groups accidentally coordinated with one another by primary group relationships. They are well aware that the army is an organization in which formally constituted agencies exercise authority over persons with whom they have no primary group relations whatsoever. The fundamental significance of command and sanction never disappears from their field of vision. They understand that whole constellations of motives and sets of institutions broader than and prior to the Army and much narrower than the Army are intertwined with formal military authority (with its powers of command and coercion) in directing the conduct of the effective soldier. They are at pains to assign to each of these different factors their proper weight, but they are hampered by the paucity of their data and to some extent by the form in which they were gathered.

The crucial data bearing directly on the limited power of expectations of coercive sanctions are relatively scanty and not entirely free from self-contradiction at certain points.[5] The appearance of contradiction is however diminished by the relative infrequency with which soldiers mention coercion and the fear of sanctions in explaining their *own* behavior in battle. It is also diminished by the insight of the Research Branch that moral considerations (*i.e.*, conceptions of duty and legitimacy), primary group sanctions and formal military sanctions in most cases move in the same direction, reinforcing one another in ways which present research techniques and conceptual schemes do not allow us easily to disentangle from

[5] Thus 72 per cent of the enlisted men agreed that "it is wrong for a soldier to break Army rules even if he doesn't get caught," while in reply to another question, 67 per cent of the enlisted men agreed that "the main reason most soldiers obey rules and regulations is because they are afraid of being punished." (Vol. I, p. 417.)

one another.[6] "One important general function of the existence of formal sanctions was . . . that when imposed they called into automatic operation informal sanctions both social and internalized. The existence of these informal sanctions gave the formal sanction much of its force."[7]

The formal coercive powers of the Army must moreover lose some of their directive force in the very situation towards which the entire military organization is directed: namely, the situation of battle. Here, as a result of the high probability of the unforeseen, the need for discretion is at a maximum and the dangers can be faced and contended with only if there is a positive self-impelled effort coming from within the general disposition of the individual soldier and reinforced by the most diverse kinds of gratifications and compensatory pressures. And it is in this very situation that formal authority changes some of its bases and formal sanctions become less effectively coercive.[8] The actual role of expectations of coercion and of specific stipulated rewards in the instigation of effort on behalf of corporate goals and their place among the other influences on behavior in corporate bodies represents a central and still unsolved problem of social science. Among these alternative or complementary influences are loyalties to general impersonal standards,

[6] Part of the difficulty of estimating the relative importance of the various factors arises from the fact that the Research Branch noted only *the* factor which each soldier considered most important to him. Since there is no indication that the soldiers thought this factor alone was important, it might have been possible to elicit from them their judgments as to the second and third most important incentive. (*cf.* Vol. II, pp. 108-109.)

[7] Vol. II, p. 114.

[8] One incidental but interesting instance of this decline in the fear and hence in the efficacy of official Army sanctions with increased experience in combat was produced in Italy. There the less battle-hardened privates, "pfc's" and noncommissioned officers, said dishonorable discharge in addition to a prison sentence was "a great deal worse—one of the worst things that can happen to a man," considerably more frequently than their more experienced comrades who had become more indifferent to the perils of disgrace.

	PRIVATES AND PFC'S WHO HAVE BEEN IN COMBAT FOR:			NON-COMS WHO HAVE BEEN IN COMBAT FOR:		
	Less Than 4 Mo.	*4 Through 6 Mo.*	*7 Mo. or More*	*Less Than 4 Mo.*	*4 Through 6 Mo.*	*7 Mo. or More*
Somewhat Worse	19	22	22	7	18	26
A great deal worse— "it's one of the worst things that can happen to a man."	39	36	31	63	41	34

From Table 3, Vol. II, p. 115.

to large collectivities such as state, nation, army, or party, and loyalty to primary groups.

One of the most significant contributions to the clarification and very tentative resolution of this problem and thereby to our knowledge of the importance of primary groups in the execution of the goals of large corporate organizations comes from certain inquiries made by the Research Branch into the soldier's own assessment of the factors which caused him "to keep going." Two major inquiries conducted on different occasions and somewhat differently phrased both indicated that the desire to avoid "letting the other fellow down" was one of the most important of all factors and was surpassed only by prayer when the "going was tough," [9] or by the "desire to get the job over with" in the second inquiry. In reply to the query: "Generally in your combat experience, what was most important to you in making you want to keep going and to do as well as you could?" addressed to infantry combat veterans in Europe, 39 per cent mentioned "ending the task"; 14 per cent, solidarity with group, "cannot let the other fellows or the outfit down"; "sticking together," "buddies depending on me"; "my friends around me"; 9 per cent, "sense of duty and self-respect"; 10 per cent, "thoughts of home and loved ones." Five per cent mentioned "idealistic reasons," 2 per cent vindictiveness, only 3 per cent indicated absence of alternatives, leadership, and discipline.[10] In another inquiry into the factors which helped when the "going was tough," Pacific and Mediterranean veterans answered as follows: "prayer helped a lot," was indicated by 70 per cent of the Pacific veterans and 83 per cent of the Mediterranean veterans; "couldn't let the other men down," by 61 per cent and 56 per cent, respectively; "had to finish the job in order to get home again," 42 per cent and 28 per cent; "thoughts of hatred for the enemy," 38 per cent and 28 per cent; "what we are fighting for," 34 per cent and 29 per cent.[11]

It will be noted that in both inquiries and in both theaters, motives connected with primary group solidarity were estimated as very important and that none of the preponderant "motives" refers to the acceptance of a formal command from a formally appointed authority although obviously a good share of their importance consists in the extent to which they furthered the execution of com-

[9] Vol. II, p. 174.
[10] Vol. II, pp. 108-109.
[11] Vol. II, p. 174.

mands or the exercise of initiative within the general framework of commands.

These data support the more complex hypothesis that primary group solidarity functions in the corporate body to strengthen the motivation for the fulfillment of substantive prescriptions and commands issued by the official agents of the corporate body, within the context of *a set of generalized moral predispositions* or *sense of obligation.* The latter need not be strongly present in consciousness but some measure of identification with the collectivity and some sense of generalized obligation and readiness to acknowledge the legitimacy of its demands in numerous particular situations must exist. Thus, for example, the soldiers who thought first of getting the job done must, in some way, have accepted the legitimacy of the "job" and felt some degree of obligation to carry it out. The general setting of their goal was given by their identification with the United States and this made for an acceptance of specific commands from their officers. But even the 39 per cent who mentioned "ending the task" as a motivating consideration might have been lax and reluctant if they had not been subject to the pressure of their comrades who, more or less hiding the same belief, added the autonomous weight of their approval and affection for those who conformed and disapproval for those who were deviant.[12] In other words then, it cannot be said that goals are set by membership in the primary group but only that efforts to achieve the legitimate, formally prescribed goals may be strengthened by such membership.[13]

However great the importance of broad communal loyalties as matrices which predispose the individual soldier to strive to achieve authoritatively commended goals, their effect in motivation does not

[12] Certainly more than one of the motives or considerations listed above must have been operative in the soldiers whose attitudes are reported above. Unfortunately our techniques for analyzing in a simple and exact way combinations and interrelations of motives, hampers the advancement of our knowledge about primary groups in corporate bodies.

[13] There is neither evidence in these studies nor very general reason for believing that genuinely new goals are created from the existence of the primary group. But it must be acknowledged in the light of the data presented in *The American Soldier* that primary groups activate and intensify certain demands or needs in their members as well as create the opportunity to gratify these needs. The striving to gratify these needs, *e.g.,* the need to demonstrate manliness (*vide infra*) might then converge on and facilitate the type of action necessary to achieve the authoritatively prescribed collective goals which are also accepted as legitimate. On the other hand the gratification of certain demands which arise from primary group existence might actually interfere with the

emerge as directly as the pressure of primary group obligations. Patriotism, and hatred of the enemy which in combat might be considered as the obverse side of patriotism, were not accorded very high rating by the soldiers themselves.[14] Feelings of vindictiveness toward the enemy did not show a very significant relationship with feelings of readiness for combat,[15] which we may be permitted to interpret as readiness to strive to achieve corporate goals. The role of hatred of the enemy soldier or hatred of the enemy people thus seems to have been relatively insignificant in the determination of combat motivation.

It is moreover noteworthy that hatred of the enemy decreased as the soldiers came into combat. Soldiers still in training in the United States or in rear areas hated the enemy more than soldiers who had actually fought against the enemy in combat situations.[16] The authors believe that "hatred of the enemy, personal and impersonal, was not a major element in combat motivation." [17]

Similarly the evidence does not support the hypothesis that devotion to patriotic ideals directly played a great part in the motivation of the soldiers in the performance of the numerous specific actions which make up the military life in battle and behind the front. Most of the soldiers attributed a relatively low order of efficacy to patriotic or political ideals in their assessment of their own experience under fire.[18] There was a strong taboo against

---

attainment of the collective goals, *e.g.*, the need to aid a wounded comrade even though it interferes with the execution of a command.

[14] Thirty-eight per cent of the Pacific veterans, 28 per cent of the Mediterranean veterans, said that "hatred of the enemy" helped a lot when the "going was tough." Thirty-four per cent and 29 per cent respectively, said they were greatly helped by the thought of "what we are fighting for." These two "variables" were fourth and fifth in a list of five. (Vol. II, p. 174.)

[15] In one veteran division in the Pacific there was only a difference of five percentage points between the "high" and the "low" vindictiveness groups (25 per cent and 21 per cent) with respect to their readiness for combat. In another division the difference was only slightly larger (67 per cent and 59 per cent). (Vol. II, p. 165.)

[16] Forty-two percent of the veteran enlisted men in the Pacific favored wiping out the whole Japanese nation as compared with 67 per cent of the enlisted men in training in the U.S. Twenty-two per cent of the veteran enlisted men in Europe favored wiping out the German nation while 29 per cent in training in the U.S. favored equally drastic measures. (Vol. II, p. 158.)

[17] Vol. II, p. 166. More intensive interviews as well as greater concentration on special combat situations (as over against comprehensive self-assessments) are required for the further exploration of this hypothesis. But even with their narrow data, the authors have promulgated and respectably supported an hypothesis of far reaching and hitherto seldom acknowledged importance.

[18] *Cf.* Footnote 14 above.

extremely patriotic expression in soldiers' circles especially in groups under combat conditions—just as there was a strong taboo on extremely disloyal remarks.[19] "The broad picture . . . is one of a matter of fact adjustment, with a minimum of idealism or heroics in which the elements which come closest to the conventional stereotypes of soldier heroism enter through the close solidarity of the immediate combat group." [20] When directly confronted with the question as to their own justification for the war most of the soldiers answered in ways which indicated a general acceptance of the war as legitimate and as a largely just basis for their risks and discomforts. Only a small fraction of the soldiers "very often" thought that the war was "not worth fighting" and although doubts were slightly more frequent among combat veterans, than among soldiers in training, even at the extremes, doubt was relatively rare.[21] "The issues behind the war were singularly unreal to [the soldier] in contrast to the issues and exigencies of his day to day existence." [22] Yet it would be a mistake to say that the tacit patriotism of the soldiers played no significant part in disposing the men to acceptance, obedience and initiative. The widespread character of their acceptance of the legitimacy of the war although in itself not a strong combat motivation must still be viewed as flowing both directly and indirectly into combat motivation. First of all, as we have already indicated above, it makes for a general readiness to accept commands and to execute them. Also, through its provision of a very general common universe of discourse, it provided the rudiments of one of the most important pre-conditions for the formation of primary groups which have a more positive and immediate function in strengthening the soldier's will to exert himself under dangerous conditions.

The careful analysis of this problem in *The American Soldier*, the respect for the data and for common sense in its interpretation leaves us with the conclusion that in the main, identification with

[19] The affectively intense hostility towards extremely patriotic language might of course be interpreted in either direction. It might mean that the soldiers regarded allegations of patriotic motivations as erroneous and hypocritical or that they were repressing strongly patriotic sentiments. Only more intensive interviewing can resolve this dilemma.

[20] Vol. II, p. 112.

[21] Seven per cent of soldiers in training often thought the War was "not worth fighting," 11 per cent of combat veterans thought the same (Vol. II. p. 152). The proportion of sceptics did not increase materially with extended exposure to battle (Vol. II, p. 153).

[22] Vol. II, p. 167.

specific secondary symbols is not enough nor are clearly defined commands enough to make a military organization an effective mechanism for moving men to action. The authors of *The American Soldier* do not possess the information necessary to analyze the general moral matrix which underlay the desire to "get the job done." The primary group has been put into its proper context and by ingenious use of material which is often tangential in its connection, they have succeeded in adding to our knowledge of how primary groups in conjunction with other factors affect the achievement of collective goals.

II

PRIMARY GROUPS AND THE INDIVIDUAL

IN November 1945, when the war was over and morale was deteriorating, a survey of enlisted men showed that nine-tenths of them believed that soldiers are greatly concerned with the opinion in which they are held by the other enlisted men in their units.[23] We may accept the results of this enquiry as a demonstration of the source of the influence of primary groups on the behavior of their members. The authors of *The American Soldier,* although they have not related the particular data which disclose this responsiveness to the opinion of others to their data on other aspects of primary groups, seem to have their point of departure in such a proposition. They assume that the favorable judgment of intimates is a major determinant of behavior, and in their interpretation of their data they draw the implications of that assumption. They have characterized the function of the primary group for the behavior of its members in the following terms: The primary group, they say, "served two principal functions in combat motivation: it *set and emphasized group standards* of behavior and it *supported and sustained the individual* in stresses he would otherwise not have been able to withstand. These are related functions: the group enforced its standards principally by offering or withholding recognition, respect and approval which were among the supports it had to offer, while the subjective reward of following an internalized

[23] Vol. I, p. 418.

group code enhanced the individual's resources for dealing with the situation." [24]

Given the individual soldier's responsiveness to the opinion of his comrades, the execution of a generally accepted command will be in part motivated by expectations of favorable responses from others who share the same goal. The grant of approval awakens favorable responses in the recipient and an affectionate relationship is established which has its own standards of mutual helpfulness and devotion. These are effective both through internalization into the soldier's own conscience and by his constantly renewed expectations concerning the responses of his comrades. Since the fear of death or injury is one of the chief deterrents of the execution of commands or the use of initiative in combat, one of the important functions of the primary group, as *The American Soldier* amply testifies, is the reduction of fear. We have already cited the soldier's own conception of the importance of his feeling of responsibility to his comrades in execution of what becomes in a well-led unit a primary group goal as well as an authoritative command. We have also cited the soldier's own testimony concerning his sensitivity to the opinion of his comrades with its clear implication of the need for comradely approval as an incentive to exertion in battle. There is also some evidence that the experience of that feeling of solidarity is a protection against fear. Soldiers who were helped in dangerous moments by their feeling of responsibility to their comrades were less likely to be frightened than soldiers who had recourse less frequently to the image of their comrades and their solidarity with them. The more fearful soldier was the one who resorted more readily to prayer than to the thought of his responsibilities to his comrades. [25]

It is of course possible that the soldiers, whose personalities were sufficiently free from anxiety prior to entry into battle, and who were able to confront threatening situations with a smaller number of fear symptoms, were psychologically more capable of entering into primary group relationships. By their lower level of anxiety and their smaller need for protection, the amount of affection and protection offered by the primary group would be adequate for their needs. Conversely, the extremely anxious soldier could not

[24] Vol. II, pp. 130-131.
[25] *Cf.* Table 20, Vol. II, p. 179. (The form in which the data are presented does not allow any certainty that the relationship might not be the opposite from that presented here. Either one, however, if well demonstrated, would constitute a proposition of extraordinary importance for the theory of primary groups.

find sufficient protection and assurance in a primary group, even where it is available, and to alleviate his distress would turn to prayer. However, another set of data supports the hypothesis that primary group solidarity reduces the need to resort to prayer in dangerous situations, and this strengthens the hypothesis that primary group membership is an independent variable in fear-reduction. In a comparison of infantrymen who came overseas with their units (and who may therefore be presumed to have formed primary groups) and those who entered their units as replacements (and who are accordingly being interpreted as less likely to be incorporated into a primary group), the replacements were more inclined to resort to prayer in combat situations when "the going was tough." [26] By their provision of affection and protection primary groups reduce fear and thus facilitate the execution of the commands of authorities.

Primary group relations help the individual soldier to bear threatened injuries and even death by increasing his self-esteem and his conception of his own potency. They help particularly to raise his estimate of his capacity to encounter and to survive deprivations. "The sense of power and security which the combat soldier derived from being among buddies on whom he could depend and from being part of a strong and winning team should . . . be regarded . . . as one way in which the resources of the individual were maintained at a level at which he remained capable of coping with the stresses of combat. . . ." The authors of *The American Soldier* go on to say, "it was surely as important as more positive factors in combat motivation." [27]

The data to support this hypothesis are once more not direct. If we are correct in our interpretation of certain morale indices as indicative of primary group formation, then we may safely assert that soldiers who came overseas with their units formed primary groups to a greater extent than soldiers who joined their units as replacements. Understanding the term in this sense, primary group members had more self-confidence (*e.g.*, felt their training had been

If we learn with some assurance that primary group membership reduces fear or that fearfulness reduces the capacity to enter primary groups—both propositions are plausible in the light of existing knowledge—a major step forward will have been accomplished. The fruitfulness of the data of *The American Soldier* in suggesting hypotheses for further investigation could scarcely be better illustrated than by this instance.)

[26] Vol. II, pp. 183-184.
[27] Vol. II, p. 149.

adequate) than those who were not so fully integrated into primary groups. Of the "primary group members," 32 per cent thought their training had fitted them "very well" for combat while only 18 per cent of the "newcomers" felt the same way; 25 per cent of the "primary group members" thought that their training had prepared them "not so well" or "not well at all" while 42 per cent of the "newcomers" believed the same.[28] The self-confidence and self-esteem which primary group members obtain from their membership is heightened by the confidence and esteem in which they hold their superiors in the group and in the corporate body within which the group exists.

The effectiveness in the execution of authoritative commands also depends on the quality of relations with the agents of authority and particularly with those agents of authority who are in close proximity to the actor. The material presented by the Research Branch provides a somewhat more reliable foundation for the widely current but undemonstrated hypothesis concerning the relationship between the readiness of soldiers (and, by implication, of subordinates in other types of bureaucratic organizations) to execute commands and the existence of primary group relations with their immediate superiors who issue or transmit the commands.

Soldiers who said their officers took "a personal interest" in their men, who regarded them as "willing to go through whatever they asked their men to go through" and under whom they would "want to serve in combat" felt very much more ready for combat than did soldiers who felt hostile toward their officers.[29] The one particularly *primary group* component in this assessment of officers, namely, "active concern," "encouragement," etc., made up more than half of the favorable comments on officers and it appears to have a positive influence on heightening the disposition of soldiers to carry out their military tasks.[30] "The officer who commanded the personal respect and loyalty of his men could mobilize the full support of a willing fellowship; he therefore had at his disposal the resources of both the formal coercive system and the system of informal group controls. If, however, the officer had alienated his men and had to rely primarily on coercion, the informal sanctions of the group might cease to bear primarily on the combat mission." [31]

[28] Vol. II, p. 282.
[29] Vol. II, p. 127, Table 7.
[30] Vol. II, p. 125, Table 6.
[31] Vol. II, p. 118.

III

ASSIMILATION INTO PRIMARY GROUPS

IN the foregoing sections we have treated the primary groups as already established entities and were interested for the most part in the effect of primary group membership on behavior in roles outside the primary group. Among the important problems in the study of primary groups, however, are those centering about the modes and conditions under which new members are assimilated into *established* primary groups. Little work has been done on these problems. Two cases of assimilation are described by Lippitt [32] and Mayo and Lombard [33] who have studied the phenomenon clinically in two California aircraft factories during the Second World War. Here and there the problem has been touched in passing.

It is, however, in *The American Soldier* in the chapter entitled "The Combat Replacement" [34] that we find for the first time a large body of reliable observations of various aspects of the process of assimilation into established primary groups. The "replacement" system of the American Army provided a continuous opportunity to study the influence on the behavior of newcomers of an already established primary group with which the newcomers were required to collaborate.

The aspects chosen for study seem to have been accidentally rather than systematically selected—as if material gathered for other purposes were being re-analyzed with respect to its potentialities for general sociological analysis. Yet, however unsystematic from a theoretical standpoint the choice of problems, the data are sufficiently rich and sufficiently coherent to permit the formulation of a number of important hypotheses.

The basic enquiry compared the attitudes of veterans in a veteran infantry division, replacements in those veteran divisions, and infantrymen in three inexperienced divisions on a number of ques-

[32] Lippitt, Ronald, "An Experimental Study of the Effect of Democratic and Authoritarian Group Atmospheres," in *Studies in Topological and Vector Psychology*, by K. Lewin, R. Lippitt and S. Escalona. *Studies in Child Welfare*, Vol. XVI, No. 3 (1940).

[33] Mayo, E. & Lombard, G. F. F., *Teamwork and Labor Turnover in the Aircraft Industry of Southern California* (1944).

[34] Vol. II, pp. 242-289.

tions. The replacements in the veteran divisions approximated the attitudes of the veterans when asked about their willingness to enter combat. The totally green men (in the inexperienced divisions) were most willing, the veterans least willing, and the replacements were more than half way toward the veterans.[35] The replacements had less confidence in their own ability as combat leaders than either the veterans who had most self-confidence or the green men who were less self-confident than the veterans. In their attitudes toward their non-commissioned officers the replacements were most favorable, the veterans second and the green men least. The replacements were most proud of their company. They were even more proud than the veterans, and both were markedly ahead of the green men. On the whole the replacements seemed to feel inferior *vis-à-vis* the established primary group into which they are not yet accepted and which had a dual source of prestige in their eyes— both as combat veterans and as an established primary group sharing intimacies and "knowing the ropes." Their feeling of inferiority, which was the product of their proximity to and probably incomplete acceptance by those who have already performed successfully some very difficult action which they had still to perform, had influenced them to value themselves less than green men did and to value their superiors more than green men did. This high evaluation of the veteran primary group which they confronted and into which they have not yet been fully assimilated gave them pride in their membership in the company in which the veteran primary group was established. Except with regard to attitudes which involved direct judgments of themselves and which aroused their insecurity and pride, they sought to "prove" themselves by taking over the veterans' attitudes, *e.g.*, conviction about the war. Accordingly in such situations they stood between the other two groups.

Further evidence of the influence of the established veterans' primary group on replacements may be seen in a series of comparisons of the attitudes of replacements in several units of veterans classified according to their morale score at an earlier period. In many respects, variations in the morale of veterans were paralleled by variations in the morale of replacements.[36]

But the variations were not uniformly parallel. Perhaps because of their relatively higher degree of cohesion, it was difficult for the

[35] Vol. II, p. 244.
[36] Vol. II, pp. 266-267, Chart II.

newcomers to judge the situation realistically and in veterans units with poor morale, the replacements tended to overestimate the degree of solidarity prevailing in the established group. Newcomers who presumably had not yet been allowed to share in the primary group life of the veterans were prouder of their company than the veterans, in units in which the veterans felt relatively little pride. The replacements were moreover not resentful of their inferiority to the veterans; they accepted it and were grateful for the help given them by the veterans. Eighty-two per cent of the replacements in another investigation thought that the veterans had given them as much help "as they could." [37]

As in other sections of *The American Soldier,* the information on group structure of the units into which the replacements came is very meager and so the important problem of the effect of the large influx of newcomers on both the established primary group and on the rate of assimilation is not directly treated. However, it is possible to put forward a very tentative hypothesis on the basis of some data which has perhaps a connection with the problem. The larger the proportion of newcomers, the greater the resistance of the established primary group to their assimilation. In units with larger proportions of replacements, both veterans and newcomers were apt to say that teamwork in their units was poorer than it was reported to be by both newcomers and veterans in units in which the proportion of replacements was smaller.[38]

IV

INDIVIDUAL NEEDS AND THE ESTABLISHMENT OF PRIMARY GROUPS

THE replacement's sense of inferiority which is manifested in his higher estimation of the value of the veteran non-commissioned officer as compared with judgments by the veteran enlisted men

[37] Vol. II, pp. 278-279.
[38] Vol. II, pp. 258-259. It is obvious that the data here would support other, contradictory hypotheses as well. This hypothesis has been chosen because of its coherence with other propositions about primary groups but even more be-

gives a clue to the grounds of soldiers' dependence on their officers. It also gives a clue to the conditions under which primary group relations are established between officers and soldiers.

The enlisted man's desire for some type of personal relationship with his officer, particularly for a protective personal relationship, is well documented. More than any other single characteristic, veteran enlisted men mentioned helpfulness toward their men, and the display of personal interest in them and their problems, in describing the characteristics of the best officer they had known in combat.[39]

As one wounded veteran said, "About officers—everybody wants somebody to look up to when he's scared. It makes a lot of difference."[40] The need to have not only personal relationships but personal relationships with a protective exemplary authority whose qualities permit identification is shown not only by this vivid remark but by the statistical data assembled by the Research Branch. In assessing the qualities of officers who helped them to cope with difficult situations, one of the most frequently mentioned was leadership "by example" in which the officer performed dangerous actions himself and displayed personal courage and coolness.[41] It is easy to understand that soldiers who are being pressed by conscience, command and the expectations of their primary group comrades will be better able to face these dangers where they can identify with an exemplary and protective leader. And identification will be facilitated by personal interest and solicitude on the part of the officer.

We shall shortly treat the effect of combat on the formation of primary groups but it is appropriate to point out here that in combat situations in which primary group formation usually reached its maximum, 61 per cent of the infantry and heavy weapons privates in the European combat zone thought all or most of their officers took a personal interest in the welfare of their men and 70 per cent

cause it illustrates the highly suggestive nature of even those data in *The American Soldier* which do not allow safely assertable hypotheses to be proposed.

[39] Vol. II, p. 134. In another enquiry into veterans' judgments of the particular leadership practices which did most to give their men confidence in tough or threatening situations 28 per cent stressed the protective personal relationship. (*Cf.* also Vol. II, p. 125.)

[40] Vol. II, p. 124.

[41] Vol. II, p. 125.

thought that all or most of the officers were willing to go through anything they make their men go through. And among troops who have not yet entered combat, the proportion who say that they would like to serve under a given company commander in combat varies directly with the proportion who think that he "takes a lot of interest in what his men are thinking." [42] Companies with high morale were characterized by far higher frequency of the belief that the officers were "interested" in their men, "understood" them, were "helpful," would "back them up"—who in other words showed to a high degree the qualities of primary group leaders.

There is nonetheless an antinomy between officer-man relations in the execution of the goals of the corporate organization and in primary group relations. Military life is deprivational and only where the officer shows his worth by protectiveness, exemplary aggressiveness and benevolence can the deprivations which he imposes be compensated. In inactive areas, especially inactive overseas areas, where the protective function is small and the deprivational function realistically and especially symbolically large, the officers are most disesteemed. Outside of combat conditions, the formation of primary groups between officers and men is hampered by the availability of specially privileged facilities for officers from which the men are excluded. In combat, however, where these opportunities are almost always lacking, this cause of resentment against officers is eliminated and the positive factors can work with less impediment. Since only one of the components of the officers' contribution to primary group formation can be effective in noncombat conditions—namely, benevolence—and since this too is probably hampered by the officers' privilege system outside of combat, there is little in non-combat areas to balance the deprivations of military life. Another indication of the plausibility of the hypothesis that the protective function is of great importance in the formation of officer-soldier primary groups is that after prolonged exposure to battle, when the deprivations have accumulated beyond the protective capacities of the officers, their status begins to decline in the eyes of their men. [43]

The dependence of good combat morale—which we equate here hypothetically with good primary group relations—on *confidence in the officer's* capacity to guide, protect, initiate and serve as a model

[42] Vol. II, p. 384.
[43] Vol. I, pp. 364-365.

might sometimes be derived to a greater extent from the soldier's needs than from the officer's propensities. Thus while in their attitudes officers seem to be more repressive and less tolerant toward their men than the non-commissioned officers,[44] the soldiers' readiness to fight seems to be more dependent on their confidence in their immediate officers than on their non-commissioned officers.[45] This would seem to be in accord with certain general hypotheses (which have even less rigorous empirical foundation) to the effect that in the personal relations of subordinates with two levels of authority, affection and trust will go to the higher level while the more proximate level which is the immediate agent of deprivations (emerging from decisions at remote reaches of the organization) will receive somewhat more negative affect.

Here we must introduce a cautionary remark similar to that made in the earlier discussion of the role of primary group membership in motivation. In this section we have presented some of the data and explanatory hypotheses to be found in or derived from *The American Soldier*. We have stressed the importance of the immediately commanding officer in the formation of primary groups among the men and the importance of primary group (although not necessarily equalitarian) relations between men and officers as a factor in the effective execution of specific commands and general tactical aims. It would be extremely shortsighted to neglect the great importance of the higher levels of the military hierarchy in setting goals, in organizing the provision of facilities and in providing many of the conditions which affectively accrue to the credit of the immediate company officer. The protection of his men, and the sense which they have of it, is not just a result of the officer's personal qualities, his courage, benevolence, aggressiveness, skill, *etc.* It is made possible by the weapons which other parts of the organization provide, by food and clothing provided by other parts of the organization and by the larger tactical and strategic dispositions which are the context of the operations of the company. Nonetheless, as far as the enlisted man's motivation is concerned, the higher command has relatively little direct significance. "Unless the higher command was personalized by a highly popular individual commander on the one hand or unless things were going very badly on the other, men

---

[44] Vol. I, pp. 408-409. Presumably junior officers are referred to here.

[45] Vol. II, p. 129. As in the study referred to in the preceding footnote, junior officers are presumably involved here.

did not give much concern to what went on above. Their confidence in their own immediate leadership was probably a more effective factor in combat motivation." [46] And this was, in many respects, a primary group affair.

In addition to a benevolent and protective leader, an aggregate of individuals, to become a primary group, must meet certain other requirements. Personality qualities seem to be rather important variables in explaining dispositions of individuals to accept or seek primary group membership or to avoid it. Here too *The American Soldier* renders it possible to formulate certain hypotheses about this problem, on the basis of the unique data on the characteristics of soldiers who went AWOL in comparison with well adjusted soldiers and a cross section of all soldiers. We shall consider mainly the AWOL's who in the winter of 1943–44 had been in the Army less than six months. These tended to be younger than the cross-section of privates (78 per cent under 24 years among AWOL's, 60 per cent among privates), more frequently unmarried (72 per cent and 56 per cent, respectively) and less well educated (84 per cent with "some high school" or less, compared to 56 per cent of privates with the same amount of education).[47] AWOL's tended to have been more isolated socially in childhood, and less inclined "to go around with a bunch" than any except psychoneurotic soldiers; as children they had been far more disposed towards truancy than any other army group. They claim to have "really liked fighting" as children more than any other group and also to have had "dates with girls" more frequently.[48]

This picture of the AWOL might be interpreted as that of a person with inferiority feelings, fearful of giving or receiving affection and yet desirous of doing so, concerned to overcome his image of his own inadequacy by demonstrating his masculinity and at the same time reluctant to undergo any test which would reveal the defects which he feels. It is the picture of a late adolescent worried about his capacity to "prove" his masculinity in an environment which would surely put it to test both by its composition and by the tasks which it would have to perform. Hypothetically this may be related to the feeling of uncertainty about heterosexual capacity and the fear of falling into a strictly male society which would

[46] Vol. II, p. 145.
[47] Vol. I, pp. 116, 118, 119.
[48] Vol. I, p. 133.

reactivate latent homosexual tendencies and thus accentuate internal conflict about heterosexual capacity. Those for whom the challenge was too great withdrew very soon simply by going AWOL. Those who suffered these feelings less acutely or for whom other conditions were more favorable, found many compromise formulations to reassure themselves and their comrades of their masculinity. Indeed much of "GI culture" and particularly "GI language" had exactly the function of asserting masculinity in a social organization which required it and which by creating an exclusively male society and by presenting very extreme challenges aroused two deep and independent sources of anxiety—namely, homosexuality and death.[49]

The male character of the army accentuated, as we have indicated, the young soldier's needs to prove his masculinity. The formation of primary groups strengthened this tendency since each member feared both the subjective and social consequences of regression to the menacing period of latency. In this way primary groups in the Army, by placing a high reaction-formative evaluation on bravery and aggressiveness [50]—the chief values of masculinity—served the goals of the organization.

In the light of these very tentative hypotheses, we might assert that assimilation into male primary groups will be more probable where the candidate is heterosexually well adjusted and has a relatively low anxiety level about his capacity to give and to receive affection without arousing either homosexual tendencies or defensive counter-tendencies.

But even where personality and leadership conditions are favorable, there are still many other variables which can impede primary group formation. We have already discussed the assimilation problem and need only repeat a few points here. Newcomers, as we have seen, tend to feel insecure and their sense of inferiority is aggravated. Both replacements (59 per cent) and veterans (48 per cent) agreed that replacements tended to feel more insecure in combat

---

[49] The data on marital status of AWOL's who have served longer in the army seem too inconsistent to permit the construction of a unifying hypothesis. Moreover, without further information concerning the nature or degree of marital adjustment, it does not seem profitable even to attempt such an interpretation.

[50] Fifty-nine per cent of the privates and "pfc's" chose courage and aggressiveness as characteristics of the best combat soldier they had known. Thirty per cent of them chose it as the characteristic of the best combat officer they had known (as compared with 24 per cent who regarded helpfulness and interest in their men as the most important quality of their best officer). Vol. II, p. 134.

than veterans and sought the protection of close association much more frequently by the serious error of "bunching up" under fire.[51] Replacements, then, because of their imperfect integration into the established primary groups hampered the functioning of the military organization by the *ad hoc* creation of militarily inefficient primary groups while under fire. The magnitude of the difference in military efficiency caused by this is obviously unknown and under present conditions unknowable, but it was probably not very large—partly because the primary group was not the only factor in military effectiveness and partly because the degree of assimilation into primary groups was very considerable.[52] Of the factors affecting the rate of assimilation, apart from those mentioned in the immediately preceding pages and in the earlier section on replacements, *e.g.*, officers' behavior, the degree of integration of the established veterans' primary group, the proportion of veterans and newcomers, *etc.*, one of the most important is exposure to combat.

It is of course ancient wisdom that groups are integrated more closely when they are faced with an external threat. The data and interpretations in *The American Soldier* have given rise to no fundamentally new hypotheses on this problem and they do not easily help us to refine and make more rigorous the old. But they do bring out certain nuances and point the way toward new research. One of the most interesting of these subsidiary hypotheses is that which asserts that the rate of assimilation of newcomers into established primary groups is accelerated by combat. There were no significant differences between the morale indices of replacements who were sent into combat nearly at once (*i.e.*, three days or a week after attachment to the unit) and those who had longer periods of pre-combat association.[53]

As to *why* solidarity should increase under combat conditions, relatively little new insight is forthcoming. Nor does it explain why hostility towards superiors declines and favorable attitudes increase

---

[51] Vol. II, p. 283.

[52] In reply to the question: "How long was it after you arrived in your present outfit before you felt you really belonged in the outfit and were an important part of it?", 14 per cent replied "after the first day;" 33 per cent, "after the first few days;" 18 per cent, "after the first week;" 9 per cent, "after several weeks," and 13 per cent, "never felt this way." (Vol. II, p. 280. *Cf.* also Vol. II, p. 281.) Nothing is stated in *The American Soldier* about the factors determining these differences.

[53] Vol. II, pp. 277-278. It would have been instructive to have a comparison of the degree of assimilation achieved by replacements attached for similar periods to units which were not in combat.

up to a point with exposure to danger—although it documents the proposition more incontrovertibly than has even been done before.[54]

Another important problem which is, however, not left entirely untouched is the disruption of primary group unity under conditions of extreme deprivation. The connection is, it is true, a roundabout one and must be pieced together from discrete bits of data. Our previous discussion has shown that some evidence exists for the proposition that increased fear places a heavy potentially disruptive burden on a primary group. Casualties occurring to primary group members will be more fearfully interpreted than those which occur to members of the group with whom an individual is less closely bound. The sight of "one or more best friends killed" by men in companies which experienced high casualties bears some positive relation to the amount of fear experienced. Thirty-nine per cent of the men who saw one or more of their best friends killed reported six to nine fear-symptoms. Only 34 per cent of those whose general context of casualties was about the same and who did not see one or more of their best friends killed fell into the same class. The difference is certainly not large but it is large enough to stimulate hypothesis-construction and further research.

One could go on indefinitely multiplying the hypotheses which might be built directly or indirectly on the data presented in *The American Soldier*. The study of primary groups has been much enriched by it and the subject has been moved forward by a sensible measure.

V

CONCLUDING REMARKS

THE fact that the Research Branch did not set out to study primary groups frontally and from the beginning means that many extremely important problems could not be formulated, to say nothing of resolved, even tentatively, on the basis of the data which they

---

[54] Vol. I, pp. 364-366. Another interesting confirmation of this proposition is the evidence that the solidarity of a group of veterans on garrison duty was regarded by its members as having declined from the level which it had reached during combat (Vol. II, p. 258).

gathered. At the end of the preceding section, for example, we have shown that hypotheses with regard to the conditions of danger under which primary groups disintegrate can not be investigated from the materials presented even though some very intriguing hypotheses could be constructed. This is to some extent the result of the failure of the Research Branch to pay sufficiently detailed attention in their questionnaires to the soldiers' own report of their experiences under combat and of the general tendency to avoid the technical and substantive problems involved in the description of group action and relationships. Only in a few cases were attempts made to discover actual performance.

But more fundamentally, the difficulties here and elsewhere arise from the fact that for many of the problems on which we would like more light the relevant variables were not observed. Those variables which were observed were almost invariably excellently observed— observed with a degree of precision and reliability seldom achieved in the history of social science. The limitations are not inherent in the techniques, nor in the authors, whose judiciousness and imagination in interpretation leaves a deeply favorable impression. The difficulties seem rather to be those which are almost inseparable from the task of arriving at empirically adequate results on fundamental problems of social structure while doing research for administrative purposes.

However, *The American Soldier* also shows that where research is scrupulously executed on problems which are of administrative importance even though there fails to be complete congruity with our scientific and theoretical needs, it cannot fail to produce data sufficiently rich and sufficiently reliable to provide many new hypotheses, some of which are fairly well supported by the data, some of which are suggested by the data and all of which are a challenge to gather data with equal skill more centrally focused on the crucial theoretical problems which have been brought to our attention. And this is the achievement of the Research Branch, for which it is entitled to a worthy and prominent place in the growth of the empirical theory of society.

ROBERT K. MERTON and ALICE S. KITT

CONTRIBUTIONS TO THE THEORY OF REFERENCE GROUP BEHAVIOR

*T*HIS paper proceeds on the assumption that there is two-way traffic between social theory and empirical research. Systematic empirical materials help advance social theory by imposing the task and by affording the opportunity for interpretation along lines often unpremeditated, and social theory, in turn, defines the scope and enlarges the predictive value of empirical findings by indicating the conditions under which they hold. The systematic data of *The American Soldier,* in all their numerous variety, provide a useful occasion for examining the interplay of social theory and applied social research.

More particularly, we attempt to identify and to order the fairly numerous researches in *The American Soldier* which, by implication or by explicit statement, bear upon the theory of *reference group behavior.* (The empirical realities which this term denotes will presently be considered in some detail. It should be said here, however, that although the *term* "reference group" is not employed in these volumes, any more than it has yet found full acceptance in the vocabulary of sociology as distinct from social psychology, reference group *concepts* play an important part in the interpretative apparatus utilized by the Research Branch.)

At two points, we deal briefly with related subjects which are not, however, part and parcel of reference group theory. We review the statistical indices of group attributes and social structure as variously adopted in these researches, and attempt to indicate, though very briefly and programmatically, the specific value of *systematically* incorporating such indices in further research. And, in equally brief fashion, we point out how data analyzed by the Research Branch from a psychological standpoint can be supplemented and usefully re-worked from the standpoint of functional sociology.

A common procedure for extracting and attempting to develop the theoretical implications of *The American Soldier* is adopted throughout the paper. This entails the intensive re-examination of *cases* of research reported in these volumes, with an eye to subsuming the findings under higher-level abstractions or generalizations. In the volumes themselves, the authors austerely (and, in our judgment, wisely) limit their analysis to the interpretation of the behavior of soldiers and to the organizational contexts in which that behavior occurred. But manifestly, the analytical concepts hold not merely for the behavior of soldiers. By provisionally generalizing these concepts, we may be in a position to explore the wider implications of the materials for social theory.

Our discussion thus grows out of an internal analysis of every research study in these volumes in which some reference group concept was used by the authors as an interpretative variable. The object of collating these cases is to determine the points at which they invite extensions of the theory of reference group behavior which can be followed up through further strategically focused research. Occasionally, the effort is made to suggest how these theoretical extensions might be incorporated into designs for empirical research which will thus build upon the findings of the Research Branch. In this way, there may be provision for continuity in the interplay between cumulative theory and new research.

The inductive re-examination of cases admits also the linking of these reference group conceptions with other conceptions prevalent in social psychology and sociology which have not ordinarily been connected with the theory of reference group behavior. In the degree that such connections are established, *The American Soldier* will have served a further function of empirical research: the provisional consolidation of presently scattered fragments of theory.[1]

Along these lines, an effort will be made to indicate the coherence between reference group theory and conceptions of functional sociology. It appears that these deal with different facets of the same subject: the one centers on the processes through which men relate themselves to groups and refer their behavior to the values of these

[1] On this function, see Robert K. Merton, *Social Theory and Social Structure*, (Glencoe, Illinois, The Free Press, 1949) Chapter III, "The Bearing of Empirical Research on Sociological Theory."

groups; the other centers on the consequences of the processes primarily for social structures, but also for the individuals and groups involved in these structures. It will be found that reference group theory and functional sociology address different questions to the same phenomena but that these questions have reciprocal relevance.

Throughout, then, this essay aims to learn from *The American Soldier* what it has to yield for the current state of reference group theory and related theoretical problems. Committed as we are to the notion that the development of social theory requires a large measure of continuity, rather than a collection of self-contained and allegedly definitive results, this means that the present re-working of some of the materials in *The American Soldier* is itself a highly provisional phase in an ongoing development rather than a stable stopping point. Nor is it assumed, of course, that each and all of the extensions of reference group theory here proposed will in fact turn out to be sound; for like any other form of human activity, theorizing has its quota of risk. Indeed, it is when every hypothesis provisionally advanced at a given stage in the development of a discipline turns out to be apparently confirmed that the theorist has cause for alarm, since a record of unvarying success may indicate a defective and overly-compliant apparatus for confirmation rather than an unexceptionably sound theory.

THE CONCEPT OF RELATIVE DEPRIVATION

OF the various concepts employed by the authors of *The American Soldier* to interpret their multiform materials, there is one which takes a major place. This is the concept of relative deprivation. Its central significance is in some measure evidenced by its being one of the two concepts expressly called to the attention of the reader in the chapter introducing the two volumes. As the authors themselves put it, after a brief allusion to the conception of varying profiles, "Other conceptual tools, notably a theory of *relative deprivation,* also are introduced to help in more generally ordering otherwise disparate empirical findings." (I, 52)

Although the concept of relative deprivation is periodically utilized for the interpretation of variations in attitudes among different categories of men, varying, for example, with respect to age, education and marital status, it nowhere finds formal definition in the pages of these volumes. Nevertheless, as we shall presently discover, the outlines of this conception gradually emerge from the various instances in which it is put to use. It is in the very first instance of such use, for example, that the authors refer to the nature of the theoretical utility of the conception and to its possible kinship to other, established concepts of sociological theory:

"The idea [of relative deprivation] is simple, almost obvious, but its utility comes in reconciling data, especially in later chapters, where its applicability is not at first too apparent. The idea would seem to have a kinship to and, in part, include such well-known sociological concepts as "social frame of reference," "patterns of expectation," or "definitions of the situation." " (I, 125)

This absence of a formal definition of relative deprivation is no great handicap. In any case, the authors escape the well-established tradition of works in sociological theory to be replete with numerous definitions which remain unemployed. In place of an explicit definition of the concept we can assemble an array of all those occasions, scattered through the volumes and dealing with seemingly unrelated types of situations, in which the concept has been put to use by the authors, and in this way we can learn something of the actual operational character of the concept.

The following list represents, albeit in much abbreviated form, every research in which some version of the concept of relative deprivation (or a kindred concept, such as relative status) is explicitly drawn upon in *The American Soldier:*

1. *With reference to the drafted married man: "Comparing himself with his unmarried associates in the Army,* he could feel that induction demanded greater sacrifice from him than from them; and *comparing himself with his married civilian friends,* he could feel that he had been called on for sacrifices which they were escaping altogether." (I, 125)

2. "The average high school graduate or college man was a clear-cut candidate for induction; marginal cases on occupational grounds probably occurred much more often in groups with less educational attainment. On the average, the non high school man who was inducted *could point to more acquaintances* conceivably no more entitled to deferment than himself, who nonetheless had been deferred on occupational grounds . . . when they *compared themselves with their civilian friends* they may have been more likely to feel that

they were required to make sacrifices which *others like them* were excused from making." (I, 127)

3. "The concept of *relative deprivation* is particularly helpful in evaluating the role of education in satisfaction with status or job, as well as in some aspects of approval or criticism of the Army. . . . With higher levels of aspiration than the less educated, *the better educated man had more to lose in his own eyes and in the eyes of his friends* by failure to achieve some sort of status in the Army. Hence, frustration was greater for him than for others if a goal he sought was not attained. . . ." (I, 153)

4. ". . . the concept of differential deprivation and reward . . . may help us understand some of the psychological processes relevant to this problem. In general, it is of course true that the overseas soldier, *relative to soldiers still at home,* suffered a greater break with home ties and with many of the amenities of life in the United States to which he was accustomed. But it was also true that, *relative to the combat soldier,* the overseas soldier [in rear areas of an active theater] not in combat and not likely to get into combat suffered far less deprivation than the actual fighting man." (I, 172)

5. "The concept of differential deprivation would lead us to look further for a reason why the actually more deprived group of soldiers seemed little more critical than the less deprived group . . . the less *the differential between officers and men* in the enjoyment of scarce privileges—the extreme case being that of actual combat—the less likely was the enlisted man to be critical of the officers and the easier it was for him to accept the inevitability of deprivation." (I, 181)

6. ". . . as would be expected . . . those soldiers who had advanced slowly *relative to other soldiers of equal longevity* in the Army were the most critical of the Army's promotion opportunities. *But relative rate of advancement can be based on different standards by different classes of the Army population.* For example, a grade school man who became a corporal after a year of service would have had a more rapid rate of promotion *compared with most of his friends at the same educational level* than would a college man who rose to the same grade in a year. Hence we would expect, at a given rank and a given longevity, that the better educated would be more likely than others to complain of the slowness of promotion. . . . A similar phenomenon appeared to operate between different branches of the service." (I, 250)

7. "From the studies of enlisted men reported previously in this chapter, it would be expected that attitudes of officers about promotion, like those of enlisted men, would reflect some relationship with level of expectation and with level of achievement *relative to that of one's acquaintances.* Thus we would expect a captain who had been in grade a long time *compared with other captains* to be less happy about the promotion situation than a lieutenant in grade a relatively short time." (I, 279)

8. "... it seems likely that both Northern and Southern Negroes may have been considerably influenced in their overall adjustment by other psychological compensations in being stationed in the South, which can be understood if we look at their situation as one of *relative status.*

"*Relative to most Negro civilians whom he saw in Southern towns,* the Negro soldier had a position of comparative wealth and dignity." (I, 563)

9. "Putting it simply, the psychological values of Army life to the Negro soldier in the South *relative to the Southern Negro civilian* greatly exceeded the psychological values of Army life to the Negro soldier in the North *relative to the Northern Negro civilian.*" (I, 564)

These nine excerpts touch upon the core interpretative statements in which the notion of relative deprivation or affiliated concepts were expressly utilized to interpret otherwise anomalous or inconsistent findings.[2] To these explicit uses of the concept we shall later add several research cases not subjected by the authors to interpretation in terms of reference group concepts which nevertheless seem explicated by such concepts.

In all these cases, it should be noted, the concept of relative deprivation serves the same theoretical purpose: it is used as an interpretative intervening variable. The researches were designed to study the sentiments and attitudes of American soldiers—their attitudes toward induction, for example, or their appraisals of chances for promotion. These attitudes are typically taken as the *dependent variables.* The analysis of data finds that these attitudes differ among soldiers of varying status—for example, older or married men exhibited more resentment toward induction than younger or unmarried men; those enjoying the status of high school and college graduates were less likely to be optimistic about their prospects for promotion in the Army. These status attributes are in general taken provisionally as the *independent variables.* Once these relationships between independent and dependent variables are established, the problem is one of accounting for them: of inferring how it comes to be that the better educated are typically less optimistic about their chances for promotion or how it comes to be that the married man exhibits greater resentment over his induction into military

[2] It thus appears, as we shall have occasion to note in some detail, that the concept of relative deprivation grows out of what has been called "the serendipity pattern" of the impact of empirical research upon theory, namely, "the fairly common experience of observing an *unanticipated, anomalous and strategic datum* which becomes the occasion for developing a new theory or for extending an existing theory." See Merton, *op. cit.,* 98.

service. At this point of interpretation, the concept of relative deprivation is introduced, so that the pattern of analysis becomes somewhat as follows: the married man (independent variable) more often questions the legitimacy of his induction (dependent variable), because he appraises the situation within the frame of reference (interpretative variable) yielded by comparing himself with other married men still in civilian life, who escaped the draft entirely, or with unmarried men in the Army, whose induction did not call for comparable sacrifice. We may thus tag the major function of the concept of relative deprivation as that of a provisional after-the-fact interpretative concept which is intended to help explain the variation in attitudes expressed by soldiers of differing social status. And since after-the-fact interpretations have a distinctive place in the ongoing development of theory, we shall later want to consider this characteristic of the concept of relative deprivation at some length.[3]

The collation of these key excerpts serves as something more than a thin summary of the original materials. Since the studies employing the concept of relative deprivation deal with diverse subject-matters, they are scattered through the pages of *The American Soldier* and thus are not likely to be examined in terms of their mutual theoretical linkages. The juxtaposition of excerpts admits of a virtually *simultaneous inspection* of the several interpretations and, in turn, permits us to detect the central categories which were evidently taken by the Research Branch as the *bases of comparison* presumably implicit in the observed attitudes and evaluations of soldiers. And once the categories of analysis employed by the Re-

[3] At this point it need be noted only in passing that it is premature to assume that *ex post facto* interpretations are *in principle* not susceptible to empirical nullification. To argue this, as Nathan Glazer does in his overly-quick rejection of the concept of relative deprivation, is to be opaque to the interplay between theory and research in the *historical development* of a discipline. As we shall see, there is no foundation for saying, as Glazer does, that the notion of relative deprivation cannot conceivably be nullified: "Thus, [with the concept of relative deprivation] a little imagination will permit us to cover any conceivable outcome. . ." And later, he claims, that the conception "cannot be refuted by facts, and it will be found to hold true whatever the outcome of a given set of data." It will presently become clear that propositions incorporating the concept of relative deprivation are readily subject to empirical nullification, if they are in fact untrue. To appreciate one reason for our stress on empirically-oriented sociological theory as an ongoing *development*, see the consequences of neglecting this fact as exhibited in Nathan Glazer, "'The American Soldier' as Science," *Commentary*, 1949, 8, 487-96.

search Branch are detected, their logical connections can be worked out, thus leading to formulations which seem to have significance for the further development of reference group theory.

If we proceed inductively, we find that the frames of reference for the soldiers under observation by the Research Branch were provisionally assumed to be of three kinds. First of all are those cases in which the attitudes or judgments of the men were held to be influenced by comparison with the situation of others with whom they were in *actual association,* in sustained social relations, such as the "married civilian friends" of the soldier in excerpt 1, or the "acquaintances" of the non-high-school man in excerpt 2.

A second implied basis of comparison is with those men who are in some pertinent respect *of the same status* or in the *same social category,* as in the case of the captain who compares his lot "with other captains" in excerpt 7 without any implication that they are necessarily in direct social interaction.

And third, comparison is assumed with those who are in some pertinent respect of *different status* or in a *different social category,* as in the case of the non-combat soldier compared with combat men in excerpt 4, or the enlisted men compared with officers in excerpt 5 (again without social interaction between them being necessarily implied).

For the most part, as we learn from this inspection of cases, the groups or individuals presumably taken as bases for comparison by soldiers do not fall simply into one *or* another of these three types, but involve various combinations of them. Most commonly, presumed comparison is with *associates* of the same status, as the grade-school man compared with friends of the same educational level in excerpt 6, or with various unassociated "others" who are of a *status similar in some salient respect and dissimilar in other respects,* such as the Negro soldier who compares himself with the Negro civilian in excerpts 8 and 9.

If these attributes of the individuals or groups serving as presumed frames of reference are arranged in a matrix, then the conceptual structure of the notion of relative deprivation (and affiliated concepts) becomes more readily visible. The schematic arrangement enables us to locate, not only the frames of comparative reference most often utilized in the interpretation of data by the Research Branch, but additional possible frames of reference which found little place in their interpretation. It thus affords an occasion for systematically exploring the theoretical nature of relative deprivation as an interpretative tool and for indicating the points at which it possibly deepens and broadens the apposite theory of reference group behavior.

In substance, the groups or individuals taken as points of reference in the nine excerpts are explicitly characterized by these few attributes. The presence of sustained social relations between the individual and those taken as a basis for comparison indicates that they are to this degree, in a common *membership group* or *in-group*, and their absence, that they are in a *non-membership* or *out-group*. When it comes to comparative status, the implied classification is slightly more complex: the individuals comprising the base of comparison may be of the same status as the subject or different, and if different, the status may be higher, lower, or unranked. The array of reference points implied in the interpretations of the Research Branch thus appears as follows:

ATTRIBUTES OF INDIVIDUALS, SOCIAL CATEGORIES AND GROUPS TAKEN AS A FRAME OF COMPARATIVE REFERENCE BY INDIVIDUALS *

IN SUSTAINED SOCIAL RELATIONS WITH INDIVIDUAL	SAME STATUS	DIFFERENT SOCIAL STATUS		
		Higher	*Lower*	*Unranked*
Yes—(membership- or in-group)	#1 married friends #2 non high school acquaintances #6 friends at same educational level	#5 officers	#8,9 Negro civilians in South	#3 friends #7 acquaintances
ORIENTATIONS OF INDIVIDUAL TO				
No—(non-membership or out-group)	#4 soldiers in U.S. or in active combat #6 soldiers of equal longevity #7 other captains	#5 officers	#8,9 Negro civilians in South	

* The numbers refer to the appropriate excerpts which are here being provisionally classified.

Examination of this matrix of variables implied by the notion of relative deprivation at once directs attention to several empirical and theoretical problems. These problems, as will presently become evident, not only bear specifically upon the concept of relative deprivation but more generally upon a theory of reference group behavior.

It will be noted from the preliminary survey of cases contained in the matrix that, at times, the authors of *The American Soldier* assume that individuals take as a base for self-reference the situation of people with whom they are in direct social interaction: primarily, the in-group of friends and associates. At others, the assumed frame of reference is yielded by social categories of people—combat soldiers, other captains, etc.—with whom the individual is not in sustained social relations. In order to highlight the connection of the concept of relative deprivation with reference group theory, these "others" with whom the individual does not interact are here designated as non-membership groups or out-groups.[4] Since both membership groups and non-membership groups, in-groups and out-groups, have in fact been taken as assumed social frames of reference in these interpretations, this at once leads to a general question of central importance to a developing theory of reference group behavior: *under which conditions are associates within one's own groups taken as a frame of reference for self-evaluation and attitude-formation, and under which conditions do out-groups or non-membership groups provide the significant frame of reference?*

[4] We recognize that this sentence is replete with implicit problems which it would be premature to consider at this point. It involves, for example, the problem of criteria of "membership" in a group. Insofar as frequency of social interaction is one such criterion, we must recognize that the boundaries between groups are anything but sharply drawn. Rather, "members" of given groups are variously connected with other groups of which they are not *conventionally* regarded as members, though the sociologist might have ample basis for including them in these latter groups, by virtue of their frequent social interaction with its conventional membership. So, too, we are here momentarily by-passing the question of distinctions between social *groups* and social *categories,* the latter referring to established statuses between the occupants of which there may be little or no interaction. It will also be noticed by some that the formulation contained in *The American Soldier* extends the formulations by such theorists of social psychology as George H. Mead who confined himself to *membership groups* as significant frames of reference in his concept of the "generalized other" and in his account of the formation of self-attitudes. All this bears only passing mention at this point since it will be considered at a more appropriate place.

Reference groups are, in principle, almost innumerable: any of the groups of which one is a member, and these are comparatively few, as well as groups of which one is not a member, and these are, of course, legion, can become points of reference for shaping one's attitudes, evaluations and behavior. And this gives rise to another set of problems requiring theoretical formulation and further empirical inquiry. For, as the matrix arrangement of cases drawn from *The American Soldier* plainly suggests, the individual may be oriented toward any one *or more* of the various kinds of groups and statuses—membership groups and non-membership groups, statuses like his own or if different, either higher, lower, or not socially ranked with respect to his own. This, then, locates a further problem: if *multiple* groups or statuses, with their possibly divergent or even contradictory norms and standards, are taken as a frame of reference by the individual, how are these discrepancies resolved? [5]

These initial questions may help establish the range of our inquiry. That men act in a social frame of reference yielded by the groups of which they are a part is a notion undoubtedly ancient and probably sound. Were this alone the concern of reference group theory, it would merely be a new term for an old focus in sociology, which has always been centered on the group determination of behavior. There is, however, the further fact that men frequently orient themselves to groups *other than their own* in shaping their behavior and evaluations, and it is the problems centered about this fact of orientation to non-membership groups that constitute the distinctive concern of reference group theory. Ultimately, of course, the theory must be generalized to the point where it can account for *both* membership- and non-membership-group orientations, but immediately its major task is to search out the processes through which individuals relate themselves to groups to which they do *not* belong.

In general, then, reference group theory aims to systematize the determinants and consequences of those processes of evaluation and self-appraisal in which the individual takes the values or standards

[5] Though this problem is reminiscent of the traditional but only slightly clarified problem of conflict between multiple group *affiliations* or multiple *roles,* it is by no means identical with it. For, as we have seen, frames of reference are yielded not only by one's *own* membership groups or one's own statuses, but by non-membership groups and other statuses, as well.

of other individuals and groups as a comparative frame of reference.[6]

From our brief preliminary examination, it appears that the researches in *The American Soldier* utilizing the concept of relative deprivation can act as a catalyst quickening theoretical clarification and the formulation of problems for further empirical study. But the precise nature of these formulations can be better seen through a detailed examination of several of these cases after we have more definitely connected the concept of relative deprivation with the theory of reference group behavior.

RELATIVE *DEPRIVATION* OR *RELATIVE* DEPRIVATION

IN developing their concept of relative deprivation, the authors of *The American Soldier* have, on the whole, centered their attention on the deprivation component rather than the relative component of the concept. They have, so to say, focused on relative *deprivation* rather than on *relative* deprivation. The reason for this seems both apparent and understandable, in view of the conspicuously deprivational character of the Army situations with which they dealt. By and large, American men viewed service in the armed forces as at best a grim and reluctantly accepted necessity:

"The vast majority of men did not come into the Army voluntarily . . . the acceptance of the soldier role probably tended to be passive in character, at least with respect to initial attitudes . . . the passive attitude toward military service implied a relative absence of identification with broad social goals which would serve to deflect attention away from the day-to-day frustrations in the new environment. Recruits were therefore likely to be sharply aware of the deprivational features of Army life." (I, 208-9)

It was, then, the patterns of response to a basically deprivational situation which most often called for study and it was primarily in the service of interpreting these patterns of response that the concept of relative deprivation was developed. As the term, relative

[6] This summary and elliptical statement will be amplified in later sections of the paper.

deprivation, itself suggests, the concept was primarily utilized to help account for feelings of dissatisfaction, particularly in cases where the objective situation would at first glance not seem likely to provoke such feelings. This is not to say that the concept was wholly confined to interpreting the feelings of dissatisfaction, deprivation, or injustice among soldiers, since the presumed practice of comparing one's own situation with that of others often resulted in a state of relative satisfaction. In the main, however, satisfactions stemming from such comparison with others are seen in the role of offsetting excessive dissatisfaction in cases of multiple comparison: for example, the dissatisfaction of the noncombat man overseas, presumably reinforced by comparison with those serving in the United States, is tempered by satisfaction with his status as compared with the combat man. (I, 173)

As the authors themselves evidently recognize, "deprivation" is the incidental and particularized component of the concept of relative deprivation, whereas the more significant nucleus of the concept is its stress upon social and psychological experience as "relative." This may be seen from the text at the point where the authors introduce the notion of relative deprivation and suggest its kinship to such other sociological concepts as "social frame of reference, patterns of expectation, or definitions of the situation." (I, 125) It is the *relative* component, the standards of comparison in self-evaluation, that these concepts have in common.

By freeing the concept of relative deprivation from confinement to the particular data which it was initially designed to interpret, it may become generalized and related to a larger body of theory. Relative deprivation can provisionally be regarded as a special concept in reference group theory. And since *The American Soldier* provides systematic empirical data and not merely discursive views on the concept of relative deprivation, the way is possibly opened for progressively clarifying crucial variables so that further cumulative research bearing on the theory can be mapped out.

All this, however, is still programmatic. Whether *The American Soldier* does indeed have these functions for reference group theory can only be determined through inspection, at closer range than we have yet attempted, of the researches in these volumes bearing upon the theory.

The analysis of these several cases is intended to document and to elaborate the emergence of those problems of reference group theory briefly foreshadowed in the foregoing pages and to indicate further related problems which have not yet received notice. Toward this end, the essential facts and basic interpretation as these are set out by the Research Branch will be summarized for each case, and followed by a statement of its apparent implications for the advancement of reference group theory.

By way of preview, it may be said that these cases generate the formulation of a wide range of specific problems which will be taken up in detail and which are here roughly indicated by the following list of headings:

> *Membership-groups operating as reference groups;*
> *Conflicting reference groups and mutually sustaining reference groups;*
> *Uniformities of behavior derived from reference group theory;*
> *Statistical indices of social structure;*
> *Reference group theory and social mobility;*
> *Functions of positive orientations to non-membership groups;*
> *Social processes sustaining or curbing these orientations;*
> *Psychological and social functions of institutions regulating passage from one membership-group to another;*
> *and*
> *A review of concepts kindred to reference group theory.*

MEMBERSHIP-GROUP AS REFERENCE GROUP

Case #1. This research deals with soldiers' evaluations of promotion opportunities as these were elicited by the question, "Do you think a soldier with ability has a good chance for promotion?" A generalized finding, necessarily and too much abbreviated in this summary, holds that for each level of longevity, rank and education, "the *less* the promotion opportunity afforded by a branch or combination of branches, the *more favorable* the opinion tends to be toward promotion opportunity." (I, 256) Within the limits of the data in hand,[7] this paradoxical response of greater satisfaction with

---

[7] It is important that we introduce this caveat, for it is scarcely probable that this relationship between actual mobility rates and individual satisfaction

opportunities for mobility in the very branches characterized by less mobility finds clear demonstration. Thus, although the Air Corps had a conspicuously high rate of promotion, Air Corps men were definitely far more critical of chances for promotion than, say, men in the Military Police, where the objective chances for promotion "were about the worst in any branch of the Army." So, too, at any given rank and longevity, the better educated soldiers, despite their notably higher rates of promotion in general, were the more critical of opportunities for promotion.

This paradox is provisionally explained by the Research Branch as a result of evaluations occurring within the frame of reference provided by group rates of promotion. A generally high rate of mobility induces excessive hopes and expectations among members of the group so that each is more likely to experience a sense of frustration in his present position and disaffection with the chances for promotion. As it is put by the authors, "Without reference to the theory that such opinions represent a relationship between their expectations and their achievements *relative to others in the same boat with them,* such a finding would be paradoxical indeed." (I, 251, italics supplied)

Theoretical implications. First of all, it should be noted that it was an anomalous finding which apparently elicited the hypothesis that evaluations of promotion chances are a function of expectations and achievements "relative to others in the same boat with them." And, in turn, the raw uninterpreted finding appears anomalous only because it is inconsistent with the commonsense assumption that, in general, evaluations will correspond to the objective facts of the case. According to common sense, marked differences in objective rates of promotion would presumably be reflected in corresponding differences in assessments of chances for promotion. Had such correspondences been empirically found, there would seemingly have been little occasion for advancing this hypothesis of a group frame of reference. As it turns out, the data suggest that men define the situation differently. But it is not enough to mention these "definitions of the situation"; it is necessary to *account for* them. And the

with mobility chances holds throughout the entire range of variation. If promotion rates were reduced to practically zero in some of these groups, would one then find an even more "favorable opinion" of promotion chances? Presumably, the relationship is curvilinear, and this requires the sociologist to work out toward the conditions under which the observed linear relation fails to obtain.

function of the concept of relative deprivation (as with other concepts of reference groups) is precisely that of helping to account for observed definitions of a situation.

In this case, it required *systematic* empirical data, such as those assembled in *The American Soldier*, to *detect* the anomalous pattern, not detectable through impressionistic observation. And this illustrates a basic role of systematic empirical research in reaching unanticipated, anomalous and strategic findings that exert pressure for initiating or extending theory.[8] The data and the hypothesis advanced to account for them open up further theoretical and research problems, which can here receive bare mention rather than the full exposition they deserve.

The hypothesis makes certain important assumptions about *the* group taken as a point of reference by the soldiers and thus affecting their level of satisfaction with promotion opportunities. This assumption is stated, as we have seen, in the form that evaluations are "relative to others in the same boat." And the data are consistent with the view that four groups or social categories have presumably been taken as a context or frame of reference: men with similar longevity, similar educational status, similar rank, and in the same branch of the Service.

Now, this hypothesis, suitably generalized, raises all manner of further questions germane to reference group theory and requiring renewed inquiry and analysis. Which conditions predispose toward this pattern of selecting people of the same status or group as significant points of reference? The idiomatic phrase, "in the same boat," raises the same sociological problems as the idiomatic phrase, "keeping up with the Joneses." Who are the specific Joneses, in various social structures, with whom people try to keep up? their close associates? people in immediately higher social or income strata with whom they have contact? When are the Joneses people whom one never meets, but whom one hears about (through public media of communication, for example)? How does it happen that some select the Joneses to keep up with, others the Cabots, or the Cassidys, and finally that some don't try to keep up at all?

In other words, the hypothesis advanced in *The American Soldier* regarding individuals of similar status being taken as frames of reference for self-evaluations at once opens up an interrelated array

[8] This "creative function" of empirical research for theory warrants greater attention than is accorded it in Merton, *op. cit.*, 98-102, 374-5.

of problems, amenable to research and constituting important further links in the development of reference group theory. When are one's membership-groups *not* taken as reference groups in arriving at evaluations? After all, many men were apparently aware of the differences between the table of organization of the Air Corps and their own branch. When would these mobility rates among men *not* in the same boat affect their own level of satisfaction? And these sociological problems, though they might have originated elsewhere, were in fact generated by the anomalous empirical findings developed and provisionally interpreted in this study.

That new systematic experience, such as that represented by the data and hypothesis of *The American Soldier*, does indeed generate the formulation of further theoretical questions is suggested by glancing briefly at the somewhat contrasting work of a notable theorist in social psychology, George H. Mead, who did not steep himself in *systematic* empirical materials. Mead was, of course, a forerunner and an important forerunner in the history of reference group theory, particularly with respect to his central conception, variously expressed in his basic writings, but adequately enough captured in the statement that "The individual experiences himself as such, not directly, but only indirectly, from the particular standpoints of other individual members *of the same group*, or from the generalized standpoint of the social group as a whole *to which he belongs.*" [9]

In this formulation and in numerous others like it,[10] Mead in effect advances the hypothesis that it is the groups of which the individual *is a member* that yield the significant frame of reference for self-evaluations. And this he *illustrates* abundantly with anecdotal instances drawn from his varied personal experience and insightful reflection. But, possibly because he was not exposed to *systematic* empirical evidence, which might prove seemingly inconsistent with this formulation *at specific points,* he was not driven to ask whether, indeed, the group taken as a point of reference by the individual is invariably the group of which he is a member. The terms "another," "the other" and "others" turn up on literally hundreds of occasions in Mead's exposition of the thesis that the development of the social self entails response to the attitudes of

[9] George H. Mead, *Mind, Self and Society* (The University of Chicago Press, 1934), 138 (italics supplied).
[10] For example, see *ibid.*, 151-156, 193-194.

"another" or of "others." But the varying status of "these others" presumably taken as frames of self-reference is glossed over, except for the repeated statement that they are members of "the" group. Thus, Mead, and those of his followers who also eschew empirical research, had little occasion to move ahead to the question of conditions under which non-membership-groups may also constitute a significant frame of reference.

Not only does the research from *The American Soldier* point directly to that question, but it leads further to the problems raised by the facts of *multiple* group affiliations and *multiple* reference groups. It reminds us that theory and research must move on to consider the *dynamics of selection* of reference groups among the individual's several membership groups: when do individuals orient themselves to others in their occupational group, in their congeniality groups, or in their religious group? How can we characterize the *structure of the social situation* which leads to one rather than another of these several group affiliations being taken as the significant context?

Following out the hypothesis advanced in the text, we note as well the problem raised by the simultaneous operation of multiple reference groups. Further steps call for study of the *dynamic processes* involved in the theoretically supposed counter-tendencies induced by multiple reference groups. For example, what are the dynamics of evaluation, and not merely the final evaluation, of the mobility system among college graduates relatively new to the Military Police: on the hypothesis advanced in *The American Soldier*, they would be moved, through reference to the status of other college graduates, toward dissatisfaction, but as comparatively new replacements and as M.P.'s they would be moved toward relative satisfaction. How are these counter-tendencies ultimately resolved in the evaluation which comes to the notice of the observer?

Turning finally to the dependent variable in this study, we note that it consists in soldiers' evaluations of the *institutional system* of promotion in the Army, and not to *self-evaluations* of personal achievement within that system.[11] The men were in effect asked to

[11] True, as the text implies, the institutional evaluations probably reflect soldiers' assessments of their own position as compared with their legitimate expectations, but this is not at issue here. The reference group hypothesis attempts to account for variations in the nature of these expectations in terms of the social contexts provided by the distribution of statuses in significant in-groups.

appraise the system of promotion in terms of its effectiveness and legitimacy, as can be seen from the carefully worded question which elicited their judgments: "Do you think a soldier with ability has a good chance for promotion?"

This introduces a problem, deserving attention which it has not yet received: do the two types of evaluations, self-appraisals and appraisals of institutional arrangements, involve similar mechanisms of reference group behavior? At this point, it is clear that research is needed to discover the structure of those social situations which typically elicit self-evaluations or internalized judgments—for example, where comparison with the achievements of specified others leads to invidious self-depreciation, to a sense of personal inadequacy—and the structure of those situations which typically lead to evaluations of institutions or externalized judgments—for example, where comparison with others leads to a sense of institutional inadequacies, to the judgment that the social system militates against any close correspondence between individual merit and social reward.

Here, as with many of *The American Soldier* researches, the implications of procedure, analysis, and interpretation are of course not confined to further studies of behavior of soldiers. They bear upon some of the more strategic areas of study in the larger social system. For example, the sociological factors which lead men to consider their own, relatively low, social position as legitimate, as well as those which lead them to construe their position as a result of defective and possibly unjustified social arrangements clearly comprise a problem area of paramount theoretical and political importance. When are relatively slim life-chances taken by men as a normal and expectable state of affairs which they attribute to their own personal inadequacies and when are they regarded as the results of an arbitrary social system of mobility, in which rewards are not proportioned to ability?[12] The concepts of relative depriva-

[12] Such questions have of course been raised on numerous previous occasions. But they have ordinarily been regarded as distinct and self-contained problems of interest in their own right and not as special problems subsumable under a theory of reference group behavior. For example, it has been suggested that conspicuously "successful" individuals who have risen rapidly in a social hierarchy and who are much in the public eye, function as models or reference-figures testifying to a mobility-system in which, apparently, careers are still open to talents. For some, these success-models are living testimony to the legitimacy of the institutional system and in this comparative context, the individual deflects criticism of the system onto himself. See R. K. Merton,

tion and of relative reward help transfer these much-discussed but little-analyzed patterns of behavior from the realm of impressionistic speculation to that of systematic research.

MULTIPLE REFERENCE GROUPS

SEVERAL researches in *The American Soldier* afford occasion for looking into theoretical problems arising from the conception that multiple reference groups provide contexts for evaluations by individuals. Two of these cases have been selected for attention here because they apparently exhibit different patterns of multiple comparison: in the first of these, multiple reference groups provide contexts which operate at cross-purposes; in the second, they provide contexts which are mutually sustaining.

Conflicting reference groups. Case #2. During the latter part of 1943 and the early part of 1944, the Research Branch conducted a series of surveys from which they developed a picture of differences in attitudes (reflecting personal adjustment) of noncombat men overseas and of men stationed in the United States. Though consistent, the differences in attitudes were not large. Among noncoms still in the United States, for example, 41 per cent reported themselves as "usually in good spirits" in comparison with 32 per cent of those overseas; 76 per cent of the one held that the "Army is run pretty well or very well" compared with 63 per cent of the other. (I, 167, Chart IV) But since other surveys found that the major concern of the men overseas was to get back home (I, 187), the authors observe that considerably greater differences in attitudes expressing personal adjustment might well have been expected.

Three factors are tentatively adduced to account for the absence of greater differences, factors operating to curb the expectable [13]

M. Fiske and A. Curtis, *Mass Persuasion* (New York: Harper, 1946), 152 ff.; Merton, *op. cit.*, 137 ff. But these observations remain impressionistic and anecdotal, since they do not provide *systematic* designs for inquiry into this behavior along the lines suggested by the researches of *The American Soldier.*

[13] Here we see again that the concept of relative deprivation (just as the notion of "definition of the situation" generally) is introduced to account for an apparently anomalous finding. In this case, the finding seemingly deviates, not

degree of dissatisfaction expressed by the noncombat soldier overseas. Of these, we attend only to the interpretative concept of "differential deprivation and reward" [14] which, it will be remembered from an earlier excerpt,

"may help us understand some of the psychological processes relevant to this problem. In general, it is of course true that the overseas soldier, *relative to soldiers still at home,* suffered a greater break with home ties and with many of the amenities of life in the United States to which he was accustomed. But it was also true that, *relative to the combat soldier,* the overseas soldier not in combat and not likely to enter into combat suffered far less deprivation than the actual fighting man." (I, 172)

Theoretical implications. In effect, the authors suggest that two contexts of comparison, operating at cross-purposes, affected the evaluations of overseas noncombat troops. What, then, can be learned from this case about the grounds on which certain contexts rather than others become pertinent for such evaluations?

It should be noted at the outset that the status of those constituting the contexts of evaluation is, in some significant respect, *similar* to the status of the men making the evaluation. Thus, the soldiers still at home are similar in that they too are not in combat, and the combat soldiers are similar in that they too are overseas. Beyond this, other similarities and dissimilarities, pertinent to the situation, affect the resulting evaluations in contrasting ways. Thus, the overseas noncombat soldier is, by the standards of Army life, worse off than the soldier at home in that he is comparatively deprived of amenities and cut off from social ties, and better off than the combat soldier in that he is not exposed to the same measure of deprivation and risk. It is as though he had said, "Bad off as we are, the

---

from common sense expectation merely, but from other facts uncovered in the course of research. It would thus seem to illustrate the type of serendipity pattern in research in which "the observation is anomalous, surprising, either because it seems inconsistent with prevailing theory or with other established facts. In either case, the seeming inconsistency provokes curiosity; it stimulates the investigator to 'make sense of the datum.'" Merton, *Social Theory and Social Structure,* 98-99.

[14] The other two are, first, physical selection since men overseas had to meet more rigorous standards and second, "a sense of the significance of one's army job." In this latter connection, the authors remark: "While the difference between theaters . . . cannot prove or disprove hypotheses, the fact that, on the average, United States-overseas differences on attitudes toward Army jobs were negligible or reversed—as compared with United States-overseas differences in personal esprit or attitudes toward the Army—is a fact not to be overlooked." (I, 173)

others are worse off," a comparison not seldom adopted by those
who would accommodate themselves to their position. His definition
of his situation is then presumably the resultant of these counter-
acting patterns of comparison.

This suggests the general hypothesis that some similarity in status
attributes between the individual and the reference group must be
perceived or imagined, in order for the comparison to occur at all.
Once this minimal similarity obtains,[15] other similarities and differences pertinent to the situation, will provide the context for shaping evaluations. Consequently, this focuses the attention of the
theorist immediately upon the factors which produce a sense of
pertinent similarity between statuses, since these will help determine which groups are called into play as comparative contexts.
The underlying similarities of status among members of in-groups,
singled out by Mead as *the* social context, thus appear as only one
special, though obviously important, basis for the selection of
reference groups. Out-groups may also involve *some* similarity of
status.

By implication, the hypothesis of the Research Branch at this
point provides a clue to the factors affecting the selection of reference groups. The hypothesis does not hold that the two categories
of men—the combat men overseas and the noncombat men at home
—constituted the *only* ones with which *any particular individual*
among the overseas combat men compared himself. He may indeed
have compared his lot with that of numerous and diverse others
—a civilian friend in a cushy job back home, a cousin enjoying life
as a war correspondent, an undrafted movie star whom he had read
about in a magazine. But such comparisons by an individual, precisely because they involve personal frames of reference, might well
be idiosyncratic. They would not provide contexts *common* to
(many or most of) the individuals in the status of overseas non-

[15] This minimum of status similarity apparently presupposed by reference
group behavior clearly requires systematic study. *Some* similarity in status can
of course always be found, depending only on the breadth of the status category. One can compare oneself with others, if only in the most general social
capacity of "human being." And more germane to the case in question, the overseas combat man could (and did) compare himself with the noncombat man back
home by virtue of their similar status as soldiers, and with civilians by virtue
of their similar status as young adult American males. The theoretical and
research problem at this point is to determine how the structure of the social
situation encourages certain status-similarities to become the basis for such
comparisons, and leads other status-similarities to be ignored as "irrelevant."

combat men. To the degree that they are idiosyncratic, they would vary at random among the various categories of soldiers. Consequently, they would not aggregate into statistically significant differences of attitudes between *groups* or *social categories* of soldiers.

In other words, the statistics of *The American Soldier* on differential definitions of their situation among combat men,[16] overseas noncombat men and men still in the United States are taken to manifest the impact of *socially structured* reference groups more or less common to men in each category. It is not mere indolence or lack of insight which keeps the sociologist from seeking to track down all the comparative contexts which hold for any given individual; it is, rather, that many of these contexts are idiosyncratic, not shared by a large fraction of other individuals within the same group or social category. The comparative statistics in *The American Soldier* are plainly not intended to manifest and cannot manifest those numerous private contexts peculiar to individuals and hence varying at random to the social category. One does not look to these sociological data for idiosyncratic contexts of appraisal.

The reference groups here hypothesized, then, are not mere artifacts of the authors' arbitrary scheme of classification. Instead, they appear to be frames of reference held in common by a proportion of individuals within a social category sufficiently large to give rise to definitions of the situation characteristic of that category. And these frames of reference are common because they are patterned by the social structure. In the present case, for example, the degree of closeness to combat provides a socially organized and socially emphasized basis of comparison among the three categories of soldiers—overseas combat, overseas noncombat, and troops back home. It is, accordingly, categories such as these which provide the *common* comparative contexts for definition of the situation among these men. This is not to deny that other contexts may be of great consequence to particular individuals within each of these social categories. But these become relevant for the sociologist only if they are shared sufficiently to lead to group differences in evaluations.

In these pages, *The American Soldier* affords a clue, and possibly an important clue, for solving the sociological problem of finding

[16] *The American Soldier* does not supply data on the attitudes of combat men at this point in the text, although apposite data are found at other places in the volumes. (*e.g.,* I, 111)

the common residual which constitutes the reference groups distinctive for those in social status category.

There is another problem implicit here about which little can be learned from this case: what are the patterns of response among members of a group or status category when they are subject to multiple reference groups operating at cross-purposes? In the present case, the net evaluation of their lot among overseas noncombat men apparently represented a compromise, intermediate between the evaluations of noncombat men at home and of men in actual combat. But it is not implied by the authors of *The American Soldier* that this is the only pattern of response under such circumstances. It is possible, for example, that when several membership groups exert diverse and conflicting pressures for self-appraisal, the individual tends to adopt other, non-membership groups as a frame of reference. In any event, there arises the large and imperfectly defined problem, previously alluded to, of searching out the processes of coming to terms with such conflicting pressures.[17] That the social scientists of the Research Branch were cognizant of this line of inquiry, emerging from their wartime studies, is suggested by the fact that the director, Stouffer, is now developing researches on the varying patterns of response to the simultaneous but conflicting demands of primary groups and of formal organizational authorities.[18]

Mutually sustaining reference groups. Case #3. In its bare outlines, this study (I, 122-130) is concerned with the feelings of legitimacy ascribed by men to their induction into service. Patterns of response to the question, "At the time you came into the Army,[19]

[17] Thus, a study of political behavior found that individuals, under crosspressure, were more likely to delay their final vote decision. And as the senior author goes on to say: "But such delay is not the only possible reaction. Other alternatives range all the way from individual neurotic reactions, such as an inability to make any decision at all, to intellectual solutions which might lead to new social movements. Many of the baffling questions about the relationship between individual attitudes and social environment may be answered when these problems of cross-pressures and reactions to them are thoroughly and properly studied." P. F. Lazarsfeld, Bernard Berelson, and Hazel Gaudet, *The People's Choice* (New York: Columbia University Press, 1948, second edition), xxii.

[18] Samuel Stouffer, "An analysis of conflicting social norms," *American Sociological Review*, 1949, 14, 707-717.

[19] Since it is not germane to our chief purpose, we have made no effort throughout this paper to report the numerous technical steps taken by the Research Branch to determine the adequacy of their data. But readers of *The American Soldier* will be well aware of the diverse and often imaginative pro-

did you think you should have been deferred?" showed that married men, over 20 years of age, who had not been graduated from high school were most likely to maintain that they should have been deferred. In this status category, 41 per cent, as compared, for example, with only 10 per cent of unmarried high school graduates under 20 years of age, claimed that they should not have been inducted at all. More generally, it is found that the statuses of age, marital condition and educational level are consistently related with willingness for military service.

Since the hypotheses advanced to account for these findings are essentially of the same type for each of the three status categories, we need concern ourselves here with only one of these for illustrative purposes. As we have seen in an excerpt from this case, the authors provisionally explain the greater reluctance for service of married men in terms of the standards of comparison yielded by reference to two other status categories. The key interpretative passage bears repetition at this point:

"*Comparing himself with his unmarried associates* in the Army, he could feel that induction demanded greater sacrifice from him than from them; and *comparing himself with his married civilian friends* he could feel that he had been called on for sacrifices which they were escaping altogether. Hence the married man, on the average, was more likely than others to come into the Army with reluctance and, possibly, a sense of injustice." (I, 125, italics supplied)

Theoretical implications. However brief and tentative the interpretation, it helps us to locate and to formulate several further problems involved in developing a theory of reference group behavior.

First of all, it reinforces the supposition, hinted in the preceding case, that it is the institutional definitions of the social structure which may focus the attention of members of a group or occupants

cedures adopted to cross-check each set of data. In the present case, for example, it is shown that the responses to this question were not merely a reflection of the soldiers' sentiments *subsequent* to induction. For "when asked of new recruits, whose report on their feelings about induction could not be colored by months or years of subsequent Army experience, the [same kind of] question discriminated significantly between recruits who *later* became psychoneurotics and other men." (I, 123n) This note is intended to emphasize, once and for all, that our summary of a research case does not at all reproduce those subtle and cumulative details which often lend weight to the data in hand. For these details, rather than the more general questions to which they give rise, a first-hand study of *The American Soldier* is necessary.

of a social status upon certain *common* reference groups. Nor does this refer only to the fact that soldiers will take the official institutional norms (the rules governing induction and exemption) as a *direct* basis for judging the legitimacy of their own induction into the service. These same rules, since they are defined in terms of such statuses as marital condition and age, also focus attention on certain groups or statuses with which individuals subject to service will compare themselves. This is, in effect, implied by the authors who, referring to the greater sacrifices entailed by induction of the married man, go on to say: "This was officially recognized by draft boards. . . . The very fact that draft boards were more liberal with married than with single men provided numerous examples to the drafted married man of *others in his shoes* who got relatively better breaks than he did." (I, 125, italics supplied) The institutional norms evoke comparisons with others similar in *particular* aspects of status—"others in his shoes"—thus encouraging *common* reference groups for these married soldiers. In addition to these common reference groups, as previously stated, there may well have been all manner of idiosyncratic reference groups, which, since they vary at random, would not have resulted in the statistically discernible reluctance for service which was comparatively marked among married men.

A second problem is highlighted by the hypothesis which uniformly assumes that the married soldier compares himself with like-statused individuals with whom he is or has been in *actual social relations: associates* in the Army or civilian *friends*. This, then, raises a question concerning reference group behavior when the frame of comparative reference is provided by *impersonal status categories* in general (other married men, noncoms, *etc.*) and by those representatives of these status categories with whom he is in *sustained social relations*. Which, for example, most affects the evaluations of the individual when these operate at cross-purposes (a problem clearly visible in the matrix of variables set out earlier in this paper)?

This question leads at once to the comparative significance of general status categories and intimate subgroups of which one is a member. Suppose, for example, that all or almost all of a married soldier's married associates have also been drafted, even though, *in general*, this status category has a smaller proportion of inductions than the category of the unmarried male. Which basis of comparison will, on the average, prove more effective? Will he compare himself with the other drafted benedicts in his clique or subgroup and consequently be the more ready to accept induction for himself, or will he compare himself with the larger status category of married men, who are in general more often deferred, and consequently feel aggrieved over his own induction? The question has, of course, more general bearing. For example, are workers' expectations regarding their personal prospects of future employment shaped more by the present employment of themselves and their associates on the job or by high rates of unemployment prevailing in the occupation at large?

This case from *The American Soldier* thus points to the need for cumulative research on *the relative effectiveness of frames of reference yielded by associates and by more general status categories.* It suggests the salient items of observation which must be incorporated in such projected studies, so that this problem, at least in its major outlines, can lend itself to research, here and now, not in some remote future. Such projected studies could readily include items of data on the norms or situation of close associates as well as data on knowledge about the norms or situation prevailing in the given status at large. Subsequent analysis would then be in terms of systematic comparison of individuals in the *same status* but with immediate *associates* who have distinctly opposed norms or who are in contrasting situations. Replicated studies including such materials would substantially advance our present understanding of the workings of reference group behavior.[20]

Third, the theory assumes that individuals comparing their own lot with that of others have some *knowledge* of the situation in which these others find themselves. More concretely, it assumes that the individual knows about the comparative rates of induction among married and single men, or the degree of unemployment in their occupation at large.[21] Or, if the individual is taken to be posi-

[20] Thus, a current unpublished research in the sociology and social psychology of housing by R. K. Merton, P. J. S. West, and M. Jahoda includes a study of the comparative effectiveness of "primary environment of opinion" (constituted by the opinions of one's close associates) and of "secondary environment of opinion" (constituted by the opinions of those with whom one is not in close association). When these operate at cross-purposes, it appears that the primary environment does take some measure of precedence.

[21] It may of course turn out that, under certain conditions, individuals extrapolate their knowledge of the situation of associates in a given social category to that social category at large. Or, it may develop that the situation of one's

tively oriented toward the norms of a non-membership group, the theory of course assumes that he has some knowledge of these norms. Thus, the theory of reference group behavior must include in its fuller psychological elaboration some treatment of the dynamics of perception (of individuals, groups and norms) and in its sociological elaboration, some treatment of channels of communication through which this knowledge is gained. Which processes make for accurate or distorted images of the situation of other individuals and groups (taken as a frame of reference)? Which forms of social organization maximize the probabilities of correct perception of other individuals and groups, and which make for distorted perception? Since *some* perceptual and cognitive elements are definitely *implied* even in a description of reference group behavior, it will be necessary for these elements to be explicitly incorporated into the theory.

A fourth problem emerging from this case concerns the empirical status of reference group concepts. In this study, as well as in others we consider here, the interpretative concept of relative deprivation was introduced *after* the field research was completed.[22] This being the case, there was no provision for the collection of *independent systematic* [23] *evidence* on the operation of such social

associates is accorded greater weight by the individual than the contrasting situation which he knows to obtain in the social category at large. These are questions amenable to empirical research and salient for reference group theory.

[22] Although the concept is after-the-fact of *data collection,* it was introduced early enough in the *analysis* to permit its use in suggesting types of tabulations which would otherwise not have been undertaken. From the interpretative standpoint, therefore, relative deprivation was not confined to use as an *ex post facto* conception.

[23] The emphasis on *systematic* data is essential, for *The American Soldier* has abundant indications that *in many cases* assumed reference groups were indeed taken as a context of comparison. For example, their text includes remarks by overseas soldiers which clearly indicate that the soldiers back home are sometimes taken as a point of reference in assessing their own situation: "I think I've had my share being overseas over two years. That's plenty for any man. . . Let them USO boys get some of this chow once in a while, then they will know what it is to sleep in the mud with mosquitoes buzzing around them like a P-38." "We should have a chance to breathe a little fresh air for a while. But I guess you better keep them USO boys back there or there won't be any USO." "It is hard as hell to be here and read in every paper that comes from home where Pvt. Joe Dokes is home again on furlough after tough duty as a guard in Radio City." "We receive letters from soldiers who have not yet left the States and who are on their second furlough." (I, 188) These remarks also contain passing allusions to the source of information regarding the situation of the men back home: "read in every paper," "we receive letters," *etc.*

frameworks of individual judgments. That a significant proportion of married soldiers did indeed compare their lot with that of married civilian friends and unmarried associates in the Army in arriving at their judgment remains, so far as the data in hand go, an assumption. These comparisons are inferred, rather than factually demonstrated, intervening variables. But they need not remain assumptions. They not only happen to square with the facts in hand, but are of a kind which can be directly tested in future inquiries employing the concept of reference group.[24] These studies can be designed to incorporate systematic data on the groups which individuals actually do take as frames of reference for their behavior and can thus determine whether variations in attitude and behavior correspond to variations in reference group contexts.

This possibility of converting the intervening variable of reference groups from assumption into fact brings us to a fifth problem. Before plunging into research on the conditions under which individuals compare themselves with *specified* other individuals or groups, it is necessary to consider the psychological status of these comparisons. For when individuals *explicitly* and consciously adopt such frames of reference, sociological researches involving interviews with large numbers of people face no great procedural difficulties. Appropriate questions can elicit the needed information on the groups, status categories or individuals which are taken as a frame of reference. But there is, of course, no reason to assume that

---

But such telling anecdotal materials are properly enough not regarded as a basis for *systematic* analysis by the authors of *The American Soldier*.

[24] A recent example of the possibility of now anticipating the need for data on reference group behavior is provided by the 1948 voting study in Elmira. Under a grant from the Rockefeller Foundation for the study of panel techniques in social research, a conference at Swarthmore on reference group concepts was arranged, with an eye to having materials bearings on these concepts introduced into the Elmira voting study. *The American Soldier* provides numerous further conceptions which can be similarly incorporated in further research. It is this process of an ongoing interplay between theory and empirical research which is overlooked by verdicts such as Glazer's that the concept of relative deprivation "cannot be refuted by facts." (See footnote 3 of this paper.) A theoretical concept emerging or developed in the course of one inquiry, if it has any empirical relevance at all, can then be utilized (and if defective, modified or nullified) in subsequent researches. If it is to be creative at all, research cannot be *confined* to the testing of predetermined hypotheses. New concepts and hypotheses emerge in the process of inquiry, and these become the basis for further inquiry. This, we take it, is precisely how continuity in science occurs. For a general statement of this view, see Merton, *Social Theory and Social Structure*, 3-16, 97-111.

comparisons of self with others are uniformly conscious. Numerous experimental studies in social psychology have shown that individuals *unwittingly* respond to different frames of reference introduced by the experimenter. To the extent that unwitting reference groups are involved in the ordinary routines of daily life, research techniques must be extended to detect their operation.

Appropriate research procedures must also be designed to discover which reference groups are spontaneously and explicitly brought into play, as distinguished from the study of responses to reference group contexts provided by the experimenter or suggested by the interviewer. Both interview and experimental studies have heretofore been largely centered on responses to reference group contexts supplied for the subjects. These studies can be further advanced by providing ordered arrays of comparative contexts, somewhat as follows:

"Compared with others on your work-team [or other membership-group], do you feel you are getting a fair income for what you do?"
"Compared with the men in the front office, do you . . . etc. . . ?"
"Compared with the president of the firm, do you . . . etc. . . ?"

Or similarly, information about the salaries of various individuals and groups could be given an experimental group and withheld from a matched group of workers to determine whether the subsequent self-appraisals and satisfactions of the experimental group are modified by possible reference groups supplied by the investigator.

But such tentative types of inquiry, in which the particular reference groups are provided, do not, of course, enter into the uncharted region of the *spontaneous selection of reference groups* in varying situations. Why will A, in one situation, compare himself with B, and in another, with C? Or, more concretely and illustratively: when do workers compare their lot with that of fellow-workers in close association, and when with others of markedly different status? which aspects of the social structure and which psychological processes limit the range of individuals and groups regarded as pertinent frames of reference? It is this type of problem—the processes shaping the selection of reference groups—that stands in most conspicuous need of research.[25]

[25] A notable beginning is found in the pioneering study by Herbert H. Hyman, *The Psychology of Status*, Archives of Psychology, No. 269, 1942. Hyman sought to have his subjects report the groups or individuals which

UNIFORMITIES OF BEHAVIOR DERIVED
FROM REFERENCE GROUP THEORY

TO this point, we have examined researches in which the concept of relative deprivation was explicitly utilized by Stouffer and his associates to interpret empirical findings. In doing so, we have attempted, first, to indicate how this concept can be incorporated in a more general, though still primitive, theory of reference group behavior and second, how these studies give rise to further empirical and theoretical problems that can become the object of new and cumulative research.

We want now to consider whether the theory of reference groups does indeed have wider applicability than the seemingly special concept of relative deprivation. Fortunately, the numerous researches of *The American Soldier* enable us to check this, at least to some degree. For some of these researches involve findings which are apparently not germane to the concept of relative deprivation —since they deal with self-images, but not with levels of satisfaction with one's lot—yet which can, we believe, be explicated by applying reference group conceptions to them. In the course of seeing whether this theory permits us to detect sociological uniformities underlying apparently disparate patterns of behavior, we shall also have occasion to add to the list of specific problems needing solution if reference group theory is to be advanced.

Case #4 (II, 242-72). Combat groups were in general subject to high personnel turnover. It is true that some outfits were trained and entered into combat with few changes in personnel, but even in these instances, casualties required frequent replacements. The Research Branch seized upon the sociologically significant fact that inexperienced soldiers thus found themselves in two distinctly different social structures: some being for a time in homogeneous outfits comprised wholly of similarly green troops, and others, in

---

they had taken for comparison with their own status. This kind of direct questioning can of course elicit only the conscious and remembered frames of comparison. But the advancement of reference group theory has suffered by the general failure to follow up Hyman's suggestive lead on spontaneously emerging frames of group reference.

divisions with combat veterans. And here the study took a decisive sociological turn. Unlike the ordinary polling studies in social psychology, which compare *aggregates of individuals of different status* (age, sex, class, etc.), they did not merely compare the attitudes of inexperienced and of veteran troops. This would have been only a comparison of aggregates of men in two distinct statuses, an important type of comparison but of severely limited value for sociology. Rather, they defined this as an occasion for studying the impact of *group contexts* upon the attitudes of types of individuals, a problem which is of course old, older than sociology itself, but which has less often been the object of systematic empirical research than of impressionistic discussion.

The Research Branch therefore centered upon the group contexts in which these troops found themselves: green troops in outfits comprised wholly by their own kind; equally inexperienced replacements in divisions otherwise composed of combat veterans; and the veterans themselves in these divisions.[26] Questions were put to these three groups of soldiers in several of what the Research Branch calls "attitude areas" (willingness for combat, confidence in their ability to take charge of a group in combat, appraisal of their physical condition, and so on). These surveys found apparently diverse *patterns of differences* in response among the three groups. In the first "attitude area," for example, veterans expressed greater reluctance to get into combat than the troops in green outfits, with the replacements being intermediate to the two. Whereas 45 per cent of the green troops were "ready to get into an actual battle zone," this dropped to 28 per cent among the replacements and to only 15 per cent among the veterans. It is, of course, the contrast between the green troops and the replacements which is most significant, since these were alike in their *individual attribute* of lack of combat experience, but different with respect to the *kind of group* in which they found themselves. This same pattern, with the replacement *intermediate* to those of the veteran and green troops, occurred in responses to questions about attitudes toward noncoms.

But, the Research Branch reports, this is only one pattern of response. Quite another pattern was found with regard to the men's

26 There is, of course, a fourth group context which might have entered strategically into the systematic comparison, namely, the divisions comprised wholly of combat veterans, except that the replacement practices of the Army did not make it possible for the Research Branch to include such all-veteran divisions in this study.

confidence in their ability "to take charge of a group of men" in combat. As some might expect on commonsense grounds, the veterans more often expressed confidence in their capacity to fulfill this role than did the green troops in green outfits. But it is of crucial significance that, unlike the first instance of willingness for combat, where the replacements were intermediate in their responses, in this case, they were consistently the least confident of the three groups.[27]

Again, on yet another type of "attitude"—toward his own physical condition—the replacement was virtually indistinguishable from the other green troops, but far more likely than the veteran to consider himself "in good physical condition."

These three sets of data, then, seem to show three different patterns of response, in the first of which the replacement responds more like the veteran than the green troops; in the second, most remote from the veteran and also unlike other green troops; and in the third, quite like his counterpart in green outfits. And since these are diverse patterns, the Research Branch has advanced diverse interpretations. With regard to the replacements' approximation to the veterans' reluctance to go into combat, it is suggested that "to some extent the replacements took over the attitudes of the combat veterans around them, whose views on combat would have for them high prestige." (II, 250) With regard to capacity for leading a group in combat, where the replacements differ most from the veterans, it is suggested that "for the veterans, experience was their strong point, and also the point at which replacements in contact with them felt the greatest inferiority, standing as they did in the shadow of the veterans." (II, 251) And when the replacement is quite like his counterpart in green outfits, as with appraisals of physical condition, this is tentatively explained by saying that these judgments probably reflect an actual (objective) difference in physical condition between veterans and others.

[27] Were there opportunity here for a full re-analysis of these data, it would be necessary to take account of problems of "question reliability," since three distinct index-questions in this "attitude area" of "self-confidence" led to somewhat different patterns of response. However, that is not essential for the purposes in hand, particularly since we are here concerned primarily with the replacements, who were *consistently* less confident than the veterans and green troops on all three items. (For figures, see II, 252.) See also the analysis of questions in this study by Kendall and Lazarsfeld, "Problems of Survey Analysis," this volume.

Theoretical implications. It will be at once granted that this poses an intriguing challenge and problem for sociological theory. For the response-behavior of the replacements seems to exhibit almost random variation, a situation distasteful to the theorist whose task it is to perceive underlying uniformities amid such apparent disorder. It is reminiscent of the situation confronting Durkheim when he found an immense variety of suicide rates, differing among the sexes, rural-urban areas, military and civilian populations, religious groups, and so on. Rather than advance new and separate interpretations of each set of differentials, he attempted to derive these numerous variations from a limited set of propositions. So here, these various patterns of response of replacements set sociological theory the task of discerning the significant variables and conditions which bring about this seeming diversity of response-behavior.

As is well known, the first step in the search for sociological order amid apparent disorder is to re-examine, in theoretical terms, the *concepts* in terms of which the data are reported. More often than not, it will be found that these concepts may profit by clarification and reformulation. That appears to be the case here. These several sets of data are all reported as *attitudes* falling into distinct "attitude-areas." The theorist might at once consider the possibility that basic conceptual differences in these data might be obscured by use of a single crudely defined concept.[28] The single blanket concept of "attitude" may also fail to direct the analyst's attention to the appropriate body of theory for interpreting the data. And finally, by tacitly including significantly different elements in the data under this one undifferentiated concept, the empirical findings may exhibit anomalies, contradictions, and lack of uniformities which are only apparent, not real.

What does a conceptual reformulation of these data show? The first variable, "willingness for combat," may indeed be usefully described as an "attitude" in the approximate sense of "a mental and neural *state of readiness,* organized through experience, exerting a directive or dynamic influence upon the individual's response

[28] In the introduction, Stouffer calls special attention to the looseness of the concept "attitude" as adopted in these studies: ". . . in the main work of the Research Branch and in most of the text of the present volumes there is no operational definition of attitudes—whence, concepts like 'attitudes,' 'tendencies,' and 'opinions' are used more or less loosely and even sometimes interchangeably. . ." (I, 42) We are here engaged in exploring some of the empirical and theoretical consequences of such initially loose formulations of concepts.

to all objects and situations with which it is related."[29] But the second variable, "self-confidence in leadership capacities," as here indexed, appears not so much a preparatory set for behavior, as a *self-image and a self-appraisal.* Two consequences flow from this provisional reformulation of a single "attitude" concept into the two concepts of attitude and of self-appraisal. First, it is no longer assumed that the data bearing on these two variables need manifest the same comparative distributions: that now becomes a moot question and not a tacit presumption. And second, the reformulation in terms of self-appraisal leads us at once to the reference group theory of self-appraisals. Reformulation of the concept in which the dependent variables are stated thus provides a tentative link with theory of the past: we are not forced to improvise wholly new hypotheses, standing alone and unconnected with a general body of theory, but can, perhaps, derive these findings from an established set of hypotheses centered about the structure, functions and dynamic mechanisms of self-appraisals in diverse group contexts. This is, moreover, the theory which incorporates the concept of relative deprivation, used elsewhere in these volumes, but not here.

With this new conceptual basis, we are prepared to re-examine the data of *The American Soldier* to see whether they do indeed exhibit the anomaly of three distinct patterns of response under the same conditions. If a general theory is to move out from these data and beyond the interpretations advanced in the text, then it should be able to incorporate these seemingly different patterns of response as expressions of an underlying regularity.

Stemming then from the theoretic background provided by James, Cooley and Mead, and by Hyman, Sherif and Newcomb, the hypothesis holds that, insofar as subordinate or prospective group members are motivated to affiliate themselves with a group, they will tend to assimilate the sentiments and conform with the values of the authoritative and prestigeful stratum in that group. The function of conformity is acceptance by the group, just as progressive acceptance by the group reinforces the tendency toward conformity. And the values of these "significant others" constitute the mirrors in which individuals see their self-image and reach self-appraisals. Applied to the specific case in hand, the significant

[29] The particular definition cited is that by G. W. Allport, but various current conceptions of "attitude" have essentially this same core-denotation.

others in the membership-group are similarly inexperienced men for the green soldier in a green outfit, whereas for the replacement, the significant others are experienced veterans, with their distinctive sets of values and sentiments.

In applying the general hypothesis, it must be anticipated that the replacements, as "outsiders" motivated to affiliate themselves with the prestigeful and authoritative stratum (the veterans), would more nearly conform to *all* of the veterans' values and sentiments here under inspection. We should be clear on this point. If its interpretative utility is to be properly assessed, the hypothesis must stand on its own feet, and not be modified or abandoned because the text of *The American Soldier* reports that the responses of replacements in these distinct "attitude areas" were in fact different. The present hypothesis gives us a set of instructions to the effect that we must re-examine these reportedly different patterns in order to determine whether they are actually different, or merely speciously so.

In a provisional way, and to the extent that the reported data allow us to say, it appears that the differences are only apparent. Underlying these manifest differences in the percentage distribution of replies to the given questions by veterans, replacements, and green troops, are regularities of response corresponding to those anticipated in the hypothesis.

Thus, first, with respect to willingness for combat, the sentiments of veterans held, in effect, that "combat is hell," and consequently, veterans most frequently expressed reluctance to enter into combat. The green troops, in contrast, who had more lately quitted civilian ranks, were likely to have at the outset the values of the wartime civilian population, with all its "conventional stereotypes" of combat as affording occasions for dramatic heroism. This is in fact borne out by the text at another place and in another connection, where it is reported that "probably the strongest group code (among combat men) . . . was the taboo against any talk of a flag-waving variety. . . . The core of the attitude *among combat men* seemed to be that any talk that did not subordinate idealistic values and patriotism to the harsher realities of the combat situation was hypocritical, and a person who expressed such ideas a hypocrite." [30]

[30] II, 150 (italics supplied). Essentially the same point of a contrast in values regarding combat between the civilian population and combat men is made at numerous places in the two volumes; *e.g.*, at II, 111-112, 151; I, 484. Notice

In this first instance, then, our hypothesis drawn from reference group theory would lead us to anticipate that the replacements, seeking affiliation with the authoritative and prestigeful stratum of veterans, will move from the civilian-like values toward the more tough-minded values of the veterans. And this, as we know, is indeed the case. For replacements, the assumed function of assimilating the values of the veterans is to find more ready acceptance by the higher-status group, in a setting where the subordinate group of replacements does not have independent claims to legitimate prestige.

But if the hypothesis is consistent with the first set of data on willingness for combat, can it also hold for the second set of data dealing with the so-called attitude of self-confidence regarding capacity for leadership, particularly since it was found that, in this instance, the replies of replacements were *remote* from those of the veterans, even more so than the replies of the green troops? Indeed, the text refers to this as a "different" or "divergent" pattern of response. To be sure, the manifest distribution of replies differs from the first. But, viewed in terms of reference group theory, it is, we believe, only another expression of the same underlying dynamic regularities of behavior in this group context.

This can be tested by applying the hypothesis. In the case of self-confidence, as we have seen, we deal with a self-appraisal rather than with an attitude in the sense of a preparatory set for action. The values and sentiments of the veteran stratum hold, in effect, that "actual combat experience is needed to prepare a private to take charge of a group of men in combat."[31] Now, if, as the hypothesis anticipates, replacements seek to assimilate *this* value and judge themselves accordingly, if they see themselves in the mirror provided by the values of the prestigeful veterans, they can only appraise themselves as, by and large, unprepared for

should also be taken of Chart VIII in Chapter 3 of volume II, showing that veterans were far more likely than inexperienced troops to say that "this war is not worth fighting." And finally, it should be said that this contrast between the definitions of the combat situation by civilians and by combat men is drawn by Brewster Smith, who also conducted the analysis of replacement behavior now under review.

[31] The statistical data of replies to the question, "Do you think you have been given enough training and experience so that you could do a good job of taking charge of a group of men on your own in combat," constitute one basis for the view that veterans hold this value. Discussions of the values of combat men, especially in II, Chapter 3, bear this out.

spontaneous leadership in battle. On the hypothesis, the replacements would, in short, behave just as they do, being most likely to say that they are *not* ready to take charge of men in combat (involving a lower self-estimate than that found among the green troops, *not* vis-à-vis the veterans). Thus, although their *distribution* of replies differs markedly from that of the veterans, leading the Research Branch to describe this as another pattern of response, the replacements are engaging in the same pattern of behavior in the two instances—when this is construed in terms of reference group theory. They are assimilating the values of the veterans, and thus presumably affiliating themselves with this authoritative and prestigeful stratum. In the first instance of "willingness for combat," this calls only for direct reaffirmation of the veterans' sentiments, leading the replacements' distribution of responses to resemble that of the veterans. In the second instance of self-confidence in leadership capacity, they also assimilate the veteran standards but since this is not merely an attitude but a self-appraisal, they apply these standards to themselves, find themselves comparatively wanting, and thus give distributions of responses to the self-appraisal questions differing from those of the veterans. Thus, a uniformity of social process apparently underlies the different patterns of manifest replies.

The same hypothesis can be tested anew on other items from these data on "attitudes" of veterans, replacements, and green troops; for example, those dealing with "attitudes toward physical condition." In this case, the green troops and replacements respond alike, with 57 per cent and 56 per cent respectively saying that they are in good physical condition, whereas only 35 per cent of the veterans make that claim. This is reported as a third pattern of response, again on the manifest empirical level of response-frequencies, leading the Research Branch to another interpretation of this apparently new pattern: the similarity of answers by replacements and green troops, it is suggested, "undoubtedly parallels similarity in the men's actual physical condition." [32]

Here, it is said, the responses represent, not an assimilation of veterans' attitudes, but more nearly a faithful reporting of objective

[32] II, 263. This refers to their "absolute" ratings in response to the question, "Do you think that you are in good physical condition?" Alternative questions which refer to "combat" conditions possibly introduce the factor of replacements' assimilated reluctance for combat; they tend to be intermediate to veterans and green troops in their responses to these.

differences in the physical condition of fatigued veterans—"beat-up Joes"—and of the fresh replacements and green troops.

But this only poses another problem for theory: under which conditions do men respond by reporting the objective situation rather than a socially reflected image? [33] Does this third, apparently different, pattern of response require a new hypothesis? It seems that, again, no additional *ad hoc* variables need be introduced, although in the absence of the required data, this must of course remain for future research to examine. It appears that the veterans do not hold poor physical condition as a distinctive and positive social *value* (except, as the text indicates, as a possible rationalization for escaping further combat) in the same sense that they hold the belief that "combat is hell" or that "combat experience equips a private to take charge of men in combat." Replacements seeking to affiliate themselves with the prestigeful and socially validated veterans will therefore not be served by asserting that they are in poor physical shape, that they, too, are in effect "beat-up Joes." If anything, this claim would only be the occasion for rejection of replacements by veterans, since it would represent, not a bid for affiliation with the group, but for equality of *status*. Moreover, the replacements' recognition of their comparatively good physical condition does not affirm a counter-value, which might also threaten their acceptance by the veterans. Within the same group context, then, there is no functional or motivational basis for replacements to reproduce the self-judgments of the veterans, and apparently objective differences in the physical condition of fatigued veterans and of fresh replacements and green troops find expression.

Insofar as differences in these three patterns of manifest response can be theoretically derived from a functional theory of reference

[33] Here, as elsewhere, a slightly more generalized formulation of the problem directs our attention to the saliency of data now presented in various, and unconnected, pages of *The American Soldier*. At several points in these volumes, recourse is had to the assumption that soldiers' replies represent "objective reporting" rather than group-conditioned judgments. But, without a general formulation, the need for collating these and for clarifying the theoretical issue is not likely to be perceived. See, for example, the interpretation of responses of "nonreturnees in predominantly returnee outfits," where it is said: "In part this agreement between returnees and nonreturnees suggests that there was *some basis in fact* as well as in attitude for the returnees' preference for and greater comfort in their own outfits. But these data may not be taken as sure corroboration of this point, since they may be, at least in part, simply evidence that the attitudes of returnees affected the opinions of the nonreturnees around them as well." (II, 515, 517)

group behavior, this case illustrates one major service of theory for applied social research: the reconstruction through conceptual clarification of apparent irregularities in data leads to the provisional discovery of underlying functional and dynamic regularities. But, as we have suggested, the avenues between social theory and applied research carry two-way traffic: not only can theory reformulate some of the materials in *The American Soldier*, but on the basis of the same materials we can specify the types of further sociological indices and observations needed to achieve continuity and cumulation in the theory of value-assimilation, the group context of self-appraisals, and the objective assessment of situations. A brief list of such indices must stand in lieu of a detailed analysis of their potential for the advancement of this theory.[34]

1. *Index of actual social relations:* There is plainly need for systematic data on the social relations actually obtaining between the prestigeful and authoritative stratum, and the newcomers to a group. Is there an empirically discoverable tendency for those in most frequent or most enduring affiliative contact to exhibit value-assimilation?
2. *Index of motivations of incoming group members:* The theory presupposes a concern among newcomers to affiliate themselves with the higher status group. For research purposes, it would of course be necessary to divide newcomers in terms of the presence, absence, or degree of such motivations. A derivative analytical procedure, moving in another direction, would consist in taking such affiliative motivations not as given, but as problematical, in turn requiring explanation.
3. *Index of social cohesion and of associated values:* Do the newcomers represent a scattered *aggregate* of individuals, or an organized subgroup? If the latter, do they have their own group values with distinctive claims to moral legitimacy? And in such instances, does

[34] The reader might be tempted to say that most of the following have been recognized as probably significant variables from the earliest days of modern sociology. But here, as at many points in this paper, it must be said that there is a great difference—in fact, all the difference—between impressionistic and sporadic references to such variables, and *systematic* incorporation of these variables into research. Only through the latter procedure will theory and research both advance. Impressionism is no adequate substitute, if only *because it is so flexible and vague in character as not to admit of decisive nullification of a provisional hypothesis.* As Nietzsche, not ordinarily one to understand the ethos of science, put it in an insightful moment, "It is certainly not the least charm of a theory that it is refutable." It is the object of systematic incorporation of variables into research to allow for nullification as well as confirmation, a rather difficult assignment for an author, wedded to a theory, and not exposed to data sufficiently incriminating to have him divorce himself from that theory.

continuous contact lead to more nearly reciprocal, rather than one-sided, assimilation? [35]

Inclusion of indices such as these, and systematic use of the panel-interview method, as well as direct observation, would encompass systematic study of the *processes* of value-assimilation as part of reference group behavior, and not only, as in the applied researches of *The American Soldier*, the study of certain net results of such processes. There could then be, for example, inquiry into the possibly circular and cumulative process through which value-assimilation furthers social contact between the groups which in turn reinforces value-assimilation, greater social acceptability and increased social contact.

An entirely different sequence of empirical and theoretical inquiry is suggested by the re-analysis of these data on group contexts of value-assimilation. Under which conditions do we find such changed evaluations of entire groups or social strata (whether this be called "perspectivistic thinking," or "false-consciousness")? Does it occur primarily when members of this group identify their fate with that of another group, so that they no longer faithfully express their own distinctive interests and values in the present? In other words, within which context of social structure does such "distortion" of group values occur, and in which is there a response more nearly appropriate to the situation?

Following out this one set of data—found on a few pages among the many hundreds of *The American Soldier*—seems to have involved the following procedures and to have had the following results:

First, a clarification of concepts has allowed an apparent disorder or variation in some reported findings to be interpreted as diverse expressions of underlying sociological uniformities, thus serving the theoretical objective of *parsimony*, found whenever several empirical generalizations are derived from a more general formulation.

Second, reconceptualization operated to this end by suggesting the relevance of a previously developed body of theoretic propositions, thus reducing the *ad hoc* nature of current interpretations and

[35] It will be noted that the materials in *The American Soldier* did not allow in general for study of the effects of replacements upon veterans, a problem manifestly involved in an extended setting of the problem. However, the Research Branch was clearly sensitive to the problem. At one point, for example, they were able to determine, roughly, if veterans' pride in their company was affected by a comparatively high proportion of replacements. (See II, 255-257)

making for *continuity* of present findings and theories of the past. In a measure, this is the same theory implied by the concept of relative deprivation which, though utilized elsewhere in *The American Soldier*, was not applied to this particular set of empirical materials.

Third, generalizing the concepts (beyond the immediate descriptive categories of veterans, replacements, and green troops), points to the possibility that these generic formulations are pertinent, not only for the specifically military situation, but for a wider range of situations corresponding to the requirements of the theoretic formulations, thus extending the *scope* of data to which these can perhaps be applied.

And finally, the very existence of such systematic data permitting provisional reconceptualization may importantly advance the development of theory, by highlighting the need for a series of sociological indices to be incorporated into research on these problems, thus providing for further *cumulation* of sociological knowledge by linking past theory, present data, and future research.

Although undertaken as an applied social research, *The American Soldier* has, then, the potential by-products of furthering the parsimony, continuity, scope and cumulation of sociological theory. And, as is not infrequently the case with applied research, the by-products may prove more significant for the discipline of sociology than the direct application of findings.

STATISTICAL INDICES OF SOCIAL STRUCTURE

BEFORE continuing with our review of problems in reference group theory, it will be useful to consider explicitly the implications of these researches for the study of social contexts. From the foregoing examination of the researches on assessment of promotion opportunities and on replacements' self-evaluations, it can be seen that *The American Soldier* is a fertile source for the development of relatively precise, statistical indices of social structure. In these and other studies, the survey data are analyzed in terms of the distribution of responses by social units (companies, divisions, branches of service). And in their analyses relating frequency distributions or rates characterizing social units to the responses of individuals and subgroups within these diverse units, they have moved well beyond the point ordinarily reached in studies of social ecology.

Like the use of statistical indicators in ecology for depicting different kinds of social units on an areal basis, *The American Soldier* provides indices of attributes of social structure, but *unlike* the ecological studies, *The American Soldier* goes on to make a *systematic analysis of the attitudes or evaluations of like-statused individuals within diverse social structures.*

This *combination* of indices suggests numerous statistical indices of group attributes or social structure which can be built into future sociological research. Moreover, the use of frequency distributions or proportions or rates as indices of social structures has the special merit of reminding us that these structures often vary in terms of degree, and not necessarily in terms of all-or-none qualities. For instance, social systems do not provide simply for mobility *or* for fixity of its members; they exhibit varying rates of mobility.[36] They are not simply heterogeneous *or* homogeneous, but have varying degrees of heterogeneity.[37] They are not integrated *or* unintegrated, cohesive *or* dispersive, but have varying degrees of integration and cohesion.[38]

Because statistical indices of such attributes of social systems have seldom been utilized in conjunction with indices of individual behavior, comparative sociology has been largely limited to loose and

[36] See, for example, the use of indices of comparative rates of social mobility in the Air Forces, Service Forces, Ground Forces, *etc.* as a social context for individual evaluations of promotion-chances. I, 251 ff.

[37] See, for example, the indices of social heterogeneity of companies provided by proportions of replacements in outfits as a social context for individual expressions of pride in company. II, 255 ff. A similar procedure has been adopted in a study of individual racial attitudes within the contexts of sub-areas in a biracial housing development which are characterized by differing proportions of Negroes and whites. (A soon-to-be-published research on the sociology and social psychology of housing by R. K. Merton, P. J. S. West and M. Jahoda.)

[38] Consider how contemporary sociology can improve upon Durkheim's early study of suicide which *assumed* varying degrees of social cohesion and integration among Catholics and Protestants, military and civilian groups, etc. As noted elsewhere, "the degree of integration is an empirical variable, changing for the same society from time to time and differing among various societies." (Merton, *op. cit.,* 28.) Statistical indicators of integration and cohesion would permit systematic study, with a rigor not possible in Durkheim's day, of the bearing of such variations of social context upon the behavior of individuals variously located within the group.

indecisive findings. Relatively strict comparison has been lacking as most of us most of the time have been confined to talking about "different" social structures rather than studying structures shown to differ in specifiable degree. When statistical indices of group attributes have been adopted—for example, variations in racial proportions among groups—these have typically not been *combined* with systematic comparisons of the behavior of like-statused people within these distinctive groups. And, correlatively, when relatively precise measures of individual attitudes have been obtained, these have seldom been combined with similarly definite measures of social structure. Thus, social psychology has in the past decade or so moved toward the systematic use of indices of individual attitudes and sentiments primarily among aggregates of mutually unrelated individuals.

The studies of the Research Branch suggest the feasibility and the importance of developing indices *both* of social structure and of the behavior of individuals situated within the structure. Their occasional comparisons of the status-structure of different branches of the Army thus involve indices of stratification similar to those provided by frequency distributions of a population among the several social classes. Once such indices are established, it becomes possible to have systematic, not anecdotal, comparisons of the behavior of people of similar class status living within differently proportioned class structures. This will result in advancing beyond the more familiar characterizations of "the middle-class man" or "the working-class man" to determine their characteristic behavior within differently constituted class systems. In the same fashion, other types of social differentiation can be indexed by the frequency distributions of various statuses (education, race, age, *etc.*) and combined with the systematic study of individuals similarly situated within these varying structures.[39]

In this respect, *The American Soldier* may represent a prelude to the immediate future in which indices of mobility rates, cultural change, group cohesion and social differentiation will be regularly and systematically incorporated into comparative studies of social structure. And once this is done, it will become possible to compare

[39] The forthcoming "Elmira study of voting behavior" makes extensive use of such procedures, providing further evidence, perhaps, of continuity in social research.

For a more detailed account of sociological indices, see Section 2 of the paper by Kendall and Lazarsfeld, this volume.

the patterns of reference group behavior of like-statused individuals within these various social systems.

REFERENCE GROUP THEORY AND
SOCIAL MOBILITY

OTHER researches reported in *The American Soldier* which do not make explicit use of the concept of relative deprivation or kindred concepts can also be recast in terms of reference group theory. One of the more rigorous and seminal of these is the panel study of relationships between the conformity of enlisted men to official values of the Army and their subsequent promotion.

This study also illustrates the widely-known but seldom elucidated point that the same social research can be variously analyzed in at least three separate, though related, respects: its documented empirical findings, its methodology or logic of procedure, and its theoretical implications.

Since the methodology and the empirical findings of this study have been amply discussed—the one in the paper by Kendall and Lazarsfeld, the other in *The American Soldier* itself—we need not concern ourselves with them here. Instead, we limit our discussion to some of its theoretical implications.

These implications divide into three related kinds. First, the implications for reference group theory as the empirical findings are re-examined within the context of that theory. Second, are the implications which enable us to connect reference group theory with hypotheses of functional sociology. And third, the implications which, once suitably generalized, enable us to see that this study bears, not only on the conformity-and-mobility patterns of American soldiers in World War II, but possibly also on more general and seemingly disparate patterns of behavior, such as group defection, renegadism, social climbing, and the like.

Tracing out these implications comprises a large order which can scarcely be entirely filled, not because of limitations of space but because of limitations of our own sociological knowledge. But even an approximation to achieving our purpose should help us recognize the theoretical linkages between presently separated types of social behavior.

We begin by following our now customary practice of briefly sketching out the chief findings of the study as these are set forth in *The American Soldier.*

Case #5 (I, 258-275). This research was concerned, not with *rates* of promotion which were determined by changes in the table of organization, but with the *incidence* of promotion: which men were the more likely to be advanced? Since the decision of the commanding officer regarding promotions was by no means based upon objective tests of capacity or performance by enlisted men, there was much occasion for interpersonal relations and sentiments to play their part in affecting this decision. Accordingly, the Research Branch advanced the hypothesis that, "One factor which hardly would have failed to enter to some extent into the judgment of an officer in selecting a man for promotion was his conformity to the officially approved military mores." (I, 259) It is noted further, and we shall have occasion to return to this point in some detail, that "in making subjective judgments, the commanding officer necessarily laid himself wide open to charges of favoritism and particularly of succumbing to the wiles of those enlisted men most skilled at 'bucking'." (I, 264)

A panel study of three groups of enlisted men was designed to find out whether the men who expressed attitudes in accord with the established military mores subsequently received promotions in proportions significantly higher than the others. This was consistently found to be the case. For example, "of the privates who in September 1943 said they did not think the Army's control was too strict, 19 per cent had become Pfc's by January 1944, while only 12 per cent of the other privates had become Pfc's." (I, 261-2) So, too, when men in the three samples are arranged according to their scores on a "quasi-scale of attitudes of conformity," it was uniformly found in all three groups "that the men whose attitudes were most conformist were the ones most likely to be promoted subsequently." (I, 263) [40]

---

[40] As the authors themselves say and as Kendall and Lazarsfeld indicate in some detail, these data do not conclusively demonstrate that conformist attitudes, rather than other correlates of these attitudes, made for significantly higher likelihood of promotion. In principle, only a completely controlled ex-

Theoretical Implications. In discussing this panel study, we want to bring into the open some of the connections between reference group theory and functional sociology which have remained implicit to this point,—an objective to which this study lends itself particularly well, since the findings of the study can be readily reformulated in terms of both kinds of theory, and are then seen to bear upon a range of behavior wider than that considered in the study itself.

The value of such reformulation for social theory is perhaps best seen in connection with the independent variable of "conformity." It is clear, when one thinks about it, that the type of attitude described as conformist in this study is at the polar extreme from what is ordinarily called "social conformity." For in the vocabulary of sociology, social conformity usually denotes conformity to the norms and expectations current in the individual's *own* membership-group. But in this study, conformity refers, not to the norms of the immediate primary group constituted by enlisted men but to the quite different norms contained in the official military mores. Indeed, as data in *The American Soldier* make clear, the norms of the in-groups of associated enlisted men and the official norms of the Army and of the stratum of officers were often at odds.[41] In the language of reference group theory, therefore, attitudes of conformity to the official mores can be described as a positive orientation to the norms of a non-membership group that is taken as a frame of reference. Such conformity to norms of an outgroup is thus equivalent to what is ordinarily called nonconformity, that is, nonconformity to the norms of the in-group.[42]

---

periment, obviously not feasible in the present instance, would demonstrate this beyond all reasonable doubt. But controlled experiment aside, this panel study, holding constant the factors of age and education which had been found to be related both to attitudes and promotion, goes a long way toward demonstrating a relationship between the incidence of conformist attitudes and subsequent advancement. In this respect, the study moves well beyond the point reached by the use of less rigorous data, indicating a static correlation between rank and conformist attitudes, inasmuch as it can show that those with conformist attitudes were more likely to be *subsequently* promoted. See I, 272-3.

[41] Although the absolute percentages of men endorsing a given sentiment cannot of course be taken at face value since these percentages are affected by the sheer phrasing of the sentiment, it is nevertheless suggestive that data presented earlier in the volume (*e.g.,* I, 147 ff.) find only a small minority of the samples of enlisted men in this study adhering to the officially approved attitudes. By and large, a significantly larger proportion of officers abide by these attitudes.

[42] There is nothing fixed about the boundaries separating in-groups from out-

This preliminary reformulation leads directly to two interrelated questions which we have until now implied rather than considered explicitly: what are the consequences, functional and dysfunctional, of positive orientation to the values of a group other than one's own? And further, which social processes initiate, sustain or curb such orientations?

Functions of positive orientation to non-membership reference groups. In considering, however briefly, the possible consequences of this pattern of conformity to non-membership group norms, it is advisable to distinguish between the consequences for the individuals exhibiting this behavior, the sub-group in which they find themselves, and the social system comprising both of these.

For the individual who adopts the values of a group to which he aspires but does not belong, this orientation may serve the twin functions of aiding his rise into that group and of easing his adjustment after he has become part of it. That this first function was indeed served is the gist of the finding in *The American Soldier* that those privates who accepted the official values of the Army hierarchy were more likely than others to be promoted. The hypothesis regarding the second function still remains to be tested. But it would not, in principle, be difficult to discover empirically whether those men who, through a kind of *anticipatory socialization,* take on the values of the non-membership group to which they aspire, find readier acceptance by that group and make an easier adjustment to it. This would require the development of indices of group acceptance and adjustment, and a comparison, in terms of these indices, of those newcomers to a group who had previously oriented themselves to the group's values and those who had not. More concretely, in the present instance, it would have entailed a comparative study among the privates promoted to higher rank, of the subsequent group adjustment of those who had undergone the hypothesized preparation for status shifts and those who had pre-

groups, membership-groups from non-membership-groups. These change with the changing situation. Vis-à-vis civilians or an alien group, men in the Army may regard themselves and be regarded as members of an in-group; yet, in another context, enlisted men may regard themselves and be regarded as an in-group in distinction to the out-group of officers. Since these concepts are relative to the situation, rather than absolute, there is no paradox in referring to the officers as an out-group for enlisted men in one context, and as members of the more inclusive in-group, in another context.

viously held fast to the values of their in-group of enlisted men. Indices of later adjustment could be related to indices of prior value-orientation. This would constitute a systematic empirical test of a functional hypothesis.

It appears, further, that anticipatory socialization is functional for the individual only within a relatively open social structure providing for mobility. For only in such a structure would such attitudinal and behavior preparation for status shifts be followed by actual changes of status in a substantial proportion of cases. By the same token, the same pattern of anticipatory socialization would be dysfunctional for the individual in a relatively closed social structure, where he would not find acceptance by the group to which he aspires and would probably lose acceptance, because of his out-group orientation, by the group to which he belongs. This latter type of case will be recognized as that of the marginal man, poised on the edge of several groups but fully accepted by none of them.

Thus, the often-studied case of the marginal man [43] and the case of the enlisted man who takes the official military mores as a positive frame of reference can be identified, in a functional theory of reference group behavior, as special cases of anticipatory socialization. The marginal man pattern represents the special case in a relatively closed social system, in which the members of one group take as a positive frame of reference the norms of a group from which they are excluded in principle. Within such a social structure, anticipatory socialization becomes dysfunctional for the individual who becomes the victim of aspirations he cannot achieve and hopes he cannot satisfy. But, as the panel study seems to indicate, precisely the same kind of reference group behavior within a relatively open social system is functional for the individual at least to the degree of helping him to achieve the status to which he aspires. The same reference group behavior in different social structures has different consequences.

To this point, then, we find that positive orientation toward the norms of a non-membership group is precipitated by a passage between membership-groups, either in fact or in fantasy, and that the functional or dysfunctional consequences evidently depend upon

---

[43] Qualitative descriptions of the behavior of marginal men, as summarized, for example, by E. V. Stonequist, *The Marginal Man* (New York, Scribner's, 1937), can be analytically recast as that special and restricted case of reference group behavior in which the individual seeks to abandon one membership group for another to which he is socially forbidden access.

the relatively open or closed character of the social structure in which this occurs. And what would, at first glance, seem entirely unrelated and disparate forms of behavior—the behavior of such marginal men as the Cape Coloured or the Eurasian, and of enlisted men adopting the values of military strata other than their own— are seen, after appropriate conceptualization, as special cases of reference group behavior.

Although anticipatory socialization may be functional for the *individual* in an open social system, it is apparently dysfunctional for the solidarity of the *group* or *stratum* to which he belongs. For allegiance to the contrasting mores of another group means defection from the mores of the in-group. And accordingly, as we shall presently see, the in-group responds by putting all manner of social restraints upon such positive orientations to certain out-group norms.

From the standpoint of the larger social system, the Army as a whole, positive orientation toward the official mores would appear to be functional in supporting the legitimacy of the structure and in keeping the structure of authority intact. (This is presumably what is meant when the text of *The American Soldier* refers to these conformist attitudes as "favorable from the Army's point of view.") But manifestly, much research needs to be done before one can say that this is indeed the case. It is possible, for example, that the secondary effects of such orientations may be so deleterious to the solidarity of the primary groups of enlisted men that their morale sags. A concrete research question might help clarify the problem: are outfits with relatively large minorities of men positively oriented to the official Army values more likely to exhibit signs of anomie and personal disorganization (*e.g.* non-battle casualties)? In such situations, does the personal "success" of conformists (promotion) only serve to depress the morale of the others by rewarding those who depart from the in-group mores?

In this panel study, as well as in several of the others we have reviewed here—for example, the study of soldiers' evaluations of the justification for their induction into the Army—reference group behavior is evidently related to the legitimacy ascribed to institutional arrangements. Thus, the older married soldier is less likely to think it "fair" that he was inducted; most enlisted men think it "unfair" that promotions are presumably based on "who you know, not what you know"; and so on. In part, this apparent emphasis on legitimacy is of course an artifact of the research: many of the questions put to soldiers had to do with their conception of the legitimate or illegitimate character of their situation or of prevailing institutional arrangements. But the researchers' own focus of interest was in turn the result of their having observed that soldiers were, to a significant degree, actually concerned with such issues of institutional legitimacy, as the spontaneous comments of enlisted men often indicate.[44]

This bears notice because imputations of legitimacy to social arrangements seem functionally related to reference group behavior. They apparently affect *the range of the inter-group or inter-individual comparisons* that will typically be made. If the structure of a rigid system of stratification, for example, is generally defined as legitimate, if the rights, perquisites and obligations of each stratum are generally held to be morally right, then the individuals within each stratum will be the less likely to take the situation of the other strata as a context for appraisal of their own lot. They will, presumably, tend to confine their comparisons to other members of their own or neighboring social stratum. If, however, the system of stratification is under wide dispute, then members of some strata are more likely to contrast their own situation with that of others, and shape their self-appraisals accordingly. This variation in the structure of systems and in the degree of legitimacy imputed to the rules of the game may help account for the often-noticed fact that the degree of dissatisfaction with their lot is often less among the people in severely depressed social strata in a relatively rigid social system, than among those strata who are apparently "better off" in a more mobile social system. At any rate, the *range of groups* taken as effective bases of comparison in different social systems may well turn out to be closely connected with the degree to which legitimacy is ascribed to the prevailing social structure.

Though much remains to be said, this is perhaps enough to suggest that the pattern of anticipatory socialization may have diverse

[44] For example, in response to the question, "If you could talk with the President of the United States, what are the three most important questions you would want to ask him about war and your part in it?", a substantial proportion of both Negro and white troops evidently raised questions regarding the legitimacy of current practices and arrangements in the Army. The Negro troops of course centered on unjust practices of race discrimination, but 31 per cent of the white troops also introduced "questions and criticisms of Army life." (I, 504, *et passim.*)

consequences for the individuals manifesting it, the groups to which they belong, and the more inclusive social structure. And through such re-examination of this panel study on the personal rewards of conformity, it becomes possible to specify some additional types of problems involved in a more comprehensive functional analysis of such reference group behavior. For example:

1. Since only a fraction of the in-group orient themselves positively toward the values of a non-membership group, it is necessary to discover the social position and personality types of those most likely to do so. For instance, are isolates in the group particularly ready to take up these alien values?
2. Much attention has been paid to the processes making for positive orientation to the norms of one's own group. But what are the processes making for such orientations to other groups or strata? Do relatively high rates of mobility serve to reinforce these latter orientations? (It will be remembered that *The American Soldier* provides data tangential to this point in the discussion of rates of promotion and assessment of promotion chances.) Suitably adapted, such data on actual rates of mobility, aspirations, and anticipatory socialization to the norms of a higher social stratum would extend a functional theory of conformist and deviant behavior.
3. What connections, if any, subsist between varying rates of mobility and acceptance of the legitimacy of the system of stratification by individuals diversely located in that system? Since it appears that systems with very low rates of mobility may achieve wide acceptance, what other interpretative variables need be included to account for the relationship between rates of mobility and imputations of legitimacy?
4. In civilian or military life, are the mobile individuals who are most ready to reaffirm the values of a power-holding or prestige-holding group the sooner accepted by that group? Does this operate effectively primarily as a latent function, in which the mobile individuals adopt these values because they experience them as superior, rather than deliberately adopting them only to gain acceptance? If such orientations are definitely motivated by the wish to belong, do they then become self-defeating, with the mobile individuals being characterized as strainers, strivers (or, in the Army, as brown-nosers bucking for promotion)?

Social processes sustaining and curbing positive orientations to non-membership groups. In the course of considering the functions of anticipatory socialization, we have made passing allusion to social processes which sustain or curb this pattern of behavior. Since it is precisely the data concerning such processes which are not easily caught up in the type of survey materials on attitudes pri-

92   *Continuities in Social Research*

marily utilized in *The American Soldier*, and since these processes are central to any theory of reference group behavior, they merit further consideration.

As we have seen, what is anticipatory socialization from the standpoint of the individual is construed as defection and nonconformity by the group of which he is a member. To the degree that the individual identifies himself with another group, he alienates himself from his own group. Yet although the field of sociology has for generations been concerned with the determinants and consequences of group cohesion, it has given little *systematic* attention to the complementary subject of group alienation. When considered at all, it has been confined to such special cases as second-generation immigrants, conflict of loyalties between gang and family, *etc.* In large measure, the subject has been left to the literary observer, who could detect the drama inherent in the situation of the renegade, the traitor, the deserter. The value-laden connotations of these terms used to describe identification with groups other than one's own definitely suggest that these patterns of behavior have been typically regarded from the standpoint of the membership group. (Yet one group's renegade may be another group's convert.) Since the assumption that its members will be loyal is found in every group, else it would have no group character, no dependability of action, transfer of loyalty to another group (particularly a group operating in the same sphere of politics or economy), is regarded primarily in affective terms of sentiment rather than in detached terms of analysis. The renegade or traitor or climber—whatever the folk-phrase may be—more often becomes an object of vilification than an object for sociological study.

The framework of reference group theory, detached from the language of sentiment, enables the sociologist to identify and to locate renegadism, treason, the assimilation of immigrants, class mobility, social climbing, *etc.* as so many special forms of identification with what is at the time a non-membership group. In doing so, it affords the possibility of studying these, not as *wholly* particular and unconnected forms of behavior, but as different expressions of similar processes under significantly different conditions. The transfer of allegiance of upper class individuals from their own to a lower class—whether this be in the pre-revolutionary period of 18th century France or of 20th century Russia—belongs to the same family of sociological problems as the more familiar identification of lower class individuals with a higher class, a subject which has lately begun to absorb the attention of sociologists in a society where upward social mobility is an established value. Our cultural emphases notwithstanding, the phenomenon of topdogs adopting the values of the underdog is as much a reference group phenomenon lending itself to further inquiry as the underdogs seeking to become topdogs.

In such defections from the in-group, it may turn out, as has often been suggested, that it is the isolate, nominally in a group but only slightly incorporated in its network of social relations, who is most likely to become positively oriented toward non-membership groups. But, even if generally true, this is a static correlation and, therefore, only partly illuminating. What needs to be uncovered is the process through which this correlation comes to hold. Judging from some of the qualitative data in *The American Soldier* and from other studies of group defection, there is continued and cumulative interplay between a deterioration of *social relations* within the membership group and positive *attitudes* toward the norms of a non-membership group.

What the individual experiences as estrangement from a group of which he is a member tends to be experienced by his associates as repudiation of the group, and this ordinarily evokes a hostile response. As social relations between the individual and the rest of the group deteriorate, the norms of the group become less binding for him. For since he is progressively seceding from the group and being penalized by it, he is the less likely to experience rewards for adherence to the group's norms. Once initiated, this process seems to move toward a cumulative detachment from the group, in terms of attitudes and values as well as in terms of social relations. And to the degree that he orients himself toward out-group values, perhaps affirming them verbally and expressing them in action, he only widens the gap and reinforces the hostility between himself and his in-group associates. Through the interplay of dissociation and progressive alienation from the group values, he may become doubly motivated to orient himself toward the values of another group and to affiliate himself with it. There then remains the distinct question of the objective possibility of affiliating himself with his reference group. If the possibility is negligible or absent, then the alienated individual becomes socially rootless. But if the social system realistically allows for such change in group affiliations, then the individual estranged from the one group has all the more motivation to belong to the other.

This hypothetical account of dissociation and alienation, which of course only touches upon the processes which call for research in the field of reference group behavior, seems roughly in accord with qualitative data in *The American Soldier* on what was variously called brown-nosing, bucking for promotion, and sucking up. Excerpts from the diary of an enlisted man illustrate the interplay between dissociation and alienation: the outward-oriented man is too sedulous in abiding by the official mores—"But you're *supposed* to [work over there]. The lieutenant said you were supposed to."— this evokes group hostility expressed in epithets and ridicule— "Everybody is making sucking, kissing noises at K and S now"—followed by increasing dissociation within the group—"Ostracism was visible, but mild . . . few were friendly toward them . . . occasions arose where people avoided their company"—and more frequent association with men representing the non-membership reference group—"W, S and K sucked all afternoon; hung around lieutenants and asked bright questions." In this briefly summarized account, one sees the mechanisms of the in-group operating to curb positive orientation to the official mores [45] as well as the process through which this orientation develops among those who take these mores as their major frame of reference, considering their ties with the in-group as of only secondary importance.

Judging from implications of this panel research on conformity-and-mobility, then, there is room for study of the consequences of reference group behavior patterns as well as for study of their determinants. Moreover, the consequences pertinent for sociology are not merely those for the individuals engaging in this behavior, but for the groups of which they are a part. There develops also the possibility that the extent to which legitimacy is accorded the structure of these groups and the status of their members may affect the range of groups or strata which they ordinarily take as a frame of reference in assessing their own situation. And finally, this panel

[45] "An official War Department pamphlet given to new recruits attempted to give 'bucking' a blessing: "'Bucking' implies all the things a soldier can honestly do to gain attention and promotion. The Army encourages individuals to put extra effort into drill, extra 'spit and polish' into personal appearance. At times this may make things uncomfortable for others who prefer to take things easier, but it stimulates a spirit of competition and improvement which makes ours a better Army." I, 264.

research calls attention to the need for close study of those processes in group life which sustain or curb positive orientations to non-membership groups, thus perhaps leading to a linking of reference group theory and current theories of social organization.

PSYCHOLOGICAL AND SOCIAL FUNCTIONS

IN our review of the foregoing case, an effort was made to distinguish between the consequences of positive orientation toward a non-membership group for the individual, the membership-group and the larger social system. If, as we assume, an established pattern of behavior typically has such diverse consequences, it can be usefully examined from both a psychological and sociological standpoint. On occasion, *The American Soldier* analyzes behavior only in terms of a psychological framework. In some of these instances, the same situation may be profitably re-examined in terms of its implications for a framework of functional sociology.[46] This is not to say that the sociological orientation is necessarily "superior" to the psychological, or that it is necessarily at odds with it. But it *is* different. And by regarding these materials from a perspective differing from that in the text itself, we may, perhaps, bring out further implications of these applied researches for social theory.

Case #6 (II, 272-84). Among the cases exhibiting a marked psychological orientation is the brief account of the experiences of men in replacement depots, those army stations through which they filtered from their training outfits to some depleted combat outfit in need of personnel. The author paints a vivid psychological portrait of the replacement depot: of the "apparently irreducible sources of psychological disturbance" characteristic of the depot, with its replacements handled in bulk and impersonally by permanent depot cadre, having only a casual status, and lacking the "sup-

---

[46] It is interesting to see how one's professional background apparently shapes one's description of *The American Soldier*. In his review of the book, Gordon W. Allport, the psychologist, refers to what he calls its "sociologistic bias." And here, a pair of sociologists are saying, in effect, that it has a marked "psychological orientation." The authors might well take comfort in the twin "charges."

port of social ties and the security of having an established niche in some organization." Probably, "the most salient psychological characteristic of depot life . . . was that the situation led to a state of anxious uncertainty without opportunity for resolving the tension." (II, 274) One consequence of the depot experience was to make the replacement "welcome many aspects of a permanent assignment." While this did not mean they welcomed combat itself, "even in this regard . . . the termination of anxious uncertainty was probably in some respects a psychological gain. The new combat man could say to himself, for better or for worse, 'This is it.' " (II, 176)

The Research Branch, then, was centrally concerned with the question: what were the effects of these experiences upon *the replacement?* But the same data involve another type of problem, this time from the standpoint of functional sociology: the problem, not of the effect of the depot upon the replacement, but upon his subsequent incorporation in a combat group.

Functional analysis of this situation would begin by conceptualizing the social role of the replacement depot, which falls into the category of an organization providing for *the movement of individuals from one group to another.* As typically follows upon a somewhat more generalized description of a situation, other situations nominally different on a common-sense level, are seen as belonging to the same general category. Materials presently scattered in the numerous pages of *The American Soldier* become cases in point of this pattern of transition from one group to another: for example, the replacement depot is, *in this respect,* essentially no different from the reassignment station as an intermediary between a combat outfit and a new domestic post. Furthermore, sociologists have long been interested in the standardized social patterns providing for passage from one group to another in various institutional areas, for example, the transition of the high school graduate to a first year at college.

The personal and social difficulties involved in such transfers are assumed to arise primarily from the dual process of breaking down old group affiliations (or of putting them into secondary place) and of building new group ties. That, in a sense, is comparable to the process of the recruit's initial absorption into his first army outfit, with all the attendant growing pains of group-formation. But in this special setting, the individual is immeasurably eased in his adjustment since it is not a problem peculiar to him. Every other member of the newly-forming group is experiencing a similar problem, whether he is a first-year college student or a raw army recruit.

Once he is a part of this group, however, transfer to another already established group is quite a different matter, as any child who is transferred from one school to another in mid-semester can report. In this case, his initial exposure to the new group is most apt to involve an intensification of old ties—his old friends, his former teachers, his old school are imbued with disproportionately great affect. This is much the same phenomenon as that of soldiers separated from their old combat outfits and settling into new domestic army stations. One study in *The American Soldier* reports that such returnees place tremendous importance on being permitted to "continue to wear the insignia of their old units" (II, 507-8),—just as the abruptly transferred school child may intensify his old group ties. Both reflect resistance to a sudden weaning from a former group affiliation. The school child, being a lone individual, presents no challenge to the unity of the new group, and in time, he is usually taken into the ranks. But should a sizeable number of new youngsters confront the group with their emphasis on old school ties, we might well find a need emerging for an "educational depot," to forestall the dysfunctional consequences of these challenges to the unity of the group. This is precisely the problem of the army situation. Being built on fragile enough grounds, the unity of an army outfit might be seriously impaired by the introduction of a sizeable number of replacements, if their former group attachment had not broken down prior to their admittance to the new outfit.

Thus from the perspective of the replacements' eventual ease of absorption into a combat group, new to them, as well as from the point of view of their potential effect upon the group they enter, there may well be a functional requirement for their *not* being transferred immediately from the training outfit to the outfit with which they will shortly serve in combat. One alternative is that which was in fact the practice utilized during the war years: filtering the newly trained soldier through replacement depots. This suggests the latent function possibly performed by the replacement depot: it may serve to loosen the soldier's previous army group ties, thus making him more amenable to ready absorption into his combat outfit. In much the same way that the sandhog adjusts to normal atmospheric pressure at the end of a day's work under water by going through de-compression chambers, so the soldier is *de-grouped* by passing through replacement depots. This would seem all the more important in view of the speed with which replacements were actually sent into combat upon joining a combat outfit. In one study, it was found that *half* the replacement infantrymen went into combat less than three days after joining their outfit.

In other words, the excessive psychological anxiety noted by the Research Branch as characteristic of depot life may also be regarded as a behavioral index of a state of suspended "grouplessness." But whichever is emphasized—the underlying sociological phenomenon of grouplessness or the external and visible psychological anxiety— the functional sociologist would seek to trace out its organizational consequences, *i.e.*, its impact on the absorption of the replacement into his most important army group, the unit with which he serves in combat.[47]

This anxiety accompanying the degrouping process may well be dysfunctional for the individual soldier at the time he is experiencing it, and for some soldiers, it may have had serious effects upon overall personal adjustment. Yet this same process of de-grouping may have functional consequences for other organizational units, particularly the combat outfit in which the de-grouped replacement is the more readily absorbed.[48] Empirical test of this hypothesis

[47] We have previously mentioned the similarity between the function of the replacement depot and that of the reassignment station through which the returnee soldier is transferred from his combat outfit to his domestic army post. An examination of the study of the returnee in *The American Soldier* (II— Chapter on problems of Rotation and Reconversion) suggests that the degrouping process of the returnee is of much longer duration, for the returnee has been removed from his most cohesive army group. Thus in a survey of returnees and non-overseas men in which the soldiers were asked about their sense of belonging to their new outfit, the returnees were much more apt to say they did not feel they belonged to their outfits than the non-returnees, *even though in a large proportion of the cases the returnees had been with the outfit longer than the non-returnees.* In the Air Force, for example, 34 per cent of the returnees and 15 per cent of the non-returnees said they did not feel they "belonged" to their outfits. The difference between returnee and non-returnee in other branches of the Army decreases slightly from the difference of 17 per cent in the more cohesive air corps to 11 per cent in the quartermaster corps. (II, 507) The rapidity and ease of the de-grouping process and subsequent re-absorption into a new group would appear to depend on the intensity of the former group ties.

[48] To note this possible function of anxiety is not thereby to *advocate* anxiety. For even as a concomitant of the de-grouping process, not all such anxiety situations are functional for the social organization. In the case of the officer candidate schools, for example, which "can be conceived of as an ordeal," one

could be provided by an extension of the procedure adopted in the study of returnees (see the foregoing footnote). For each level of men's attachment to their previous outfit, it could be determined, first, whether the longer the period that men have spent in a replacement depot, the more effectively they have divested themselves of their previous group solidarity, and second, whether those men who had been thus "de-grouped" were the more effectively incorporated into their new combat outfit. To the extent that this was found to be the case, it would have bearing on the more general problem of factors and processes affecting the passage from old to new membership groups. And, in some measure, this would supplement the perceptive analysis of the replacement depot provided by *The American Soldier.*

consequence of a high anxiety situation was to strip the officer candidate of any vestige of his former enlisted man's values, which apparently militated against his subsequent ability to see the enlisted man's point of view. After an analysis of the "ordeal" of an officer candidate school in case-study terms, it is said: ". . . there is enough plausibility in this account of the transmission of culture to suggest that we have in this process an explanation of why so many officers, themselves formerly enlisted men, seemed to fail as officers to carry over their enlisted experience and try to see the enlisted man's point of view in handling their men. (I, 391) From the hierarchy-conscious perspective of the Army, this may or may not be considered objectionable. But the evidence seems clear that enlisted men—products of a culture system which expounds the worth of democratic equality—functioned best when they believed the gap between themselves and their leaders was not inflexible, when they felt their officers had relatively few special privileges they did not have, and so on. (I, 369) But, in other cases, the functional consequences of the de-grouping process for the Army's objectives may far outweigh the temporary dysfunctional consequences to the individual exposed to the replacement depot. From the standpoint of a narrowly defined conception of social engineering, this might lead to recommendations for the extension of "de-grouping" through explicit provision for such transitional organizations or statuses in various institutional orders. But this would presuppose an exclusive concern with organizational objectives—*e.g.*, increased efficiency of a fighting machine—which one need not be ready to advocate. In this instance, for example, one's values may lead one to conclude that organizational efficiency, through de-grouping with its attendant anxieties, exacts too high a price. This is scarcely the first time that such moral problems of social engineering have occurred. It might be found, as so many 19th century writers asserted, that hunger, acute anxiety and insecurity are powerful incentives for work. Were this confirmed, it scarcely follows that the sociologist would *advocate* hunger as a prod to work.

CONCEPTS KINDRED
TO REFERENCE GROUP THEORY

FROM allusions scattered throughout the foregoing discussion, it is evident that certain facts of reference group behavior were noted long before the term, reference group, was coined by Hyman in his important study of 1942.[49] Thus, half a century ago, DuBois noted that "A white Philadelphian with $1,500 a year can call himself poor and live simply. A Negro with $1,500 a year ranks with the richest of his race and must usually spend more in proportion than his white neighbor in rent, dress and entertainment."[50] But though the specific fact that self-appraisals are *relative* to "the" group frame-

[49] H. Hyman, *The Psychology of Status, op. cit.*
[50] W. E. B. DuBois, *The Philadelphia Negro*, 1899, as quoted by E. F. Frazier, *The Negro in the United States* (New York: Macmillan, 1949, 299n). Frazier develops the observation further to indicate the cross-pressures to which the Negro professional man is subject. "The Negro professional man or clerical worker often feels under great compulsion to keep up the requirements of upper-class behavior in the Negro group and at the same time act in the role of a middle-class professional or white collar worker in the community at large." And he goes on to say, in effect, that changing networks of social relations—increasing integration "into the larger community"—shift the balance of pertinent reference groups, when he remarks that "As the Negro becomes increasingly integrated into the larger community, the professional man or woman or clerical worker is escaping from the obligations of the upper-class role in the Negro community and *can orient his behavior with reference to* his middle-class status." *Ibid.*, 300, italics supplied.
    Interestingly enough, technical problems in developing samples for public opinion polls *forced* attention to the same fact that economic status is relative to the income distribution of the environing community. Thus: "The owner of a small shoe store in Dubuque, Iowa, who is married, has no children, and enjoys an income of $5,000 a year, finds himself thrown with the prosperous people of the town. . . He finds himself, economically, close to 'the top of the heap' in Dubuque. His association with other prosperous people inclines him to regard his fate as being rather intimately bound up with that of the prosperous people elsewhere. . . Give the same $5,000 a year income to an assistant sales manager who lives in New York City and has two daughters of school age, and you will find that he does not regard himself as belonging to the same economic level as the Dubuque shoe dealer, nor does he think or vote like that man on many important subjects." Elmo Roper, "Classifying respondents by economic status," *Public Opinion Quarterly*, 1940, 4, 270; see also, S. S. Wilks, "Representative sampling and poll reliability," *ibid.*, 263: "A $3000-a-year salary in a small Arkansas town means one thing and a $3000-a-year salary in New York City means something entirely different. The problem of economic status in sampling is handled at present on what amounts to a relative basis in each sampling locality. . ."

work was often remarked, it was not conceptualized in terms general enough to lead to systematic research on the implications of the fact. Such a term as "reference group" is useful, not because the term itself helps explain behavior, but because it does not easily allow us to overlook this component in self-appraisals. The very generality of the term leads to the perception of similarities beneath apparent dissimilarities of behavior.

But apart from these isolated observations, there have been several lines of development in sociology and social psychology which now give promise of merging in a functional theory of reference group behavior. Each of these has, after its own fashion, made major contributions, but in retrospect, the impressive fact is that, in large measure, their mutual implications have not yet been consolidated. As is generally known, these are the conceptions of in- and out-groups set forth by Sumner, the ideas regarding the social self developed by James, Cooley and Mead, the more recent systematic researches on reference group behavior represented by the work of Hyman, Sherif and Newcomb, and the very numerous special studies on concrete problems of human behavior such as those dealing with acculturation, assimilation, the marginal man, social mobility, multiple roles, conflicting loyalties, cross-pressures, and the like.

The general and, in this truncated form, uninstructive fact that men are variously oriented to groups besides their own was captured in the terminology invented by Sumner to distinguish between "ourselves, the we-group, or in-group, and everybody else, or the others-groups, out-groups." [51] Sumner proceeded to describe the relations between these types of groups. Essentially, these somewhat premature observations held that conditions of amity and order obtain in the in-group whereas the relation to out-groups is that of hostility, plunder and exploitation. That this is the case (under unspecified conditions) Sumner was able to show through numerous *illustrations* drawn from history and ethnology. But in adopting a descriptive, rather than an analytical, outlook on the facts of the case, he inevitably blurred and obscured the otherwise conspicuous fact that, under certain conditions, the out-group becomes a basis of *positive*, not merely hostile, reference [52] and that

[51] W. G. Sumner, *Folkways* (Boston: Ginn, 1906), 12.
[52] This case of discontinuity in reference group theory is all the more significant since Sumner of course recognized, in other contexts, that what he

the science of sociology is thereby committed to determine the conditions under which one or the other orientation to out-groups obtained. In short, the initial distinction put Sumner well on the way toward opening up a series of problems regarding reference group behavior. But this avenue to the development of a theory of reference group behavior, in principle open to those who would explore it since the appearance of *Folkways* in 1906, was not followed up by systematic research.

With only the slight exaggeration inevitable in having a single sentence summarize a large number of facts, it may be said that the anticipations of reference group theory by James, Cooley, and Mead also remained almost wholly undeveloped for a generation or more. Particularly among sociologists their conceptions were treated, not as a beginning but as a virtual conclusion, repeatedly quoted and illustrated with new examples of multiple selves, the looking-glass self, responses to the significant gestures of "others," and so on. And because the words of the forefathers became final words, little was built upon their insightful suggestions. They were honored, not in the manner in which men of science do honor to their predecessors, by extending and elaborating their formulations on the basis of cumulatively developed problems and systematic researches bearing on these problems, but in the manner in which littérateurs honor their predecessors, by repeatedly quoting "definitive" passages from the masters' works.

Certain social psychologists, among whom Hyman, Sherif, and Newcomb [53] are representative, have somewhat advanced this theory

---

called "imitation" or "emulation" of out-group patterns of behavior did occur. But these observations were not systematically linked with his prior distinctions between in- and out-groups in such a way that they resulted in a series of analytical problems regarding the diverse patterns of reference group behavior under varied conditions. So, too, he commented on the parvenu (107) who is, of course, passing from one in-group to another, but again without developing the theoretical and analytical questions highlighted by such shifts in group membership. He has, in short, numerous observations pertinent to problems of reference groups, but these remain scattered and unconnected rather than analytically drawn together and seen as cognate.

[53] Hyman, *op. cit.*; M. Sherif's *Psychology of Social Norms* (New York, Harper, 1936) moved toward a conception of reference groups more fully developed in his later book, *An Outline of Social Psychology*. T. M. Newcomb's monograph, *Personality and Social Change* (New York, Dryden Press, 1943) represented a major step forward in this development, and his just-published *Social Psychology* (New York, Dryden Press, 1950) includes more recent researches.

by designing empirical researches which would feed back into theoretical formulations of reference group behavior. And since their data were systematic rather than anecdotal, they soon found themselves confronted with many of the same theoretical problems which emerge from the researches of *The American Soldier*. Newcomb's study, in particular, centered not only on the reference group contexts of attitudes, perceptions, and judgments, but also considered the social organization which affected the selection of reference groups.

The researches of *The American Soldier* belong to this last line of development, consisting of numerous empirical studies of ostensibly different types of behavior, which nevertheless involve similar social and psychological processes. Since social scientists are equipped with some, though not nearly enough, methods for the study of reference group behavior in the ordinary course of everyday life, they need not look only to the contrived situations of the social-psychology laboratory, which leaves outside its walls the established social relations which comprise the organization of groups in society. An Army private bucking for promotion may only in a narrow and theoretically superficial sense be regarded as engaging in behavior different from that of an immigrant assimilating the values of a native group, or of a lower-middle-class individual conforming to his conception of upper-middle-class patterns of behavior, or of a boy in a slum area orienting himself to the values of a settlement house worker rather than the values of the street corner gang, or of a Bennington student abandoning the conservative beliefs of her parents to adopt the more liberal ideas of her college associates, or of a lower-class Catholic departing from the pattern of his in-group by casting a Republican vote, or of an eighteenth century French aristocrat aligning himself with a revolutionary group of the time. However these may differ in detail, they are not necessarily unconnected forms of behavior "belonging," respectively, to the jurisdictions of the sociology of military life, race and ethnic relations, social mobility, delinquency (or "social disorganization"), educational sociology, political sociology and the sociology of revolution.

Such conventional divisions in terms of superficially distinct spheres of human behavior serve to obscure the similarity of social and psychological processes with which more abstract conceptions, such as those of reference group theory, are concerned. As can be seen from the matrix of variables in the first part of this paper, the combination of elements may differ, thus giving rise to overtly distinctive forms of behavior, but these may nevertheless be only different expressions of similar processes under different conditions. They may all represent cases of individuals becoming identified with reference groups to which they aspire or in which they have just achieved membership. And to the extent that this is so, the observed behaviors can, in principle, be derived from a few relatively general conceptions holding for them all, rather than having their similarity obscured by varying terminologies, such as promotion, assimilation (and acculturation), class striving (and overconformity), socialization, social deviation, renegadism, or again, relative deprivation, role conflict, cross-pressures and false consciousness.

The early development of reference group conceptions is studded with instances in which particular historical occurrences in the society led sociologists to focus on spheres of social behavior in which patterns of reference group behavior happened to be conspicuous. Thus, studies of assimilation, clearly a process in which there is reference to the culture of non-membership groups, were precipitated by waves of immigration to this country and the subsequent throes of absorption of people of diverse cultural background. So, too, growing sociological interest in mobility between social classes and in "false consciousness" whereby men identify themselves with classes "to which they do not belong," seems in part a response to open public discussion of classes, and to a possibly heightened sense of class conflict. In such instances, the sociologists' choice of subject-matter was more nearly dictated by concrete practical problems than by the requirements of systematic theory. As a result, there was a marked tendency for the interpretative conceptions to remain *particularized* to the special sphere of behavior under consideration. Distinctive concepts appropriate for each sphere were developed as separate and almost isolated tools of analysis, and their theoretical overlappings and connections were often lost to view. Specialization of inquiry in terms of the concrete practical problems generated by social change sometimes developed at the expense of a more general body of theory. Special cases usurped attention and special concepts were introduced, but the task of their theoretical consolidation was only barely begun.

Though our brief examination of cases has provided only intimations to this effect, they are perhaps enough to lend weight to the possibility that these are not unrelated forms of social behavior but concrete manifestations of underlying patterns of reference group behavior.[54] It seems probable that if special inquiries trace out the theoretical connections between these forms of behavior, they will develop one of those theories of the middle range which consolidate otherwise segregated hypotheses and empirical uniformities. The wider, more inclusive conception would mean, for example, that research on the adjustment-patterns of immigrants would contribute its share to the same theory that helps direct research on, say, factors in social mobility. And these steps toward consolidation would result in a more rapid cumulation of reference group theory, since research on diverse departments of human behavior would become mutually stimulating and sustaining. At least, that seems to be the import of this preliminary review of reference group conceptions in *The American Soldier*.

[54] A historian of science has commented on comparable problems of theoretical consolidation in the natural and physical sciences: ". . . of all forms of mental activity the most difficult to induce . . . is the art of handling the same bundle of data as before, but placing them in a new system of relations with one another and giving them a different framework, all of which virtually means putting on a different kind of thinking-cap for the moment." H. Butterfield, *The Origins of Modern Science* (London, Bell, 1949), 1.

HANS SPEIER

THE AMERICAN SOLDIER AND THE SOCIOLOGY OF MILITARY ORGANIZATION

*T*HE sociology of military organization must be based on an analysis of the administrative rules and practices which govern the life of the organization. Account must be taken of the way in which decisions are planned, made and executed. Not only the organization itself requires study but also its relations with other organizations, *i.e.* especially the functional interdependence of military and civilian agencies and the distribution of power and responsibility among them. Finally, there are problems arising out of coalition warfare which affect the performance of all national military organizations fighting a common enemy. Intelligence, security, staff planning, command functions, logistics and communications, administrative procedures varying from nation to nation, coordination and mutual support of various national units,—these and numerous other matters complicate unification of effort in coalition warfare and modify the life of the military organizations in each allied nation.

At present, only a fraction of the data necessary for an adequate sociology of American military organization during World War II is available. There are factual accounts and analytical studies dealing with selected aspects of the subject. In addition, valuable material is contained in memoirs written by military and civilian leaders. On the whole, however, our knowledge of German and Japanese military organizations during World War II is, at least potentially, superior to our knowledge of American military organization, because a large amount of unique information about the enemies has come to light in the various war crimes trials.

The two volumes on *The American Soldier* can fill many gaps in our knowledge of American military organization. They contain, as Professor Stouffer points out, "a mine of data, perhaps unparalleled in magnitude in the history of any single research enterprise in social psychology or sociology." (I, 29) It will be noted, of course, that the Research Branch, Information and Education Division, U.S. Army, ascertained primarily the attitudes of military personnel (excluding sailors and marines), or more exactly the responses to questions from which these attitudes were inferred. *The American Soldier* presents research on the American soldier rather than the U.S. Army and was not undertaken for the purpose of providing information on American military organization. It contains nevertheless a great deal of material which is indispensable for assessing the human implications of the U.S. Army as a social organization during the second World War.

The following comments cannot do justice to the large variety of problems, related to the sociology of military organization, which are raised in the two volumes and to the solution of which they contribute. A severely selective treatment is forced upon anyone who ventures to comment on this publication within the confines of a brief chapter.

I shall discuss first the question as to what place these volumes occupy in the history of the sociology of war and military organizations.

Next, I shall ask what lessons can be learned from *The American Soldier* about the moral fabric of American society during the second World War and about the personal commitment of Americans to national causes.

Third, *The American Soldier* contains many challenges to peacetime social research. Singling out one of these challenges for comment I shall discuss the leads which the work gives to studies in the field of sociology of knowledge.

Finally, I shall conclude this chapter with a few observations on the question as to what is, or what can be, the relationship between policy making and attitude research.

THE SOCIOLOGY OF WAR AND MILITARY
ORGANIZATION

IN the past American sociology has shown little interest in analyzing military institutions and the social aspects of war. American sociologists have almost entirely devoted themselves to studying society in times of peace.

This has in part been the result of fortunate circumstances. War has been on the whole a more remote experience to the American community than to any other big nation in the world. The main American conquest has been that of nature; nor has the main national effort to protect the integrity of the Republic been made against foreign invaders, as has for centuries been true of all countries on the continent of Europe. With very few notable exceptions the interest of American sociology has been absorbed by domestic social problems rather than international affairs. To the extent that American sociology subscribed to the theory of progress, moreover, wars were regarded as enterprises of a more or less barbarous past. Advances in science, industrial production, trade, and thus in civilization were expected to increase the pacification of international affairs. It is perhaps understandable that in these circumstances the valuable contributions of early European sociology to the analysis of war and military institutions have been as widely neglected in American sociology as have been later contributions by historians and military scientists.

The American Soldier thus represents a major research effort in a field largely unfamiliar to American sociology. Through its reliance on methods of opinion research the work continued a *methodological* tradition, and developed it far beyond past achievements, but there was no solid basis of accumulated sociological knowledge in recent American literature on which the authors could build.

After reading *The American Soldier* it is interesting to look back at some older writings on military matters and to compare their performance with that of modern social science. Obviously, older authors could rely neither on large research staffs nor on the modern refined methods of attitude research. They studied military institutions in the light of varying historical circumstances and political conditions; the evidence they offer for their propositions does not always live up to modern scientific standards. The historical perspective which they provide and, most of all, their keen awareness of the political context in which military organizations function, make their writings nevertheless worthwhile reading. For all its advanced methods and techniques of investigation, modern sociology has on the whole a weak sense of the interconnections of the problems it investigates, and it is chiefly in this respect that older writings can be useful to us.

The volumes on *The American Soldier* present research undertaken as "a practical engineering job, not a scientific job." (I, 5) In sifting and analyzing the enormous wealth of data that had been gathered the authors acknowledge their debt to dynamic psychology, learning theory, social anthropology, and to various sociological contributions, especially those concerned with the understanding of social role and social class, social institutions, social control and change. (I, 31) At the same time, the original frame of reference for the investigation was pre-established by Army needs, and the authors do not fail to point out that theirs had been "no operation in an academic ivory tower." (I, 11)

In view of the constraints and limitations that sometimes prevail outside ivory towers it could not be expected that military institutions would be studied from the independent and detached point of view, which is to be found in the best writings of the past. Instead, the authors were inevitably restricted in their postwar analysis by the initial orientation of their wartime studies. Given these restrictions it is remarkable that the value of many of their findings has outlasted the need which they satisfied; various contributions beyond immediate social engineering requirements have been made and are of general significance in an attempt to understand contemporary society. The general significance of the work can perhaps be even increased if in the future some of the suitable data are further studied in the light of research by earlier sociologists and historians. Although it will not be possible to test with the data on hand every hypothesis that can be derived from earlier analyses of military organization, it should be possible, in the one or the other case, to refine the interpretation of the new data.

By way of illustration, let us examine in some detail the following statement in *The American Soldier* which deals explicitly with the nature of military organization.

"The Army was a new world for most civilian soldiers. Of its many contrasts with civilian institutions, three may be cited:
1. Its authoritarian organization demanding rigid obedience.
2. Its highly stratified social system, in which hierarchies of deference were formally and minutely established by official regulation, subject to penalties for infraction, on and off duty.
3. Its emphasis on traditional ways of doing things and its discouragement of initiative." (I, 55)

One might first consider the desirability of certain qualifications of these statements. As to "authoritarianism," is it not true that military life provided in some respects at least a compensatory *release* from other forms of subordination to which many soldiers had been exposed in their civilian past? So far as the so-called "caste system" of the Army is concerned, modern mass armies are institutions in which many of the civilian status differences are effectively disregarded and levelled off and in which many civilian obstacles impeding the development of close comradeship among persons of different civilian status are inoperative. In view of this process, which Max Weber spoke of as "negative democratization," the parallel drawn by the analysts in *The American Soldier* between relationships in the Army and "the social relations of whites and Negroes, especially in the South" appears to be overdrawn. (I, 46) Finally, although mass armies, like all large bureaucratic mass organizations, develop standard operating procedures and routinize life, their "discouragement of initiative" should certainly not be so complete as to prevent the execution of military tasks, particularly in certain types of modern combat, which demand initiative of a very high order. Nor should it be forgotten that military life offers many opportunities for dangerous excitements which, for better or worse, are lacking in civilian life.

Apart from these relatively minor qualifications, however, it will be noted that none of the three characteristics of military organization which are said to constitute important contrasts with civilian institutions—authoritarianism, stratification, and traditionalism—takes account of the political *function* of military organizations. Military organizations safeguard of course, in case of outside attack, the survival of a society and the values cherished in it. The three characteristic features mentioned are denials of freedom, equality, and individual initiative, *i.e.* values which are cherished in our society by civilians and military alike, with minor exceptions to be found again among civilians as well as the military. Yet military organizations fighting for the realization or maintenance of these desirable values are certainly not organized primarily for the purpose of maximizing freedom, equality, and initiative within their own bounds but for the purpose of minimizing inefficiency; by the same token censorship in wartime may be necessary, while the war may be fought for the establishment of political conditions which will guarantee freedom of expression.

If the distaste for the negation of liberal and democratic values within military organizations is expressed without regard to the requirements of military efficiency, such distaste reflects, at least in part, "the anti-military inclinations of modern populations," to use Auguste Comte's phrase. Now much of the traditionalism of the Army undoubtedly reduces efficiency, and *The American Soldier* contains proof to that effect. But in analyzing the data on soldiers' attitudes, the authors made no attempt to distinguish clearly between functionally necessary and gratuitous or functionally detrimental negations of freedom, equality, and initiative in the Army. Similarly, the analysts took no account of the possibility that many soldiers might have complained about lack of freedom, equality, and opportunity for initiative in the Army without thereby indicating that reasons for such complaints do not exist in civilian life. In other words, the cited contrasts between military and civilian institutions may in part result from the fact that in our civilization the gap between reality and professed values exists in civilian as well as in military life, but is observed more easily and criticized more readily in military organizations. Viewing the problem in historical perspective, Comte was of the opinion that the system of conscription itself proved the existence of anti-military inclinations; he remarked that "the masses constituting the armies are in principle opposed to military life which has become for them a purely temporary burden borne by everyone who has to carry it only in the continuous expectation of imminent and inevitable dismissal." (*Sociology*, Chapt. 12)

Many of the observations contained in the earlier literature, pertinent to the question under review, are presented in terms which modern science looks at with condescension. They could nevertheless be translated into language that would be useful in current research. Adam Ferguson, in his *Principles of Moral and Political Science* (1792), as well as in his *Essay on the History of Civil Society* (1767), dealt with the dependence of popular moral notions upon the major activities prevailing in a given society. He held that men esteemed those qualities most highly which in the prevailing circumstances were the most necessary. Trade and commerce could progress only at the expense of aspirations necessary for other pursuits. This meant, according to Ferguson, that the esteem of courage would shrink in modern society where men have to be rich rather than brave, in order to be great. As he therefore believed the military spirit to be weakened in modern society, Ferguson foresaw that the much praised reforms of modern society might prepare civilized mankind for submission to a rule of force if the sword were ever entrusted to those who detest civilized life.

These doubts, which were shared by many other political scientists and early sociologists, were usually resolved in two ways. Either it was held that the advance of industrialism would lead to an era of peace among the industrial nations and that Ferguson's problem would therefore become insignificant; or it was held that industrial progress in the techniques of destruction would alleviate the danger of subjugation by backward nations. Adam Smith, who called the art of war "the noblest of all arts," held this view.

Those who doubted that progress in industrialization would pacify international relations among industrial societies viewed the characteristic development of anti-military mores in modern liberal societies with alarm and sometimes—in the pursuit of ulterior designs—with satisfaction (as was true of the Fascists).

S. B. McKinley in his book on *Democracy and Military Power* (1934) presented, in historical perspective, his challenging thesis that the rise and survival of democracy depended on the predominant importance of the foot soldier on the field of battle and that the advance of a highly intricate military technology would doom the democratic form of government because of the opportunities for monopolistic elite control of the most efficient means of destruction. Harold D. Lasswell, in his essay on "The Garrison State" (1939), too, called attention to the political consequences of the development of highly specialized and highly skilled personnel in the exertion of violence. The volumes on *The American Soldier* contain a great deal of material that sheds much light on this politically important problem but the authors do not utilize their data in a manner which a greater sensitivity to these problems would have permitted. The striking differences in attitudes between airmen and infantry soldiers, which the Research Branch found to exist, are especially pertinent in this context, although the data do not allow a clarification of all aspects of the problem.

If the available data were to be thus used in combination with lessons to be learned from the memoirs of persons who were placed in positions of great civilian or military responsibility, it should be possible to give a far more accurate picture of the similarities and contrasts between military and civilian organizations than has ever been true before.

If the *function* of military organizations rather than the *attitudes* of civilians toward military practices are taken as the point of departure, it is evidently the expectation and the demand to destroy and to kill as well as the greater risk of suffering death by violence which distinguish the soldier from the civilian. This point, rather than authoritarianism, inequality, and traditionalism would seem to deserve the main attention of the analyst. Military life is more serious than civilian life because it is more deadly and because soldiers are required both to die for the community as a whole and to kill in the interest of its preservation. Older writings never fail to focus on this point. In modern studies its implications have been explored most fully by psychiatrists and by some alert military students of warfare.

In his field studies of the rate of fire among about four hundred infantry companies in the Central Pacific and European theatres of men in combat, based on interviews of the men in the presence of their commanders and junior leaders, Colonel S. L. A. Marshall found that not more than 15 per cent of the surviving men "had actually fired at the enemy positions or personnel with rifles, carbines, grenades, bazookas, BARs, or machine guns during the course of an entire engagement." (*Men Against Fire,* 1947, p. 54) Attempting to account for this startling result, Colonel Marshall comments,

"The average firer will have less resistance to firing on a house or a tree than upon a human being. . . . The average, normal man who is fitted into the uniform of an American ground soldier . . . is what his

home, his religion, his schooling, and the moral code and ideals of his
society have made him. The Army cannot unmake him. It must reckon
with the fact that he comes from a civilization in which aggression, connected with the taking of life, is prohibited and unacceptable. The teaching and the ideals of that civilization are against killing, against taking
advantage. The fear of aggression has been expressed to him so strongly
and absorbed by him so deeply and pervadingly—practically with his
mother's milk—that it is part of the normal man's emotional make-up.
This is his great handicap when he enters combat. It stays his trigger
finger even though he is hardly conscious that it is a restraint upon him."
(*Ibid.*, p. 78)

Perhaps Colonel Marshall's explanation has been made more convincing by application of depth psychology to the examination of
psychiatric casualties, and it might be difficult to increase our understanding of such phenomena through the use of opinion research methods. But given the specific advantages of the latter
techniques in the observation of mass phenomena, the authors of
The American Soldier might find it in any case worth their while
to develop their findings on the nature of military organizations
further in the light of these suggestions which earlier sociologists,
psychiatrists, and military writers are able to offer.

I should like to add another remark to the observation that the
specific social function of the Army has not received as much attention in *The American Soldier* as it seems to deserve in a sociological appraisal of a military organization.

The authors of *The American Soldier* have not fully explored the
implications of the fact that armies are, as it were, *male societies*.
It may be surmised that each author knows far more about the
behavioral consequences of this fact than is reflected in the two
volumes. Nor is it surprising that the opportunities of the Research
Branch to investigate sexual deprivations and indulgences and
their effects upon morals and manners were severely limited by
taboos, considerations of expediency, patriotic feelings and by the
technical obstacles which survey methods would have encountered
when applied to this subject.

The problem can be briefly stated as follows. Since all members
of a social organization belong to many other groups as well and
participate in the many-faceted life of society, their basic loyalties
and demands upon life are so diversified as to create special problems to the integration of soldiers into an efficient military team.

A modern soldier may also be a husband, an engineer in civilian life, a Swedish-American, a Republican, *etc.* Hence, the identifications and loyalties of this man are manifold in content and intensity. As a soldier, he is expected to subordinate all other loyalties to his identification with the armed forces. Conflicts among the various demands upon life and loyalties which tie him into the larger social network are likely to arise and in serious cases to interfere with his military performance. The requirements of military discipline and the demands for readiness to face the risks of combat unswervingly, with professional sang-froid, and in fact, with enthusiasm, are best met in closely knit military groups that have a highly developed and frequently fiercely exclusive esprit de corps.

There are many historical instances which suggest that the exacting demands to suppress or condemn all other loyalties in conflict with this spirit of exclusiveness are most readily met under certain specific conditions. The social forces likely to be most averse to military discipline and the development of a military esprit de corps are strong family ties and strong religious beliefs in the sinfulness of killing. Conversely those military organizations have been most closely knit which succeeded in amalgamating military and religious loyalties, as was true, for example, in the case of military religious orders like the Templars, or of Cromwell's Army. Similarly, the rise of modern military discipline in the Sixteenth Century was so closely related to Protestant religious beliefs that the new discipline became known in Europe as the Protestant discipline. As to the relation between military esprit de corps and family bonds, rich historical evidence suggests that the most closely knit military elite corps achieved their extraordinary cohesion by adherence to celibacy or homosexualism. The Janissaries in the prime of their history are an outstanding illustration of the first practice and—if one shuns more recent illustrations—the armies of ancient Greece illustrate the second. The third general possibility of reconciling the requirements of military organizations as male societies with the natural demands of its members upon life is by way of tolerating organized prostitution and sporadic sexual license.

In modern, civilized societies these problems of military organization are not often faced intrepidly and rarely discussed without passion or indignation, because the mores of civilian society do not permit candor in this regard. The data bearing on this subject, contained in *The American Soldier,* allow only limited insights. It would have been possible, nevertheless, to recognize and define the problem which under modern conditions is essentially one of a compromise between the avowed standards of conduct in peacetime society and conflicting forces operative in wartime military organizations. The tangentially important materials, which the volumes do contain on this subject, could then have been examined for further insights into these problems.

PERSONAL COMMITMENT AND THE
MORAL FABRIC

THE data in *The American Soldier* on the personal commitment and on the orientation of soldiers toward the war present a gloomy picture. While some of the individual parts of the picture almost certainly result from the use of methods which do not permit any delicate probing into motivations and convictions, the composite picture leaves no doubt that the American soldier had neither any strong beliefs about national war aims nor a highly developed sense of personal commitment to the war effort. He did not think much about the meaning of the war as a whole and displayed a tendency to "accept momentarily any plausibly worded interpretation of the war." (I, 431) There was tacit acceptance of the war as a necessity but a marked reluctance to state its meaning in terms of principles or causes. (I, 433 ff.) This passivity and disillusionment extended beyond the strong "taboo against any talk of a flag-waving variety" among combat men (II, 150): there seems to have been a widespread disinclination to any talk of any variety concerning American war aims. When the men were asked to state freely their own understanding of American war aims in writing, more than half of them either did not respond at all or gave "one word, slogan-like concepts—'Freedom,' 'Peace' and the like—" in reply. Only 7 per cent of the sample answered realistically that the war was being waged in order to protect national security. (I, 436)

On the basis of other data, the Research Branch nevertheless came to the conclusion "that the men were relatively satisfied with respect to their understanding of the issues of the war." (I, 438) The sense of national danger did not seem to persist long after Pearl Harbor; early in 1943 only 1 per cent of the soldiers conceded that the enemy had a chance of winning the war, and throughout the conflict American soldiers grossly under-estimated the probable duration of the war. The desire to go home among soldiers overseas was very strong. Early in 1944, for example, only 30 per cent of a sample taken in the South Pacific agreed with the statement, "Men talk a lot about going home but most men would not really want to go back until Japan is defeated." (I, 187) The men believed that they could be replaced without impairing the war effort and "that 18 months to 2 years of overseas service was all the men could stand." (II, 456) There are very many other data corroborating the findings I have cited.

If the United States had lost the war, there can be little doubt that these findings would have been drawn upon to explain the defeat. It is indeed exceedingly difficult to understand, on the basis of the research here reviewed, why the American armed forces fought as well as they did.

The answer to this puzzling question is probably only in part supplied by the rich evidence contained in *The American Soldier* pointing to the extraordinary importance of primary group relations in sustaining morale. It would be erroneous, I believe, to treat as separate and independent the factor of generalized convictions and that of primary group relations in assessing the causes of high morale. There is no reason to doubt that strong generalized convictions about the war or a high sense of commitment would affect the nature of primary group relations and that passivity, disillusionment or haziness in the orientation toward the war impoverish not only the individual's rational understanding of the world he lives in but also the intellectual and moral life of the primary group to which he belongs.

Unfortunately, no comparable data are available on the personal commitment and orientation toward the war of soldiers in other national armies; nor do we have comparable data from earlier wars, although it should be possible to undertake such studies on the basis of letters, diaries, and similar material. It would of course be particularly important to know whether or not there has been a secular trend toward increased passivity and, if so, whether or not this trend has been accompanied by an increased vulnerability to deprivations. The reliance on primary groups for security and comfort may also have been subject to a great many variations; for example, the individual may have become more dependent upon identifications with his group members or with group leaders, as broader convictions and beliefs have faded.

"Military institutions are intimately bound up with that state of culture which the nation has attained," the German General von der Goltz once said, and this has been amply proved by early sociologists like Ferguson, Comte and Spencer; historians like Delbrück, Omar, and Ferrero; military writers like Clausewitz, Jomini, Fuller and many others. It would be quite erroneous, however, to conclude that the orientation of soldiers toward a war which they fight is merely a matter of the national culture to which they belong.

There are at least two or three other major factors which influence and enter into this "orientation" and may render any prediction based merely upon a knowledge of national culture hazardous and unreliable. Despite the continuity of the culture, forecasts about the orientation toward a war in the future cannot safely be derived from past experiences, and the experience of American military organization in World War II in particular offers no safe guidance to what might happen in the case of a third world war.

First, it appears reasonable to assume that the orientation toward war is influenced by what happens to the homeland. If part of the second world war had been fought on American soil or if enemy bombs had been dropped on American cities, popular notions of the war would in all likelihood have been severely affected. It is not possible to say whether in such circumstances pre-occupation with safety would have reduced even further the concern with "ideological" issues, whether the emotional involvement in the war effort would have gained in importance and been channeled in the direction of heightened ferocity, or whether the more direct and concrete experience with war at home would have led to greater intellectual concern with the issue of the war as a whole. We can only guess about the nature and the direction of the morale effects of deprivations greater than those suffered during the last war, and yet it may be precisely problems of such order which social scientists might be called upon to answer in the future.

Second, the nature of the enemy, or more exactly the image held of the enemy, born of traditions and influenced by enemy action and home propaganda, affects the "orientation toward the war." The popular image of the enemy influences both the conduct of soldiers and any popular definitions of war aims, which in turn enter into the conception of the war. Experiences in World War II illustrate this point. The attitudes of American soldiers toward the Germans differed markedly from attitudes toward the Japanese; although the Japanese were less well armed and in that sense weaker than the Germans, the latter were less fiercely hated, according to evidence contained in *The American Soldier,* than the former. Similarly the Germans behaved differently toward the French and the Poles. Even the same national enemy may, for special reasons, be fought according to different "conceptions" in different theaters of operation. For example, the bloody fighting with Rommel's Africa Corps approached the character of a "gentleman's war" more closely than any other campaign fought against the German Armed Forces during World War II.

In this connection it may be suggested that not one of the least important implications of cold war activities would appear to be their effect upon the popular image of the potential enemy in case of war. In view of these considerations it might be particularly misleading to assume that the orientation of American soldiers toward the last war can be regarded as indicating orientation toward a war in which the United States were to face different enemies.

Third, the orientation toward a war is in part dependent upon definitions of the war, its meaning and aims, given by national leaders. It cannot be expected that the "conception of the war" will be the result of an unaided intellectual effort on the part of each individual. Comprehending the issue of a war is a matter requiring a high degree of political interest, knowledge and intelligence. When the Research Branch, in August 1942, administered its questionnaire concerning soldiers' conceptions of the war it introduced eight statements regarding each of which the respondents were asked to indicate agreement, disagreement or indecision: "Here are some quotations from speeches or the press representing many different views expressed by different people. You will agree with some and disagree with others." (I, 432) It is entirely possible that the percentages of disagreement with statements characterized by the authors as "cynical" or "superficial" would have been higher if those statements which reflected "the defensive necessity of the war" had been the stirring words of a great national leader. The ultimate effect of such leadership upon the popular notions of the war should not be regarded merely as a matter of propagandistic manipulation. If hosts of propagandists were called upon to spread a "consistent, favorable, intellectual orientation to the war," there would still have to be a voice which they can echo and a spirit in which they partake.

The American Soldier nowhere suggests that its authors would disagree with these comments, which call attention to some of the general conditions under which the reported attitudes and opinions were formed. In the absence of a comparative analysis of these conditions, their causal significance remains largely concealed and is not fully appreciated in *The American Soldier.*

The fact that we have recently come to appreciate more fully and more precisely the importance of participation in small groups for the cohesion of the social fabric, combined with our experience of victory in a war to which large masses contributed without much concern for matters of conviction about the war, should not lead us to assume that the strength and nature of convictions will not matter in a future crisis.

EMPIRICAL CONTRIBUTIONS TO THE SOCIOLOGY OF KNOWLEDGE

THE war-time findings of the Research Branch will contribute to a better understanding of many social relations in civilian peacetime life; the authors point out on several occasions that their data are of interest to current research. In this connection a word might be said about the usefulness of *The American Soldier* to students of the sociology of knowledge.

Karl Mannheim and some of his followers have speculated a

great deal about "perspectivistic thinking" of various social classes. "Perspectivistic thinking," varying according to class position and interest, comprises a great variety of mental processes which Mannheim did not clearly distinguish, *e.g.*, explanations of social reality, policy preferences regarding the most desirable state of affairs, expectations as to the future course of events and demands upon oneself and others. Mannheim contended moreover that not only axiological but also methodological and epistemological aspects of thinking differ according to the "perspective" afforded by given class positions in society. Unfortunately, Mannheim never succeeded in defining social class in terms that would permit a test of his theory. Nor did he give a satisfactory account of the nature of the relationship between the individual who has an opinion about social or other phenomena and the social class to which he is presumed to "belong" or, as in the case of the "intelligentsia," not to belong. Finally, the "ideological" material which he imputed to various class positions was not analyzed according to specific content characteristics, his distinction between "ideology" and "utopia" being the only precarious effort in this respect.[1]

Advance in the sociology of opinion will depend on empirical studies, in which opinions are classified according to theoretically relevant content characteristics and examined as to the frequency of their association with various social roles and ranks. It should be possible to exploit the contribution to opinion research, which *The American Soldier* makes, along these lines.

There are many tables in *The American Soldier* showing that differences in attitude and opinion are associated with marital status, education, age, regional origin, combat experience, branch of service, *etc.* From the point of view of both the sociology of military organization and the sociology of opinion the association of opinions with race and rank are of particular interest.

For example, the well known social perspectivism associated with race can be illustrated by responses to the question, "Do you think that most (Negroes) (white people) are doing *more* than their share or *less* than their share to help win the war?" The percentage checking the response "they are doing more than their share" was

---

[1] See my review of Mannheim's *Ideology and Utopia* in *The American Journal of Sociology*, July 1937, pp. 155-166 and "The Social Determination of Ideas," in *Social Research*, May 1938, pp. 182-205.

considerably higher in both the Negro and the white sample of respondents with respect to the in-group than it was with respect to the out-group. (I, 511)

The opinions in this case were concerned with both in-group and out-group behavior separately, but the hierarchical relationship of the two groups, which the respondents presumably felt to prevail in some more or less vague sense, was not involved in the question which they answered, unless one were to regard the words "their share" in the wording of the question as alluding to this relationship. Furthermore, the question did not call for judgments about the behavior of the out-group *toward* the in-group and of the in-group *toward* the out-group. If questions had been asked directly concerned with the status of whites and Negroes or with the treatment of Negroes by whites, *etc.*, even larger differences in group opinions might have resulted. It is entirely possible that the "social perspectivism" reflected in the cited instance does not hold generally, representing a constant perspective for each group, regardless of the subject matter on which opinions are expressed.

In other words, just as the two groups will not be expected to display any "social perspectivism" on, say, simple arithmetic (although they may well differ in arithmetical knowledge and skill), their views on other aspects may differ somewhat and on still other aspects may indeed be strikingly "perspectivistic." Instead of searching for an immutable perspective associated with social position, it might be more fruitful to assume a continuum of degree of opinion differences associated with social position and to determine the changing "perspectives" from a given social position with reference to specific subject matters.

In attempting to put these subject matters into a rank order of ascending importance to the social perspectivism of status groups, the following gross distinctions may be made:

I. Non-social subjects (*e.g.*, the weather)
II. Social subjects (*e.g.*, cooperation)
   1. not involving the hierarchy of which the groups are a part
   2. involving this hierarchy.

Non-social subjects comprise both matters entering immediately and concretely into human experience and more remote or abstract matters. Since the experiences of groups differ according to their functions in society, their views of non-social subjects also differ widely; farmers as a group "know more" about rain than city people and "evaluate" it with reference to different needs. Similarly, the comprehension of abstract relations or remote causes, *e.g.*, meteorology, presupposes expert knowledge typically possessed by specialized groups of particular training and function in society. Such differences are here disregarded, as we are concerned with the dependence of the opinions of *status* groups upon the subject matter on which their views converge or differ. It is assumed that the unequal distribution of power, privilege and prestige among status groups does not in itself affect their views on non-social subjects, much as unequal education may do so. Of the many subcategories which can be introduced in category II-1, it would seem especially pertinent to include subjects which involve the self as distinguished from subjects which do not do so. Similarly, an especially pertinent distinction within category II-2 would appear to be that between the hierarchy itself, including rules and practices associated with it, and the qualities and behavior of the component groups of that hierarchy. Thus:

II. *Social Subjects*
   1. which do not involve the hierarchy of which the groups are a part:
      (i) Subjects which do not involve the (collective) self, *i.e.* either the individual who expresses an opinion or the status group to which he belongs. (Examples: the nature of a common enemy, the chances to defeat him, *etc.*)
      (ii) Subjects which involve the (collective) self, *i.e.* either the individual who expresses an opinion or the status group to which he belongs. (Example: my hatred of the enemy)
      (iii) Subjects which indirectly throw light on the implications of the hierarchy merely by virtue of the fact that the opinions of one status group about a subject pertaining to itself can be compared with the opinions of another status group about the same subject. (Example: the enlisted men's working habits as viewed by both enlisted men and officers.)
   2. which involve the hierarchy of which the groups are a part:
      (i) Subjects which pertain to this hierarchy as a whole, its characteristics, merits, *etc.* (Example: rewards and punishments viewed as part of the system, not as given or received by other groups.)
      (ii) Subjects which pertain to the behavior, characteristics and merits of any status group in interaction or comparison with other status groups. (Example: confidence in leadership of superiors.)

We could propose the hypothesis that the difference between opinions on the same subject matter expressed by groups high or low in power, privilege or prestige will increase as the subject matter is more closely and directly related to the status characteristics and relations of the group.

It should now be noted, however, that this hypothesis rests on the assumption of latent or overt conflict between the groups within the hierarchy. Differences in opinion on social subject matters, and particularly on those involving hierarchy, may imply, even if this is not explicitly expressed, divergent opinions about the justice of the prevailing order or about the justice of social practices and rules. If a lower status group "accepts" the existing stratification, does not contest the distance separating it from the higher group, emulates its superiors or regards the existing order as divine, similarity rather than difference in opinion concerning the social system is likely to prevail. In this sense, difference in opinion may be a sign of social disorder. The more severe this disorder, the more diversified are the subjects on which opinions differ. Obviously, a particularly alarming sign of social disorder would be differences of opinion on social subjects *not* involving the hierarchy when these differences reflect conflicts about status.

Since the socially prevailing notions of justice enter into many moral judgments, it is to be expected that opinions involving moral values will be more susceptible to perspectivism than factual judgments. This distinction between factual and moral judgments can be introduced into any of the categories of class II, but it is difficult to say whether factual opinions on subject matter low in the rank order are more or less susceptible to perspectivism than a moral judgment on subjects of high rank. For example, officers and men may disagree more in their (factual) opinions about officers' privileges (II-2-ii) than in their (moral) views of fairness in the Army (II-2-i) or of enemy treachery. (II-1-i)

In Table I thirty-nine subject matters on which opinions were expressed by both officers and enlisted men have been selected from *The American Soldier* and arranged with the initial hypothesis in mind. The arrangement roughly approximates the rank order of subjects which has just been discussed. Six classes of opinions, A-F, have been distinguished and the average difference between the percentage of officers and that of enlisted men expressing each stated opinion has been computed for each class of opinions.

TABLE I—DIFFERENCES IN OPINIONS OF OFFICERS AND
ENLISTED MEN ON VARIOUS SUBJECT MATTERS[2]

A. *Opinions about reality not involving Army as a whole, self or relations between officers and enlisted men*

ITEM NO.	PAGE REF.	OPINION (SPECIFIC SUBJECT)	DIFFERENCE Absolute	Ratio
	II, 198-9	The shell shocked should be treated as sick men		
1		Division B	— 3	1
2		Division C	5	1.2
3		Division D	5	1.1
4		Division E	7	1.1
5		Division F	— 4	1.1
	II, 147	It will be tough to beat the Japanese		
6		Pacific theater respondents	— 7	1.1
7		European theater respondents	— 5	1.1
		It will be tough to beat the Germans		
9		Pacific theater respondents	— 11	1.1
9		European theater respondents	— 9	1.1
	II, 146	All or most of our equipment better than		
10		that of Japanese	— 2	1
11		that of Germans	6	1.1
	II, 294	(Other) men in rear doing as much for front as could be expected in circumstances		
12		Division A (Pacific)	8	1.1
13		Division B (")	10	1.2
14		Division C (")	5	1.1
15		Division D (")	16	1.1
16		Division E (Europe)	28	2.2
		AVERAGE A	8.2	1.2

B. *Opinions about the individual self, not involving hierarchical relations: feelings of officers and, respectively, enlisted men in combat*

	II, 174-5	When the going was tough (Pacific theater)		
17		prayer helped a lot	8	1.1
18		it helped a lot to think that you couldn't let the other men down	— 24	1.4
19		it helped a lot to think that you had to finish the job in order to get home	11	1.3

[2] See Appendix to this Chapter.

TABLE I—DIFFERENCES IN OPINIONS OF OFFICERS AND ENLISTED MEN ON VARIOUS SUBJECT MATTERS [2]

ITEM NO.	PAGE REF.	OPINION (SPECIFIC SUBJECT)	DIFFERENCE Absolute	Ratio
20		I was helped a lot by thoughts of hatred for the enemy	− 8	1.2
21		it helped a lot to think of what we are fighting for	6	1.2
		AVERAGE B	11	1.2

C. Opinions, not involving moral judgment, about the behavior of enlisted men

22	I, 417	Main reason for soldiers' obedience is fear of punishment	21	1.7
23	I, 421	Most soldiers usually work hard enough to get by	4	1.1
24		Most soldiers usually put all they have got into their work	5	1.1
25	I, 418	An enlisted man is usually more concerned with what other enlisted men think than with what his officers think	11	1.1
		AVERAGE C	10.2	1.3

D. Opinions about the Army as a whole

26	I, 423	Army mostly does not keep promises	35	1.9
27	I, 422	Promotion depends on whom, not what, you know	20	1.3
28	I, 419	Army places too much importance upon military courtesy	51	3.8
29		Army places too much importance upon spit and polish	34	1.9
30	I, 394	Military discipline is about right at this post	− 20	1.5
31		In most ways I have gotten a square deal from the Army	− 24	1.6
32	I, 422	Army does not try its best to praise and reward the exceptionally good soldier	20	1.4
33	I, 421	The harder a man works the better his chance of success	− 35	2.2
	I, 396	Soldiers have good reasons to gripe about:		
34		too strict discipline about petty things	28	2.2
35		not getting enough passes and furloughs	25	1.9
36		wrong men get the breaks	25	1.9
37		too much "chicken" to put up with	22	1.5

TABLE I—DIFFERENCES IN OPINIONS OF OFFICERS AND ENLISTED MEN ON VARIOUS SUBJECT MATTERS [2]

ITEM NO.	PAGE REF.	OPINION (SPECIFIC SUBJECT)	DIFFERENCE Absolute	Ratio
38		work too hard and hours too long	14	2.5
39		promotions frozen or too slow	1	1
40		wrong job assignment	5	1.1
		AVERAGE D	24.9	1.8

E. *Opinions, involving moral judgments, about the behavior of enlisted men*

41	I, 420	It's all right for a man to goldbrick if he doesn't get caught	27	7.8
42		It's all right for a man to goldbrick if he doesn't make more work for the men	23	2.7
43	I, 419	Most soldiers lose respect for a man who is always trying to goldbrick	— 11	1.1
44	I, 420	Most soldiers lose respect for a man who is always bucking for promotion	12	1.2
45	I, 419	Most soldiers lose respect for a man who is too GI	30	1.6
		AVERAGE E	20.6	2.9

F. *Opinions about relations between enlisted men and officers*

46	I, 394	*Disagree* that Army would be a lot better if officers and men were more friendly with each other	— 32	3.1
47		All or most officers would be willing to go through anything they ask their men to go through	— 55	2.5
48	I, 374	If enlisted men have to observe curfew, officers should too	49	2.4
49		Officers deserve extra privileges because of their responsibility	— 44	2.9
50	I, 398	Regular civilian reader of B-Bag would get untrue picture of the problems of most soldiers in European theater	— 42	3.6
		AVERAGE F	44.4	2.9

Class A includes items (#10 and 11) dealing with equipment, *i.e.* "non-social subjects" (rank order: I), and no item lower than II-1-i in the rank order.

Class B is composed of items belonging in category II-1-ii.

The items in class C, dealing with behavior of the enlisted men, fall into category II-1-iii and are factual rather than moral in quality.

Class D contains moral and factual opinions falling into category II-2-i. Items #34-40 have been regarded as part of this class despite the reference to the "griping" of the enlisted men in the wording of the opinion, under the assumption that the distribution of opinions was predominantly dependent upon the specified content of each complaint, which clearly belongs into this class.

Class E comprises moral items of category II-1-iii.

Finally, class F contains only items falling into the last category of the rank order (II-2-ii).

The results of Table I as summarized in Table II show:

(1) There is no constant social perspective associated with social status; instead, there are various social perspectives associated with social status depending on the subject matter to which the opinion pertains.

(2) There is virtual agreement among the two status groups on matters not involving the hierarchy of which they are a part (opinion classes A-C) with the partial exception of category II-1-iii. (see (3) below)

TABLE II—SOCIAL PERSPECTIVISM ACCORDING TO RANK ORDER OF SUBJECT MATTER

CLASS IN TABLE I	RANK ORDER OF SUBJECT MATTER	DIFFERENCE Ratio	Absolute
A	I to II-1-i	1.2	8.2
B	II-1-ii	1.2	11
C	II-1-iii (factual)	1.3	10.2
D	II-2-i	1.8	24.9
E	II-1-iii (moral)	2.9	20.6
F	II-2-ii	2.9	44.4

(3) When officers' and enlisted men's opinions about the enlisted men are compared, it appears of great importance whether these opinions are factual or moral in character. (classes C and E) Such moral opinions appear to be subject to a high degree of perspectivism otherwise associated only with subject matters that involve hierarchical relations more directly, as is true of classes D and F.

(4) Opinions on hierarchical relations are particularly sensitive to perspectivistic "distortion." (Classes D and F)

(5) It should be stressed once more that the absence of social perspectivism for relatively wide areas of reality testifies to, and reflects the fact that the Army was a well functioning social organization, particularly in its dealings with the environment and the enemy.

Noticing that officers grossly overestimated the favorable attitudes of their men toward many aspects of military life, the Research Branch was led to suggest that "one of the elements in this habit of officers" "was a product of the tendency to project one's own attitudes upon the men." (I, 393) It is not possible to explore on the basis of the available data whether or not the theory of projection is equally applicable to the views which the men held of the officers. Nor was it possible to decide whether or not this explanation held for the officers only in a situation in which the justice of privileges was subconsciously questioned by them or consciously considered to be in conflict with the principles of civilian society. Further peacetime research that would help to answer problems of this kind could proceed from the pertinent findings and interpretations in *The American Soldier* and add to our knowledge of social stratification as well as of the sociology of opinions. Continuous research on peacetime social organizations along the lines here sketched might in time develop an index of social integration which would have high diagnostic and predictive value.

POLICY MAKING AND ATTITUDE RESEARCH

SINCE the work of the Research Branch was undertaken "to provide the Army Command quickly and accurately with facts about the attitudes of soldiers which, along with other facts and inferences, might be helpful in policy formation," it is to be hoped that the authors of *The American Soldier* will some time in the future examine systematically the conditions under which attitude research can be of assistance to policy makers. There is no other group of social scientists in this country, if anywhere, as well prepared by experience for this task. References to this question are scattered throughout the two volumes, and the authors have not failed to indicate some of the resistance they met in high quarters, particularly in the initial phases of their work. In the absence of an analytical summary of their experiences and thoughts on this subject, let me close with a few observations on this point.

To begin with, the nationally most important policy decisions during a war can obviously not be derived from the results of surveys. Questions as to whether hostility should continue or an armistice be negotiated or unconditional surrender be enforced are not for the individual soldiers or the individual citizens, for that matter, to decide. According to the Constitution, such decisions are happily left to the democratically constituted organs of the Republic which have the authority to make them.

Similarly, strategic decisions to reach the objectives of national policies cannot be made on the basis of polls among soldiers. The decision to defeat Germany first and thus not to give priority to the Far Eastern theaters was taken regardless of the opinion of General MacArthur in September 1942 that movements into North Africa would be "a waste of effort," and "that we should stop building up an army that we could not use,"[3] not to mention the fact that according to the surveys made early in 1944 67 per cent of the enlisted men in the United States wanted to see the whole Japanese nation wiped out, whereas only 29 per cent chose the corresponding reply from the multiple choice offered to them by the Research Branch regarding the German nation. (II, 158) Similarly, the strong and widespread desires of soldiers to get home or their preference for war work rather than service in the armed forces could not influence national policy decisions during the war. At least, it may be surmised that such desires will influence decisions only in very extreme situations bordering on, or constituting, mutiny, in which case no survey is needed.

If the question of the relation between policy and research of the kind under review must therefore at the beginning be confined to decisions of relatively lesser importance, it also appears that military decisions, taken against the enemy, cannot be influenced by opinion research. Even minor tactical moves of small units can obviously not be subject to preferences by soldiers. The realm in which attitude research conducted among personnel of the armed services during a war may affect decisions seems to be, above all,

[3] General H. H. Arnold, *Global Mission* (Harper), New York 1944, p. 344.

that of military management, possibly including such matters as demobilization, and perhaps training.

In addition, opinion surveys are most useful for providing information about response to policy decisions, which is particularly important when the execution of the policy requires the cooperation of the respondents. Finally, a major usefulness of opinion research to policy makers consists in the ability of such research to call their attention to managerial problems which they may otherwise fail to detect.

A systematic analysis of the conditions which increase the chances of opinion research findings to affect decisions should be able to specify the problem in terms such as the uncertainty of the decision maker as to what the right course of action is; his awareness of the need for specific action; the availability of information to the decision maker from other sources; the predictive ability of attitude research; the affect of the decisions on the power and prestige of the decision makers themselves; the incisiveness of the change effected by the decision, etc. Speaking generally, the importance of attitude research in the decision making process would seem to lie in its informational rather than its plebiscitarian aspects, particularly when the information obtained by attitude research cannot be obtained directly in other ways.

APPENDIX

Note on TABLE I

Table I has been computed from a large number of surveys undertaken by the Research Branch and reported in *The American Soldier*. Each item refers to a particular percentage difference between the opinions of officers and men in checking a specific response to a question. Only one of various possible responses was selected for inclusion in Table I. For example, in the case of items #1-5, the question asked by the Research Branch was worded, "In your opinion what should be done with men who crack up in action, that is, men who get shell-shocked, blow their tops, go haywire?" The Research Branch reported the percentage distribution of four responses, namely, "Most of them" (1) "should be treated as sick men," (2) "should be treated as cowards and punished," (3) "should be treated some other way," and (4) "no answer." The opinions of officers and enlisted men of five separate divisions can be compared for each of the four responses. In the table only the percentages of officers and men giving the first response have been included. Answers in response to other multiple choices have been reported in a similarly selective way. This procedure appears justified, since we are not interested in the distribution of different possible responses to the same question, but in the frequency differences of the same response as given by officers and enlisted men, *i.e.*, the two groups whose "perspectivism" we want to examine. Moreover, in a few cases, for example item #46, the Research Branch itself gives the figures for only one of the possible answers.

In items #10 and 11, two answers reported by the Research Branch have been combined into one ("all" agree and "most" agree). The wording of the question is not always reproduced verbatim but can be checked at the page referred to in column 2 of Table I.

The differences between the percentages of responses given by enlisted men and officers are reported as *absolute* and *relative* differences. In item #2, 67 per cent of the officers and 72 per cent of the men checked the answer "should be treated as sick men"; the absolute difference is therefore +5, the ratio being 1.2. The ratio has been computed in *all* cases by putting the larger percentage in the denominator regardless of whether the percentage of officers or that of enlisted men was larger. Otherwise the average for each class of opinions would not reflect the average *size* of the difference. Absolute differences are listed with a minus sign, however, whenever the percentage of enlisted men was smaller than that of officers. Thus the *direction* of each individual difference can be examined in the Table. In computing the average absolute differences for each class of opinions, all differences have again been treated as positive values.

PATRICIA L. KENDALL and PAUL F. LAZARSFELD

PROBLEMS OF SURVEY ANALYSIS

*T*HE initial steps of survey procedures—sampling, questionnaire construction, and interviewing techniques—have been fairly well codified in recent social research literature. By examining these writings a student can gain proficiency in some phases of the research trade. But such is not the case for the terminal steps of a survey. There is very little discussion of the art of analyzing material once it has been collected.

This neglect results from a variety of factors. For one, surprisingly few surveys are published and consequently there is little material available for demonstration. Then, there is a belief that good analysis is a matter of intuition, and can neither be systematically codified nor effectively taught. Finally, we have a kind of ambivalence toward the type of "secondary analysis" with which this paper will be primarily concerned. From a dogmatic point of view research proceeds in the following way: We have an hypothesis; we determine what kind of material would be likely to prove or disprove the hypothesis; we collect the pertinent data; we analyze them in the light of the original purpose of the study. Such use of empirical data might be called "primary analysis," and there is no doubt that in a well-advanced science it is the dominant procedure. At their present stage of development, however, the social sciences cannot insist on this paradigm. Our thinking is rarely far enough progressed to enable us to start out with a sharply formulated hypothesis; most studies are exploratory, directed toward the general examination of a field in order to develop theoretical formulations. Furthermore, even if the original problem was well thought through, the actual study often has new and unanticipated implications. In other cases, the situation is even more complicated. Many studies grow out of practical needs. Only after they have served their pragmatic purposes can they be explored for whatever theoretical content they contain. In these circumstances, then, secondary analysis becomes very important. It is essentially an effort to extract from given empirical data the maximum of theoretical generalizations.

Primary analysis of data is almost entirely governed by the original purpose of the study. Secondary analysis has rules of its own. These are rarely articulated because we do not like to admit how dominant a role secondary analysis still must play in current social research. It is therefore fortunate that there is now a text which not only demonstrates the merits of secondary analysis, but which is also so rich that some of the rules of analysis can be extracted and exemplified.

The American Soldier [1] is based almost exclusively on secondary analyses. That the reported findings were often obtained from surveys designed for very different practical purposes can be easily determined by tracing the biographies of separate studies through the two volumes. Thus a survey identified as a study of "attitudes toward redeployment and demobilization" is used variously to examine:

—Level of adjustment according to combat experience and service overseas. (I, 111, 159, 160) [2]

—Feelings of personal commitment to the war according to combat experience, overseas service, length of time in the Army and various demographic factors. (I, 440, 455, 456, 509)

—Willingness to fight the Japanese according to race and theater of present service. (I, 521)

—Attitudes toward civilians in the United States according to closeness to the front-lines. (II, 321)

—Resentment by combat men of rear-area troops. (II, 302)

—Self appraisal of health by rotational returnees. (II, 461)

—Willingness of returnees for further overseas service. (II, 469)

[1] We shall confine our attention to the first two volumes in the series, *Adjustment During Army Life* (Stouffer, Suchman, DeVinney, Star, and Williams) and *Combat and Its Aftermath* (Stouffer, A. Lumsdaine, M. Lumsdaine, Williams, Smith, Janis, Star and Cottrell). For a general orientation toward these studies, see Paul F. Lazarsfeld, *"The American Soldier*—an Expository Review," *Public Opinion Quarterly*, XIII (1949), 377-404.

[2] References to the two volumes are handled in the following way. The first and second volumes are referred to as I and II respectively. Chapter numbers are also indicated by subsequent Roman numerals; page numbers, by Arabic numerals.

—Changes in branch of service among returnees. (II, 482)

—Distribution of rank according to race and education. (I, 500)

—Distribution of enlisted grades according to education and length of time in the Army. (I, 248, 249)

—Number of campaign decorations awarded in different service branches. (II, 346)

—Incidence of psychoneurotic symptoms according to combat experience, branch of service, length of service, physical condition, and demographic characteristics. (II, 429, 437, 440, 442, 446, 448)

—Feeling that one's theater of war and army job are important, compared with the same feelings observed at another time. (I, 449)

—Estimates of the length of the war given at different time periods. (I, 449)

In order that the exploitation of survey materials can become a standard practice, some of the techniques for achieving it should be spelled out. It will require a great deal of systematic thinking to complete this task. But the volumes of *The American Soldier* provide such a wealth of material that a beginning in this direction is now possible. We shall focus our attention on two sets of problems which seem of major importance. The first of these is the logic of accounting for statistical relationships; the second deals with certain problems of "measurement" and classification in survey research.

PART I

ACCOUNTING FOR STATISTICAL RELATIONSHIPS

IN many ways the analysis of survey results can be described as the clarification of relationships between two or more variables.

There can be little doubt that we are interested primarily in relationships, rather than in the description of single variables. It may be an interesting fact that *x* per cent of a sample subscribed to a particular opinion or reported certain activities. But inferences of practical or theoretical significance usually emerge only from a study of the demographic characteristics, the previous experiences or attitudes to which the opinions and activities are related.

The clarification of these statistical relationships proceeds in two directions. In the first place, we want to determine how legitimate it is to draw inferences of cause and effect. Secondly, we want to examine the process through which the assumed cause is related to its effect. Both types of clarification involve a logic and a series of analytical procedures of their own. Part I of this paper is devoted to spelling these out.

Section 1—APPROXIMATIONS OF SURVEY RESULTS TO CONTROLLED EXPERIMENTATION

Even when not explicitly stated, the presentation of a relationship between two variables suggests a causal connection between them. We do not report that combat veterans are more dissatisfied than non-veterans with certain Army policies without implying that somehow the experience of combat changes the perspectives and attitudes of soldiers.

The scientific model designed to study cause-and-effect relationships of this sort is the *controlled experiment*, in which the responses of an experimental group, exposed to the crucial stimulus, are compared with those of an exactly equivalent control group, from which the stimulus has been withheld. The difficulties of carrying out such experiments in the social sciences are well known.[3] It is important, therefore, to consider the kinds of approximations provided by survey materials.

Sub-group comparisons

The type of approximation most often used in survey analysis involves a comparison of the frequency with which groups *characterized in different ways* express a certain attitude or indicate a particular behavior. Thus in *The American Soldier* we find that:

—There was a marked relationship between job satisfaction and chance to choose one's Army job. Those who asked for and got their Army jobs were much more satisfied than those who did not get the jobs they asked for, or who did not get a chance to ask. (I, Chap. VII, Chart II and Table 1.)

—There was a relationship between the theater in which the soldier served and his personal adjustment. For example, men stationed

[3] Stouffer and his associates indicate at a number of points where experimentation would have been necessary to provide final answers to the questions which they raise, and why such experimentation was impossible. See, for example, II, 205, fn. 14.

overseas reported themselves in less good spirits than did men stationed in the United States. (I, 155-189. See especially Table 1.)

In the first example it is the experience of having asked for and obtained the job they wanted which distinguished soldiers in the "experimental" group from those in the "control" group. In the second case the distinction is in terms of the soldier's location. To what extent can we attribute differences in job satisfaction, on the one hand, and different levels of personal adjustment, on the other hand, to these "stimuli"?

There are two main difficulties in equating the simple cross-tabulations of survey materials to real experimentation. One of these is the danger that spurious factors are present in the relationship. The second is the difficulty of establishing clearly the time sequence of the variables involved.

Spurious factors: To illustrate the problem of spurious factors, let us consider the relationship between theater of service and answers to the question, "In general, how would you say that you feel most of the time, in good spirits or in low spirits?" We recall that men stationed overseas reported themselves in less good spirits than did men stationed in the United States who had not yet been overseas. One possibility which occurs to us is that length of service might operate as a spurious factor in this relationship. It might be that men stationed overseas had, on the average, served for longer periods of time, and that men with records of long service had lower morale. If this were the case, we would not be justified in saying that personal esprit was determined by theater of service. Experimentally, this would express itself in the following way: two groups of soldiers, equated according to length of service, would show no differences in morale even when one group was shipped to an overseas theater.

In order to minimize the danger that spurious factors of this kind remain undetected, we employ analytical procedures which enable us to examine the relationship between the assumed cause and the assumed effect *when the influence of the possible spurious factor is eliminated.*[4] We divide the sample into different groups according to length of service in the Army. Within each of the groups we examine the relationship between theater of service and personal

---

[4] At the present time, we shall make no effort to state more precisely what we mean by a spurious factor. A refined definition will be provided in a later section. (See p. 158 below.)

esprit. In this way we are able to observe the original relationship when the possible spurious factor is "controlled" or "held constant." Often it is not enough to introduce only one control. There are a number of other possible spurious factors in the relationship which we have considered. For example, the men overseas probably held higher rank and served in different branches of the Army. There might also have been educational differences between the two groups. All of these are factors which could have produced differences in the proportions saying that they were in "good spirits"; consequently, all of them must be controlled. For these reasons, it is necessary to carry out the comparison between men stationed overseas and men stationed in the United States in a large number of subclasses. But this leads to a problem. It is obvious that if we consider four controls, each divided into three classes (if we controlled branch of service we might divide our sample into Infantrymen, Air Corps men, and all others), we would end up with 81 separate comparisons. As we extend this process of controlling possible spurious factors, the number of cases in any one subclass becomes very small.

To cope with this difficulty the author uses the following technique throughout the volumes. First of all he divides his total sample (or samples) into small homogeneous sub-groups, using the relevant control factors to achieve his stratification. Within each sub-class he then makes the crucial comparison. He does not consider the size of the differences, but only their direction. His final conclusion is based on the *consistency* with which a specified relationship is found. In the example which we have been considering, the relation between overseas service and good spirits, the analyst had available 138 small but homogeneous sub-groups in which he could make his basic comparison. In 113 of these, men stationed overseas reported less good spirits than men in the United States not yet overseas; in 23 of the sub-groups the relationship was reversed; and in the remaining 2 there was no difference in the proportion of overseas and United States soldiers reporting themselves in good spirits. (I, 157, Table 1) Because the crucial relationship persists in the large majority of homogeneous sub-classes, the presumption that overseas service leads to a deterioration in morale gains some credence.[5]

[5] We place even more confidence in the result if men stationed overseas exhibit lower morale in connection with other questions which, despite variations in wording, are all concerned with "personal esprit," for example, "In general, what sort of time do you have in the Army?"

This technique, combining results from many different but homogeneous sub-groups, is used at a number of points in *The American Soldier;* it is a procedure which deserves careful study.[6]

It is possible, then, to guard against spurious factors, and thereby make our survey results approximate more closely those that would be obtained through experimentation. But these results will always remain approximations to, and never the equivalents of, controlled experiments. We can never be sure that it is impossible to find another factor, not included among our controls, which would disqualify the main result. If we want to study the relationship between overseas service and lowered morale through controlled experimentation, we would proceed in the following way. Half of a group of soldiers, selected at random, would be shipped overseas, while the other half remained in the United States. After a lapse of time the morale of both groups would be compared. If it turned out that the group randomly selected for shipment overseas showed significantly lower spirits, we would have the necessary evidence that it was overseas service which brought about a decline in morale.

As long as we can only control factors after the fact, however, our findings are always open to doubts. If we study the relationship through a statistical analysis of survey materials, rather than by experimentation, we can, at best, control four or five factors. Let us assume that we consider length of service in the Army, rank, branch of service and education to be important factors. It might be that none of these is important, and that we overlook the really relevant spurious factor. Perhaps certain soldiers were less popular than others; their lack of popularity might be reflected in low spirits, and it might also mean that their officers were more likely to put them on lists for shipment overseas. In this case, both overseas service and low spirits are the result of personality differences, and there is no causal connection between them. The Research Branch analysts are clearly aware of this danger and they constantly caution the reader against it. (See, for example, I, 48; II, 35, 127, 163, 226, 403, and 507.)

In actual survey analysis, the control of spurious factors requires a constant weaving back and forth between speculations as to the possible factors and examination of the data when the influence of each factor has been eliminated. There is one particularly important

[6] For other examples, see I, 109, Table 1 and I, Ch. V, Tables 3, 4, and 5.

result in *The American Soldier* which illustrates this process very well.

> —The closer the contact of white with Negro soldiers, the greater the willingness of the whites to serve in mixed Negro-white companies. (I, 594, Chart XVII) [7]

This relationship is one in which typically we might suspect that spurious factors are operating. Whenever we deal with a variable like "amount of contact" or "closeness of contact" we have a feeling that the persons who are found at various points along these continua made their way there voluntarily. That is, we suspect the presence of "self-selection" factors; those who have close contact with Negroes may do so because of initially favorable or "tolerant" attitudes. If this were the case, it would not surprise us to find that their attitudes following contacts with Negroes were also favorable.

The way in which the Army's "racial experiment" came about reduced the likelihood that these self-selective processes were at work. The Negro platoons were placed *at random* within Infantry companies needing replacements. While the Negro men had volunteered for combat service, men in the white companies were not consulted about their willingness to serve in mixed companies.

While the real-life situation seemed to meet those conditions required for controlled experimentation, the Research Branch sought additional checks. For example, the companies which had suffered the greatest casualties, and were therefore most likely to receive replacements, might have become more tolerant toward other men as a result of their combat experience. If this were the case, the men in mixed companies could be expected to have initially more favorable attitudes toward service with Negroes. In order to check this possibility, the Research Branch made use of a retrospective question: The soldiers in mixed companies were asked to recall how they had felt about serving with Negroes prior

[7] One of the frustrations in any analysis, but perhaps a particular problem in secondary analyses, is the fact that one is frequently forced to base important cross-tabulations on very few cases. Thus in the chart just cited, there were only 80 men who had served in a company which had a Negro platoon, only 68 who had served in an unmixed company in a regiment with mixed companies, and 112 who served in all white companies within a division containing mixed companies. The more elaborate the cross-tabulations, the more serious this limitation of vanishing cases. Thus in a table showing the incidence of anxiety symptoms at different time periods, holding constant age and education, we find percentages based on 9, 21, 22, and 32 cases, clearly too few to yield significant or reliable figures. (See II, 431, Table 8)

to the actual experience of doing so. The results indicated an even more *un*favorable attitude initially than was observed among men not serving in mixed companies.[8]

Another possibility is that the persons in charge of assigning replacements put the Negro platoons in companies which they felt would receive them more favorably. There was undoubtedly some leeway in deciding which companies got which replacements, and the officers responsible for those decisions may not have distributed the troops at random. Again, if this were the case, we would conclude that the original relationship was a spurious one. Partial evidence that it was *not* the case is seen in the fact that there were as many Southerners serving in the mixed as in the unmixed companies.[9]

The interweaving of speculations about possible spurious factors and actual analysis of the data emerges very clearly from this example. The original relationship was one which is typically suspect as being spurious. But the results were obtained in a situation which seemed to reproduce, in real life, the conditions required in controlled experimentation. There was more reason to believe, therefore, that the original relationship was a reasonable approximation of what might have been found through actual experimentation. But the analysts did not lose sight of the possibility that spurious factors were in operation. They introduced suitable controls and checks. Even though these did not destroy the original relationship, we cannot say that the causal connection between contact with Negroes and favorable attitudes toward them has been demonstrated. The connection is more *probable* after the checks have been introduced than it was beforehand, but it is never quite certain.

The time order of variables: Clearly to be distinguished from the problem of spurious factors is the second difficulty in approximation procedures. In order even to consider whether the statistical relationship between two variables is a causal one, the variables must stand in a determinate time relation, with the assumed cause *preceding* the assumed effect. (When we say that Variable A precedes Variable B in time, we mean that A was *acquired* or *developed* first.)

[8] This result is not reported in the text of *The American Soldier*. Stouffer refers to it in a recent article, "Some observations on study design," *American Journal of Sociology*, LV (1949-50), 355-361.

[9] *Ibid.*

Often the time order between two variables is quite clear. If we relate formal educational level to rank in the Army, we can be quite sure that education precedes rank. Or, if we study the relation between civilian occupation and type of Army job, there is little doubt that Army job follows after civilian occupation in time.

There are some instances in which the same attribute is used as an index of different phenomena, so that its time order, rather than being fixed, is determined by the particular problem being considered. Suppose, for example, that we related each man's rank to the length of time which he had been in the Army. Now "length of time in the Army" can stand for a variety of different phenomena. We might consider it an index of the time when the soldier entered the Army; given this meaning, it would *antecede* promotion. We would then look at the relationship to see whether those who had entered the Army during early stages of the war were more likely to be promoted. But "length of time in the Army" can also indicate the amount of experience which the soldier has at the time that he is interviewed. Looked at in this way, length of service is a characteristic which follows *after* the soldier has acquired his rank. We then ask whether those with particular ranks are more experienced than others.

Finally, there are some instances in which the time sequence of two or more variables is indeterminate. One such case is the relationship between attitudes toward one's officers and willingness for combat. (II, 126, Table 7)[10] Which of these attitudes developed or was acquired first? Does a soldier reluctant to go into combat "rationalize" his feelings by saying that his officers are not good? Or does a soldier with favorable attitudes toward his officers develop a feeling of confidence which makes him willing for combat? Because of our inability to answer these questions, because we do not know and cannot know which of the attitudes developed first, we cannot discuss whether there is a causal connection between them. (As we shall see in the next section, panel techniques often enable one to circumvent these difficulties.)

It is very difficult to answer these questions of time sequence with

[10] In all but one or two instances, Stouffer and his associates successfully resisted the temptation to discuss the relationship between two untimed attitudes as if one might be a cause of the other. That a correlation between untimed attitudes cannot ever reveal a causal connection does not mean, however, that such correlations are not of interest. Often they help in clarifying the meaning of one of the attitudes.

the materials of only one survey. But it is possible that in some cases clues to the time order will be found. In *The American Soldier,* for example, the authors are interested in the relationship between marital status and rank. They found (I, 118-120, see especially Chart V) that married men were more likely to have higher rank, even when age and length of service in the Army were controlled. But which came first, marriage or promotion? Is it that married men are more likely to be promoted, or that promotion encourages the soldier to marry? With knowledge only of marital status and rank, very little can be said. But fortunately Research Branch analysts obtained one other bit of information which provided some clue to the time sequence: they knew whether the soldier had been married prior to his entrance into the Army or whether he had married after becoming a soldier. These data enabled them to make the following observations. They noted that there was very little relationship between rank and having been married prior to entering the Army. On the other hand, there was some relationship between rank and marriage taking place after induction. This leads them to suggest that "marriage was even more likely to be a *resultant* of promotion or of expected promotion than to be a factor *predisposing promotion.*" (I, 120, authors' italics.) The clue to the sequence of the variables was the fact that where the time order was known, one kind of relationship existed; where it was unknown, another relationship, suggesting another time sequence, prevailed.[11]

Panel techniques

While the data of one survey may sometimes suggest the time order of variables whose sequence is apparently indeterminate, they give us nothing more than clues to be checked by other means. So-called panel techniques provide the relatively best device for establishing a time sequence of two variables. In a panel study, the same respondents are interviewed at different time periods. In those cases where the respondent changes between successive interviews,

[11] But note that even where clues to the *direction* of the relationship can be found, we cannot be sure that the relationship is not a spurious one. Thus it may be that there is a particular personality type, let us call it "stable" or "dependable," which predisposes an individual both to marriage and to being promoted. Indeed the two problems exist independently of each other: knowledge of the time sequence indicates nothing about the persistence of the relationship when control factors are introduced; conversely, confidence that the relationship is not a spurious one tells nothing of the time sequence of the variables.

it is possible to determine when a particular attitude or behavior pattern developed.

These techniques contribute many new analytical devices.[12] While it is not possible to discuss all of these here, reference to one finding in *The American Soldier,* of substantive interest as well as methodological value, may give a general idea. It was found that non-commissioned officers had more conformist attitudes toward Army discipline than did privates. This relationship could be explained in a variety of ways. The non-com might have a better understanding of the importance of discipline or he might endorse disciplinary measures in order to bolster his own position. It could also be, however, that a private with what one might call an authoritarian personality has a better chance of being promoted. One of the panel studies carried out by the Research Branch shows that this latter relationship is involved in the original result. On the first interview the analysts divided the respondents according to their answers to a number of questions on discipline. Then a few months later they ascertained what proportion of the original respondents had become non-coms. Some of the findings are as follows: (See I, 265, Chart XI)

TABLE A

DISTRIBUTION OF CONFORMITY SCORES AMONG PRIVATES IN NOVEMBER, 1943	Number of Cases	Percentage of These Cases Promoted by March, 1944
Relatively high score	68	31
Medium score	138	28
Relatively low score	112	17

Through their analysis of these panel materials, the investigators were able to establish that privates who held conformist attitudes were more likely to be promoted during a subsequent six months period than were their relatively more rebellious barracks mates. As Table A shows, among those who had indicated a relatively high degree of conformity in the Fall of 1943, nearly one-third had been promoted by the following Spring, as compared with only one-sixth of the men who had originally received a low score on the conformity index.

[12] See Paul F. Lazarsfeld, "The Use of Panels in Social Research," *Proceedings of the American Philosophical Society,* 92 (1948), 405-410. The Bureau of Applied Social Research of Columbia University is currently working on a project to codify and evaluate these analytical devices.

The Research Branch of the Army was aware of the desirability of panel studies in investigations of changing attitudes or behavior.[13] Because of the peculiar conditions under which the Research Branch operated, however, it was possible for them to set up only two full-scale panel studies. One of these, from which the preceding result was taken, was a study of Infantry recruits. It is called on at various points in the two volumes: it is used to show that the better adjusted soldiers, those who reported themselves in good spirits, accepted their Army role, were satisfied with their Army jobs, and so on, consistently had better chances to be promoted at a later date (I, 147-154); data from the same study reveal the stability of response to the type of question used in gauging levels of adjustment (I, 163 and I, 208, Table 6); it also is called on to show that, compared with "normal" soldiers, a sample of recruits subsequently diagnosed as psychoneurotic were significantly less well adjusted during the early stages of their Army careers. (II, 414, Table 1)

The second panel study will be considered in detail in later sections of this paper. (See pp. 179-180; 192-193.)

In other instances, the analysts could only state that panel studies would have been appropriate had they been available. In discussing the relation of job choice to job satisfaction, for example, the authors indicate that a panel study would be required to eliminate all doubts about the relationship. (I, 289) Similarly, in their discussion of the deterioration in the effective force of formal sanctions as related to time in combat, they point out the need for a panel study. (II, 114) In all, there are a dozen points where the authors indicate that their results would have been better founded had they been based on panel materials.[14]

[13] See especially I, 198. This and the following few pages contain a very lucid and thoughtful discussion of the methodological problems involved in studying trends in attitudes, or in other words, using time as a variable. (I, 197-206)

[14] For other examples, see I, 344-346; II, 149, 207-208, 240, 436 and 625. In other sections the need for panel studies, while not explicitly stated, is implicit. See, for example, the discussion of personal adjustment as related to combat experience (I, 195-229) and the analysis of changes in attitudes at the conclusion of the war. (II, 562 ff.) It is also interesting that in his recent review of the second volume, three of the four specific findings which George Murdock points to as having special importance were obtained from these two panel studies. (The fourth was obtained in a controlled experiment.) See *The American Sociological Review*, 14 (1949), p. 815.

Retrospective questions

One of the main difficulties in a panel study is keeping the original sample intact. This is a problem even in studies of civilian populations: respondents move; some become ill and unable to participate further in the study; others become bored and refuse to participate. The enormity of these difficulties in studies of soldiers during a global war is obvious.

Because of these handicaps we sometimes use *retrospective questions* as a substitute for panel techniques. By asking the respondents to recall what their attitudes were at some earlier period (generally prior to a crucial experience whose effect we are trying to study), we attempt to reconstruct what would have been observed had there been a previous interview. We ask, "How did you feel about *y* before *x* took place?" We remember that the Research Branch used a question of this kind in checking the relationship between service in bi-racial companies and the willingness of whites to serve with Negroes. In addition to stating their present willingness to serve in mixed companies, the respondents were asked to recall what their attitudes had been before Negro platoons were put in their companies.

There are a number of grounds on which one might object to the use of retrospective questions as a substitute for panel techniques. First of all, it is difficult to know how accurate respondents are in their retrospection. Do they tend to remember selectively? Do they discount the extent to which they have actually changed their attitudes or habits? Secondly, there is the problem of specifying the exact time period to which the subjects should retrospect. "Before *x* took place" covers a wide time range.

Wherever possible, then, the accuracy of the retrospections should be checked. This was done in an interesting way at one point in *The American Soldier*. In investigating the effects of combat on the incidence of psychosomatic symptoms, the researchers used a number of different procedures. First of all, they cross-tabulated such variables as nearness to combat and length of time in combat with questions about psychosomatic symptoms. In one study of combat veterans, however, they included a retrospective question. In addition to asking, "Since you have been on active combat duty, are you ever bothered by (hand tremors, stomach disturbances, fainting spells, nightmares, shortness of breath, and pressure in the head)?"

they also asked, "During your civilian and military life, but before you went on active combat duty, were you ever bothered by . . . ?" Comparison of the retrospective form of the question with the post-combat form reveals a marked increase in the proportion of men experiencing many anxiety symptoms. (II, 449, Table 17)

But how accurate were these retrospections? As a check, the analysts compared the pre-combat answers of the veterans with those given by Infantrymen in training in the United States. The close correspondence of the answers provided some assurance that the combat veterans did not distort their answers, either consciously or unconsciously, to any extent. (II, 448, Table 16) [15]

These, then, are perhaps the major procedures through which the data obtained through surveys and utilized in secondary analyses can be made more nearly equivalent to experimental results. [16]

Section 2—INTERPRETATION AND ITS PLACE
IN A GENERAL SCHEME OF ELABORATION

Once we have satisfied ourselves that a particular statistical relationship is an adequate approximation of experimental results, we raise a somewhat different series of questions. We explore the relationship further, elaborating and clarifying it.

The general process of elaboration takes a variety of specific forms. It also can be described in quite formal terms. Before discussing either of these points, however, let us outline the general

[15] There is one caution to be noted in connection with this kind of check on the accuracy of retrospections. At Time II we ask respondents to recall their attitudes of Time I. If these retrospections are checked, it should be with data collected at Time I. In a highly dynamic situation, checks based on data obtained at Time II may introduce a distortion. Let us consider what this distortion might have been in the Research Branch study. The authors note that the Army adopted a permissive attitude toward fear and anxiety symptoms among the troops. (II, 196 ff.) But this attitude might have been more apparent at later stages of the war, so that soldiers were more willing to express their anxiety at Time II, let us say, than they had been at Time I. If this were the case, and if the checks had been based on data obtained only at Time II, then the actual extent of increase in anxiety symptoms would have been underestimated. (Actually the checks were based on material collected both at "Time I" and "Time II".)

[16] In a recent article ("Some Observations on Study Design," *American Journal of Sociology*, LV, 1949–50, 355-361), Stouffer himself suggests a general scheme through which the interrelationships of controlled experiments, panel studies, surveys, and so on, can be shown. His paper is an elaboration of pp. 47-48 in the first volume of *The American Soldier*.

argument of one type of elaboration—interpretation. When we interpret a result we try to determine the process through which the
assumed cause is related to what we take to be its effect. How did
the result come about? What are the "links" between the two
variables? Answers to these questions are provided in the interpretation of the result.

The general argument of an interpretation

The interpretation of a statistical relationship between two variables involves the introduction of further variables and an examination of the resulting interrelations between all of the factors.

To illustrate the steps which one goes through in interpreting a
result, and to indicate the types of material which are required, we
shall start with one relationship in *The American Soldier* for which
an interpretation is suggested. On one index of personal commitment, "At the time you came into the Army did you think you should
have been deferred?", the analysts found a positive correlation between education and favorable responses: the higher the education
of the soldier, the more likely he was to say that he had volunteered
or that he should not have been deferred. (I, 124, Table 3)[17] This
finding was somewhat surprising in view of the general tendency of
better educated soldiers to be more critical of the Army. The authors interpret the results in terms of the concept of "relative deprivation," which they define in the following way:

"Becoming a soldier meant to many men a very real deprivation. But
the felt sacrifice was greater for some than for others, *depending on their
standards of comparison.*" (I, 125, authors' italics.)

The analysts suggest that the lower educated soldiers, coming
mainly from skilled labor occupations which accounted for many
exemptions from service in the Army, compared their lot with that
of their friends, many of whom had been deferred because of the
importance of their jobs. On the other hand, "The great mass of
professional, trade, and white-collar occupations were not deferable.
. . . The average high school graduate or college man was a clear-cut
candidate for induction . . ." (I, 127) In other words, lower
educated soldiers, coming from an environment in which deferments
were relatively frequent, were more likely to experience their induc-

[17] This relationship held even when age and marital status on entering the
Army were controlled.

tion as a personal sacrifice than were the better educated soldiers, fewer of whose friends had received deferments.[18]

How would one go about studying this interpretation? To simplify our discussion of the actual procedure, we should perhaps first restate the interpretative statement, so as to see the statistical relationships which it implies. It might read as follows:

—Better educated soldiers are more likely to accept their inductions, because better-educated soldiers come from an environment in which deferments are infrequent, and coming from an environment in which deferments are infrequent leads to more willing acceptance of induction.

When we rephrase the statement in this way, we note that one characteristic of any "complete" interpretation is that the interpretative variable, the "test factor" as it might be called, is related to each of the original variables. The Research Branch interpretation implies (a) that the test factor, relative frequency of deferment in the environment from which the individual soldier comes, is negatively related to education, and (b) that the same factor is also negatively related to the dependent variable in the original relationship, the soldier's acceptance of his induction into the Army.

But this characteristic is not the only one. If we extend our reformulation of the interpretative statement, we note another aspect of "complete" interpretations.

—If it is true that the relationship between education and attitudes toward one's own induction can be explained entirely by the frequency of deferments in one's civilian environment, then when soldiers are classified according to this test factor, when they are separated into different groups according to the frequency of deferments in the environments from which they come, there should no longer be any relationship between education and attitude toward induction.

Stated in somewhat more technical terms, we expect that when the population is stratified according to different values of the test factor, the partial relationships between the two original variables will vanish. If we can classify men according to whether or not they came from an environment in which deferments were frequent, we

---

[18] Interestingly enough, however, out of a cross-section of soldiers, only about one-fifth of those who said they should have been deferred mentioned the importance of their jobs as the reason. (See I, 123, Table 2.) In a later section we shall discuss another case, similar to this one, in which the respondents appeared to conceal their motives. At that point we shall consider some of the checks which can be introduced to guard against evasions.

shall find, within any of the homogeneous groups thus obtained, that there is no relationship between education and acceptance of induction. The well-educated soldiers who come from an environment in which deferments were common will be just as disgruntled about their inductions as are poorly educated men from similar backgrounds; conversely, the less well educated soldier from an environment in which there were few deferments will be as likely to accept his own induction as is the better educated man in the same kind of situation. In other words, if the partial relationships between education and attitudes toward induction disappeared when soldiers were classified according to the frequency of deferments in their civilian environments, we would conclude that one's previous environment completely interpreted the original relationship.

In order to test the interpretation, then, we need to know something about the rate of deferment in the civilian environment of each man. This information, apparently not available in the Research Branch study, might have been obtained from answers to a question like, "Have some of your friends or acquaintances been deferred because they are in indispensable civilian occupations?" [19] Let us assume, for the sake of illustration, that such a question actually was asked, and that about half of the soldiers answered "yes." The next step would be to see whether this test factor actually is related to the two original characteristics, education and attitude toward induction. Again we must invent the two relationships if we want to end up with the full scheme for testing interpretations. We shall assume, finally, that, had information on this test factor been available, it would have provided a complete interpretation of the original result. Then we would have found a set of tables like those in Table B. The figures on the left represent the original relationship, taken from actual data reported in *The American Soldier*. (See I, 124, Table 3) The figures on the right are italicized because they were invented for the sake of our schematic illustration. On the left-hand side of the table, we find a relationship between education and attitudes toward induction: among the better edu-

[19] It would be preferable, of course, to have some objective measure of the deferment rate. Answers to a question like the one suggested are sometimes colored by present attitudes. We disregard this difficulty at the moment, however, since we are interested only in outlining the steps involved in an interpretation.

TABLE B

			FRIENDS OR ACQUAINTANCES DEFERRED			NO FRIENDS OR ACQUAINTANCES DEFERRED		
	High Education	Low Education	Total	High Education	Low Education	Total	High Education	Low Education	Total
Volunteered or should not have been deferred	1556	1310	2866	210	939	1149	1346	371	1717
			=			+			
Should have been deferred	205	566	771	125	545	670	80	21	101
	1761	1876	3637	335	1484	1819	1426	392	1818

cated men, the ratio of favorable to unfavorable attitudes toward induction is more than 7 to 1, while among the less well educated men, that ratio is less than 3 to 1. In the two partial tables on the right side of the "equals" sign, however, there is no relationship between the soldier's education and acceptance of his induction: in each table, the ratio of favorable to unfavorable replies on the attitude question is the same in both educational groups, even though the ratio differs in the two tables. Other aspects of Table B will be discussed in the following section.

If a particular test factor actually does interpret the relationship between two variables, we shall find that the relations between all three are characterized in the following ways:

I. The test factor is related to the assumed causal variable in the original relationship.
II. The test factor is also related to the assumed effect.
III. When the sample is stratified according to the test factor, the partial relationships between the original variables are smaller than the original relationship.

In this preliminary discussion we have outlined, in somewhat systematic fashion, the steps which one goes through in interpreting a result. Interpretation will receive an even more formal definition if we relate it to other elaboration procedures.

The process of elaboration

Let us begin this more general discussion of the process of elaboration by considering a number of results from *The American Soldier*, two of them already familiar to us:

(1) We recall that the analysts found a relationship between morale and theater of service. In order to make sure that this original relationship was not a spurious one, they examined it after holding constant branch of service, length of time in the Army, and rank. (I, 155-189. Especially Table 1.)

(2) The Research Branch also found that better educated men accepted their induction more willingly than did less well educated soldiers. The authors suggested that this might be interpreted in terms of the lower rate of deferment among white collar workers, which made the induction of the better educated man less of a personal sacrifice when he compared his lot with that of his friends and acquaintances.

(3) In another study of enlisted men, the analysts noted that there was an inverse relationship between rank and tolerance toward men who went AWOL: the non-coms were considerably more critical than were the privates and Pfc's. (II, 116, Table 4) In exploring this relationship further, the analysts found that the original relationship persisted only among men who had not seen much combat. Among battle-hardened soldiers, the non-coms were almost as lenient toward AWOL's as were the soldiers of lower rank.

However different these three results may appear to be, they have one characteristic in common. In all three we started with the relationship between two variables, and sought to clarify this by the introduction of a third variable. In the first example, we started with theater of service and personal adjustment; the relationship between these was elaborated by a number of "third" factors, among them branch of service, length of service, and rank. In the second example, education and attitudes toward induction were our starting variables; rate of deferment in the civilian environment of the soldiers was the third factor introduced into the analysis. In the final example, we started with rank and attitudes toward AWOL's; introduced into the relationship between these two variables was a third factor, length of time in combat.

What happens when this third variable is added? Essentially it results in a number of new relationships. First of all, we are able to study the relationship between the test factor and each of the variables with which we started. Secondly, we have the partial relationships between the original variables when the sample is stratified according to different values of the test factor.

Once these new relationships have been obtained, there is a rather startling development. When arranged in appropriate combinations, these new relationships can be equated to the result with which we started. The equation by which this is achieved is as follows: [20]

$$[xy] = [xy;t^+] \oplus [xy;t^-] \quad \oplus [xt][ty] \dots\dots\dots\dots(1)$$

All of the terms in Equation (1) can be found in the hypothetical example presented on page 151.

[xy] ....the original relationship, is found in the four-fold table on the left of the "equals" sign.

$[xy;t^+]$, and
$[xy;t^-]$ ......the two partial relationships, are found in the two four-fold tables on the right of the "equals" sign. (Which table is which depends on how the test variable has been defined.)

[xt] ....the relationship between the "independent" variable and the test factor, is found in the *totals rows* of the two partial tables. Thus:

FRIENDS OR ACQUAINTANCES DEFERRED:

	High Education	Low Education	
Yes	335	1484	1819
No	1426	392	1818
	1761	1876	

[ty] ....the relationship between the test factor and the "dependent" variable, is found in the *totals columns* of the two partial tables. Thus:

FRIENDS OR ACQUAINTANCES DEFERRED:

	Yes	No	
Volunteered or should not have been deferred	1149	1717	2866
Should have been deferred	670	101	771
	1819	1818	

[20] The full equation for the three-attribute case can be found in Yule and Kendall, *An Introduction to the Theory of Statistics* (London: J. B. Lippincott Co., 12 ed., 1940) Chapter 4. The equation can vary according to what coefficient is used to express the various interrelationships. It is important to keep in mind that the distinctions which will be made in the course of the present paper are, in general, not affected by the choice of any specific coefficient. The application of the formula to an analysis of interpretation as a research operation was first presented by Paul F. Lazarsfeld at the 1946 meetings of the American Sociological Society. If more than one test factor enters into the analysis, the basic formula becomes more complicated.

Having located the different terms in Equation (1), let us restate it verbally. It says that the original relationship between two variables, designated here as "*x*" and "*y*," is equal to the sum of the partial relationships betwen *x* and *y* when the sample is stratified according to the + and − values [21] of the test factor, *t*, plus a term which is the product of the relationship between *x* and *t*, on the one hand, and between *t* and *y* on the other.[22] (The plus signs in Equation (1) have been circled to indicate that the summation is not quite so simple as we suggest here; in order to work out the equation arithmetically, one must take into consideration certain weighting factors which we have ignored.)

Two types of elaboration: the M and P types

One important feature of Equation (1) is that the terms on the right-hand side can vary independently. Thus a specified magnitude of [xy] ([xy] $\neq 0$) can come about in a variety of ways.

There are two situations which interest us particularly. The first of these occurs when the test factor is unrelated to one or both of the original variables. Then the last term in Equation (1), the "marginal" term, reduces to 0. The original relationship between *x* and *y* is then a weighted average of the two partial relationships. Stated symbolically,

$$[xy] = [xy;t^+] \oplus [xy;t^-] + (0)[ty], \text{ or}$$
$$[xy] = [xy;t^+] \oplus [xy;t^-] + [xt](0) \quad \dots\dots\dots\dots (1a)$$

We shall designate the situation represented in Equation (1a) the "partial" or *P type*, since the original relationship is reduced to the values of the partial relationships.

The second situation in which we are especially interested comes about in the reverse fashion. In this case it is the partial relationships which disappear. Then the original relationship is seen to be the result of the marginal terms—the product of the relationships

---

[21] For the sake of simplicity, we shall confine ourselves to dichotomous items, recognizing that the same logic which applies to them also applies to continuous variables.

[22] The similarity of Equation (1) to standard formulae for partial correlation is obvious. The main difference is that here, instead of having only one overall measure of the partial relationship, we have two partial terms, one associated with the positive and the other with the negative value of the factor being partialled out.

between the test factor and each of the original variables. Symbolically,

$$[xy] = 0 + 0 + [xt] \, [ty] \dots\dots\dots\dots\dots\dots\dots\dots\dots (1b)$$

This case will be called the "marginal" or *M type,* depending as it does on the marginal relationships between the three variables.

In actual practice it is rare to find pure P or M types. Usually we find that the terms which should be 0 according to Equations (1a) and (1b) have values which are not precisely 0. Our interest, in the two cases, then, is not that they represent common empirical situations, but rather that *they represent, in schematized form, certain familiar research procedures and types of analysis.* They translate into symbolic terms those mental processes which together make up much of what is called analysis.

When we approach the distinction between the P and M types from the point of view of the different mental processes which they represent, rather than the different mathematical relationships which they assume, we note that the primary distinction is one of emphasis. In the P type of analysis, we are primarily interested in the *relative size* of the partial relationships. We want to see whether the relation between rank and attitudes toward AWOL soldiers is different among those who have been in combat a long time and those who have not. (See the third example on page 152.) Under what conditions are non-coms very much more critical than privates and Pfc's in their attitudes toward AWOL's, and under what conditions do the two groups seem to have relatively similar attitudes? This type of elaboration will be discussed further in the following pages.

In the M type, on the other hand, our main interest is to see whether, after the introduction of a test factor, the partial relationships between the variables with which we started are smaller, on the average, than the original relationship. Thus we examine whether, after men are classified according to the rates of deferment among their civilian friends and acquaintances, the partial relationships between formal educational level and attitudes toward induction are as large as was the original relationship between these two variables. If they are not, if they are smaller, then we say that the test factor, rate of deferment, interprets the original correlation. Or we study whether, when men are stratified according to their length of service in the Army, the partial relationships between theater of service and personal adjustment are smaller than the original relationship had been. If they are, then we say that length of service in the Army operated as a spurious factor in the relationship originally reported.

In the terms of our equation, these last two examples are exactly alike; in both we observe what happens to the average value of the partial relationships once the test factor is introduced. Nonetheless, we experience them as psychologically different. Had the partials been reduced in our example of interpretation, we would have experienced it as a positive contribution to our knowledge. We would have felt that it added something to our information about how attitudes are formed. If, on the other hand, the partial relationships are reduced when we are exploring the possibility that spurious factors operate in a statistical relationship, then our reaction is quite a different one. We no longer experience the analysis as a positive contribution; rather we think of it as the clarification of a misleading result.[23] It tells us what is *not* the case, and thereby leaves us where we started.

Why do we react differently to the two types of M elaboration? The answer lies in differences in the time order of x and t. (The concept of the time order was introduced in a previous section. See pp. 141-143.) In interpretation, the test factor lies *between* x and y in time, or, in other words, it follows *after* x.[24] Only those factors which *precede* x in time, however, can be spurious factors. For the sake of convenience, we shall label these two time orders. A test factor which follows after x will be referred to as an *intervening variable*, while one which precedes x will be called an *antecedent variable*.

[23] In some cases, this type of elaboration not only clarifies misleading results but "explains away" absurd findings. There are some classic examples of this kind. One can show statistically that there is a positive correlation between the number of storks in a given area, and the birthrate in that area. Does this mean that storks bring babies? No, because the result is a spurious one. If one separates the different areas according to their degree of urbanization, and then examines the original relationship within the rural and within the urban areas, one finds that the partials have vanished. A second absurd result of this kind is that there is a positive relationship between the number of fire engines present at a fire and the amount of damage resulting from the fire. Here again we have a finding which seems to us paradoxical and which can be "explained away" by the introduction of a third factor. The spurious factor in this case is the seriousness of the fire.

[24] In all of this discussion we assume that x precedes y in time. This emphasizes once more the importance of being able to determine the time order of the variables with which we deal.

This difference is an important one, for, when it is not kept clearly in mind, we are apt to confuse the two types of elaboration despite their very different objectives. In the example of interpretation which we considered, the time relation of x and t is clear: there can be little doubt that an individual's formal education precedes in time the number of deferments among his friends and acquaintances. In other words, the test factor is an intervening variable. If the rate of deferment is a relevant test factor, its relevance is as an interpretative variable, providing a *link* between education and acceptance or rejection of one's induction. In contrast, when Research Branch analysts sought to make sure that the relationship between contact with Negroes and willingness to serve with them in mixed companies was not a spurious one, the factor which they introduced as a check—various measures of initially favorable attitude—was one which was clearly *antecedent* to the assumed cause.

We have thus distinguished three different types of elaboration: [25]

I. *The M type* in which one is interested in noting whether the partial relationships become smaller than the original relationship. This can be further sub-divided according to the time relation of x and t.
   A. *Interpretation* in which the test factor is an intervening variable.
   B. *Explanation (or control for spurious factors)* in which the test factor is an antecedent variable.

The distinction between interpretation and explanation can be represented schematically in the following way:

Interpretation	*Explanation*
$x \rightarrow t \rightarrow y$	$\swarrow \; t \; \searrow$
	$x \qquad y$

II. *The P type* in which interest is focused on the relative size of the partial relationships in order to specify the circumstances under which the original relation is more or less pronounced. This type of elaboration will be called *specification*.

We are now in a position to review much of our preceding discussion. In the first section of our paper, we talked of the way in which we control for spurious factors. This, as we now see, is one type of a more general system of elaboration, that type which we

[25] We want to stress the irrelevance of the particular labels which are attached to each type of elaboration. In the literature, every one of these words has been used in every sense. The objective of our analysis is to distinguish and describe the different analytical processes without regard to what they have been called in the past or what they will be called in the future.

have called explanation. In our earlier discussion, we talked quite
loosely about spurious factors, but promised then that they would
receive a precise definition once the different processes of elaboration had been outlined. (See p. 137 above.) The definition which we
have arrived at in the course of our discussion is as follows: a
spurious factor is an antecedent variable which, in the M type of
elaboration, reduces the average of the partial relationships.[26]

In the opening parts of the second section we turned to a kind
of analysis which we have called interpretation. We based our discussion on an example suggested in *The American Soldier* and,
using hypothetical figures, indicated the conditions to be met if the
interpretation were to be a complete one. These conditions received
more formal statement when the general process of elaboration was
dealt with systematically.

What remains to be discussed, then, is the type of elaboration
which we have labeled specification. While we have indicated
briefly the questions which one attempts to answer through the
specification of a result, we have not shown the kinds of findings
which are obtained through this analysis.

Before turning to specification, however, there is one further point
which merits our attention. *The American Soldier* does not present
any example in which the full scheme of interpretation, as outlined
above, is utilized. The authors instead introduce interesting variations and abbreviations. It is to these which we turn now.

Interpretation in The American Soldier

Let us see how Stouffer and his associates went about interpreting
the results which developed out of their analyses. We shall start
with one of the strangest findings in the two volumes: the combat
motivations of pilots consistently varied inversely with the size of
the aircraft which they flew. On all questions fighter pilots turn out
to have the highest combat motivations; pilots of heavy bombers

[26] The notion of explanation provides an analytic basis for defining clearly
a causal relationship between two variables. *If the partial relationships never
disappear, even when every conceivable antecedent test factor is introduced,
then the original relationship is a causal one.* This definition reproduces in
statistical form the situation existing in all true controlled experiments. Through
matching procedures, one automatically eliminates the relationship between
the antecedent test factor and the stimulus, or x variable. That is, the experimenter creates a situation in which $[xt] = 0$ for every antecedent t. Thus, if
$[xy]$ exists, the partials must also exist.

the lowest. (II, 404, Chart XVIII) The authors suggest one possible interpretation of this relationship in the following sentences:

"If this relationship were to be interpreted solely on the basis of the differences among pilots shown in Chart XVIII, one might be inclined to hypothesize that the degree of responsibility for other crew members is the effective variable. This interpretation is plausible because the size-of-aircraft rank order is identical with a rank order in terms of the number of combat air crew members who were directly dependent upon the skill and good judgment of the pilot." (II, 403-405.)

In order to determine whether it was a feeling of responsibility for many other men which made heavy bomber pilots less eager for combat, the analysts selected a group who clearly could not have comparable feelings of responsibility—the enlisted men in the combat air crews. In studying the relationship between size of aircraft and combat motivation among these flyers, the analysts were, in effect, examining the partial relationship between the original variables for the group characterized by the negative value of the test factor, degree of responsibility.

The analysis showed that, even in the group which did not have any direct responsibility for other men, the same relationship between size of aircraft and combat motivation existed. (II, 406, Chart XIX) The authors therefore conclude:

"However, since the results for enlisted crew members tend to parallel the corresponding results for pilots, it is clear that the relationship cannot be explained solely on the basis of the increased degree of responsibility of pilots in the larger aircraft." (II, 405)

Thus, because the original relationship between size of plane and combat motivations exists, both for those who are and for those who are not responsible for other crew members, the authors conclude that it is not this feeling of responsibility which interprets the relationship. They have to look for some other interpretative variable.

Other statistical interpretations in *The American Soldier* take an interesting form. As one can see from Equation (1), if the marginal terms exist at all, and if their product has the same algebraic sign as the original relationship, then the *average value* of the partial relationships must, by simple arithmetic, be less than the value of the original relationship:

$$[xy;t^+] \oplus [xy;t^-] = [xy] - [xt] [ty]$$

Because of this fact, it is possible to argue that, if the marginal terms exist, the test factor which was introduced actually does provide an interpretation for the original result. In other words, one does not actually examine the partial relationships, but rather infers what happens to their average value by examining the marginal terms. This type of argument, which we shall call an *abbreviated interpretation,* is used at a number of points in *The American Soldier.* For example, having noted and discussed the differences in adjustment achieved by men who differed according to such characteristics as age, education and marital status, the authors try to show that these variations in adjustment can be explained by certain childhood experiences, such as familial stability, extroversion, physical condition as a child, and so forth. In the words of the analysts, these childhood experiences may serve as "*intervening variables* to throw light on some of the differences in adjustment . . ." (I, 131, authors' italics)

That there were differences in adjustment according to background characteristics is amply documented in the first three sections of Chapter IV in Volume 1. These, then, are the "original relationships" which the authors are attempting to interpret. Section 4 of Chapter IV (I, 130-146) is devoted to this task.

The analysts go about checking their interpretations by showing that the childhood experiences are related both to adjustment and to background characteristics. Thus we find in Chart VI that while 69 per cent of a sample of soldiers classified as "best adjusted" report that they were very healthy as children, this is true only for 51 per cent of a cross-section of soldiers and for only 21 per cent of a sample of psychoneurotics. We find also (see I, 137) that 52 per cent of the high school graduates said that they enjoyed very good health as children, while this was reported by 46 per cent of the men with less education. This is the pattern of analysis followed by the authors in their efforts to interpret the relationships with which they started. For each additional experience they show (a) that it is related to adjustment, and (b) that it is related to the several background characteristics. On the basis of the relationships, they conclude:

"Thus we get some evidence from intervening factors, like pre-Army family background, school habits, sociability, and participation in sports, which suggests links between our demographic categories and adjustment." (I, 146)

The links are those provided by an abbreviated interpretation. The analysts have not actually seen that the partial relationships between the demographic characteristics and adjustment were reduced when the childhood experiences were introduced; they have just inferred that reduction on the basis of the marginal relationships.[27]

In another case, the abbreviation is even greater. In the very remarkable chapter on the Negro soldier (I, Chap. X), the analysts indicate that Negro soldiers showed more interest in their Army jobs than did whites. (I, 537) They suggest, as one intepretation, the soldiers' belief that their Army jobs will be helpful in post-war careers. Thus they introduce a third variable, belief in the future utility of one's Army job, to interpret the relationship between race and job satisfaction in the Army:

"One source of interest in an Army job might be the fact that from it one might learn something which would be useful after the war. In March 1943, in answering the question, 'Do you think that after the war the training you are getting in the Army will or will not help you get a better job than you had before you went into the Army?' among Negroes 61 per cent checked the response 'Will help me get a better job' as contrasted with 39 per cent among whites." (I, 537)

In the first sentence, which sets forth the interpretation, the analysts suggest that the test factor is related to the dependent variable in the original relationship, job satisfaction; they do not actually show that this relation exists, however. In the latter part of the paragraph, the authors present evidence to show that there was indeed a relationship between their interpretative variable and the independent variable of the original relationship, race. In other words, on the basis of one relationship which has been demonstrated and another which has been assumed, the analysts infer that the partials would be reduced, and therefore the original relationship interpreted.

Sometimes an abbreviated interpretation is unavoidable. Many important relationships are not anticipated, but emerge as windfalls after the field work has been completed. Only then can we think of the test factor which might interpret the result. But if we have not previously seen the relevance of this factor, then it is im-

---

[27] A further difficulty in these examples is one already considered briefly. In order that a variable may serve as a *link* between two other variables, *it must intervene between them in time.* But the time relationship of some of the variables considered in this series of interpretations is not so clear. It seems likely that some of the variables offered as links between the demographic characteristics and adjustment, childhood health, for example, actually preceded in time some of the background factors, marital condition, for instance.

possible to study the partial relationships.[28] The most that we can hope for is that in some other survey we shall find data bearing on the marginal relationships, and that this information will enable us to infer the probable reduction in the partials.

Wherever it is possible, however, we should examine the partial relationships, and base our conclusions regarding the relevance of the interpretative variable on what we find there. There are a number of reasons why it is inadvisable to rely exclusively on an abbreviated interpretation. First of all, it is difficult to judge the exact reduction in the average value of the partials from knowledge only of the relationship between the test factor and each of the original variables. As we indicated previously, the partials are assigned specific weights so that their average value is a *weighted* average of the actual reduction in value. The second problem is that, in an abbreviated interpretation, we can only infer what happens to the *average value* of the partial relationships, but can infer nothing about what happens to the individual partials. In most cases it is probably legitimate to infer that, if the average value is less than the original relationship, so are the separate partials. But there might be situations in which the average is 0, while the individual partials are *larger* than the original relationship. (That is, they have opposite signs, and cancel each other out in the averaging process.) If we relied on an abbreviated interpretation, we would mistakenly infer that the test factor provided a complete interpretation of the original result.

In summary, then, an abbreviated interpretation provides only relatively imprecise information on which to base our inferences concerning the relevance of the interpretative variable. Wherever possible, therefore, we should not rely on this scheme of interpretation, but should examine the partials to see what actually does happen to them when the test factor is introduced.

[28] It is to be hoped, of course, that as we learn more about regularities of social behavior, students will be better able to anticipate what test factors will be needed. This should be especially true for relationships where attitudes, expectations, and similar "dispositions" are needed as test factors. A special review of some of these which were revealed in *The American Soldier* will be found in Lazarsfeld's review, *op. cit.*, pp. 386-390. For two examples of full interpretations, where all of the necessary data were available, see Lazarsfeld, Berelson and Gaudet, *The People's Choice* (2nd ed., New York: Columbia University Press, 1948) Charts VX and XVI; and George Katona, "Effect of Income Changes on the Rate of Savings," *Review of Economics and Statistics*, XXXI (1949), pp. 95-103.

Specification—the P type of elaboration

In the final type of elaboration which we shall consider here, we focus our attention on the relative size of the partial relationships. We want to see whether the original relationship is more pronounced in one sub-group than in the other, when the total sample is divided by the test factor. Thus, we try to specify the conditions of the original result.

Because the P type of elaboration is so different from the M type, it may be instructive to give a numerical example of what is meant by specification. In studying social mobility within the Army, the Research Branch found that there was a positive relationship between formal educational level and rank among enlisted men: the better educated the soldier, the more likely he was to have higher rank. (I, 249, Table 7) This relationship is presented in the following four-fold table: [29]

TABLE C

EDUCATIONAL LEVEL

Rank:	HIGH SCHOOL GRADUATE OR BETTER	LESS THAN HIGH SCHOOL GRADUATE
Non-com.	61%	43%
Pvt., Pfc.	39	57
Total cases	3222	3152

If we use as a crude measure of the relationship between education and rank the difference .61 − .43 (which we can symbolize by "f"), the relationship here is .18.

But as is so frequently the case when one deals with relationships of this sort, it occurred to the analysts that the relationship might be more pronounced under varying conditions. The time at which one entered the Army, for example, might affect the correlation between education and rank. It might be that not even the better educated men had much chance to be promoted if they came into the Army at a late date, when tables of organization were pretty well fixed. Accordingly, length of time in the Army, indicating the

[29] As with other numerical examples taken from *The American Soldier,* this four-fold table is a great simplification of the table in the text. We have "collapsed" the original table so that we can deal with three dichotomies.

time at which one had been inducted, was introduced as a test factor. The partial relationships thus obtained were then examined:

TABLE D

Rank:	HAVE SERVED FOR LESS THAN 2 YEARS			HAVE SERVED FOR 2 YEARS OR MORE	
	HS grad or better	*Less than HS grad*		*HS grad or better*	*Less than HS grad*
Non-com.	23%	17%	Non-com.	74%	53%
Pvt., Pfc.	77	83	Pvt., Pfc.	26	47
Totals	842	823		2380	2329
	f = .06			f = .21	

The f coefficients for these two partial tables are very different, indicating varying degrees of relationship between education and rank. Among late entrants into the Army, the better educated men had only slightly greater chances for promotion than did less well educated soldiers. Among those who had come into the Army at an earlier stage in the war, however, the better educated had considerably greater chances of being promoted.[30] In other words, the relationship between education and rank is a conditional one, depending on the time at which the soldier entered the Army.

Most specific examples of statistical analysis will be described by one or more of these different kinds of elaboration. Either we try to "explain" the result, by showing that it is spurious, or we "interpret" it, or we "specify" it. In general, our analysis will follow a definite pattern. We start out with a simple association between two variables. Our first concern is whether or not the relationship is a spurious one; consequently our initial efforts of elaboration are usually of the explanatory type. Once we have gained some assurance that the original relationship is not a spurious one, we try to interpret the result or to specify it.[31] We ask ourselves what

[30] It will be noted that the relationship between education and rank was closer among those who had been in the Army a long time than it was for the total sample. That is, one of the partial relationships was larger than the original one. This is always the case in the pure P type, of which this is an example. When the test factor is unrelated to one or both of the original variables, the marginal term is 0 and the original relationship is a weighted average of the two partials. Thus, unless the partial relationships are equal in size, one of them must be larger than the original relationship.

[31] We must stress that the failure of one antecedent test factor to disqualify the causal connection between two variables is in no way a definitive demonstration of that causal relationship.

variables might provide the links between the "cause" and the "effect," or what conditions might show the original relationship to be even more pronounced than we originally saw it to be. The elaboration of a particular result can go on almost indefinitely. We are limited only by our lack of ingenuity in thinking of factors by which to elaborate the result, by the absence of data to check the relevance of factors which we have thought of, or by the difficulties of dealing with few cases as the process of elaboration is extended.

Qualitative elaboration

When we have no quantitative information about a test factor which we consider relevant, we cannot carry out the procedures of statistical elaboration. What we do then is try to find appropriate qualitative data which will enable us to carry out a kind of hypothetical elaboration. But whether we deal with quantitative or with non-quantitative data, the essential modes of analysis are exactly the same. Much of what is generally called "qualitative analysis" is the argument, on the basis of non-quantitative data, that the relationships characteristic of the different types of elaboration actually do exist. Again, *The American Soldier* provides interesting illustrations of this point.

Let us start with a somewhat paradoxical result. In one Research Branch study of problems of malaria control, it was found that the proportion of men saying that they always took their atabrine, a drug to protect against malaria, was actually higher in outfits *without* close checkups than in outfits which did have regular inspections. (I, 176) The relationship was actually the opposite of that expected by the analysts. It is these paradoxes which most frequently call forth explanations and interpretations. If a finding is anticipated, or "plausible," there is rarely much urgency to account for it. But if the result contradicts previous findings or common sense assumptions, then there is a great psychological need to find some explanation which will bring it in line. In the present case, the explanation was found in the observation that different conditions prevailed in the various outfits studied:

"However, further analysis showed that the outfits with a less close checkup were located in spots where the need was most obvious to the men, whereas the outfits where the command was trying hardest to enforce taking atabrine, and with less success, were located in spots held longest by our troops and in which sanitation measures for mosquito control had been most effectively carried through. It was troops in the latter localities who were most likely to be careless." (I, 176)

On the basis of their observations, then, the analysts uncovered a test factor which seems to them to explain the original result. They argue that this factor, the recognized need for taking atabrine, is related negatively to the existence of some system of inspection, and positively to the men's actual behavior. They imply, furthermore, that had it been possible to classify the men according to their recognition of the need for protecting themselves against malaria, the partial relationships between systems of checking and taking atabrine would either have disappeared or become positive. Through this qualitative analysis, then, they suggest that the original negative relationship was a spurious one.[32]

In our first example, qualitative analysis suggested the spurious character of the original result. In a second case, the qualitative materials provided a possible interpretation for the statistical finding. One of the most consistent empirical generalizations uncovered in Research Branch studies was that enlisted men in rear areas overseas or in inactive theaters of war were considerably more critical of their officers than were front-line troops. (See especially I, 366, Chart 1.) There are a number of possible interpretations for this. It could be, for instance, that through some selective process, the "better" officers were assigned to command front-line troops. But qualitative materials obtained in a study of the Persian Gulf Command suggested another interpretation—that the men in rear areas were especially resentful of the special privileges which officers reserved for themselves. (See I, 370-372) In front-line areas there were no special facilities or comforts which officers could monopolize, while in rear areas or inactive theaters such opportunities were generally abundant;[33] and, where officers enjoyed special privileges, the enlisted men were more critical of them. If this interpretation is correct, then if the enlisted men were classified into those whose officers had special privileges and those whose

[32] In this example, the sign of the partial relationships is the reverse of that in the original relationship. We consider this an M type elaboration because interest is focused on what happens to the average value of the partials rather than on their relative size.

[33] These speculations were confirmed in a later study which included a question designed to probe directly enlisted men's feelings about officers' privileges. Most of the men saying that officers "get about the right number of privileges" or "too few" were in front-line combat units. (I, 373)

officers did not, we would no longer find a marked relationship between the area in which one was stationed and attitudes toward officers.

In these examples, the process of elaboration has been carried out on a qualitative level. From their qualitative materials, the analysts were able to develop some idea as to what might prove to be relevant test factors. They have then argued that, had statistical information been available, the relationships characteristic of different types of elaboration would actually have been found.

In other instances, it is not possible to think of relevant test factors immediately. We recall, for example, that the inverse relationship between size of plane and the combat motivations of flyers was never interpreted satisfactorily. What is needed in such cases is a procedure which maximizes the likelihood that relevant test factors will be uncovered. The *analysis of deviant cases* is designed to serve precisely this purpose. While *The American Soldier* provides no example, we might say a few words about this type of analysis. One takes as a starting point the empirical fact that virtually no statistical relationship, particularly in the social sciences, is a perfect one. While it is generally possible for us to find patterns of attitudes or behavior, it is inevitable that we shall find individuals who deviate from these patterns—the veterans who were eager for further combat, the soldiers who chose their own jobs in the Army and were still dissatisfied, and so on. The assumption underlying the analysis of these deviant cases is that, by focusing our attention on them, by trying to find explanations for their apparently discrepant behavior or attitude, we can extend our information about the pattern or relationships existing for the majority of cases.[34]

However they are uncovered, these test factors play a crucial role in social research. If we were to summarize in one sentence the main theme of Part I, it would be that the analysis of survey materials means essentially a clarification of the relationship between two variables in the light of one or more additional factors. While the different types of elaboration which we have discussed here vary in objective and in detail, all involve the examination of the new interrelations obtained by the introduction of additional variables.

[34] For a further discussion of the objectives of deviant case analysis, and illustrative examples, see Patricia Kendall and Katherine Wolf, "The Analysis of Deviant Cases in Communications Research," *Communications Research, 1948–49* (ed., P. F. Lazarsfeld and F. N. Stanton) New York: Harper and Brothers, 1949.

PART II

THE TREATMENT OF COMPLEX PHENOMENA

PART I dealt with logical procedures for analyzing the statistical relationships found in survey materials. In discussing these procedures we wanted to avoid any debate about the nature of the related variables; we therefore confined ourselves intentionally to simple attributes such as age, length of time in the Army, educational level and the like.

In Part II we turn to a more controversial topic, namely the study of complex phenomena. Perhaps the main progress in social research during the last few years has been precisely in this direction. Several decades ago, for example, we were content to count the numbers of non-coms and men of lower enlisted rank, and to construct pyramids representing the social structure of the Army. But, as we made progress in our research techniques, we became less interested in these simple enumerations and more interested in relatively complex phenomena. Through procedures variously called "index formation," "measurement," and the like, such phenomena as attitudes, motives, values and social processes are progressively brought within the reach of the investigator. Thus, for example, we might study whether those with different rank answer differently to a single question on personal esprit. Or, combining a number of different questions, we might examine variations in levels of personal adjustment according to rank. Finally, on a still more complex level, considering a group rather than an individual phenomenon, we might accept the rate of interaction between those of different rank in a particular Army unit as an index of the amount of cohesion within that unit.

These efforts to study more complex phenomena have not gone unchallenged, however; they are perhaps the most frequent target of external criticism. We are warned that there are many pitfalls in the investigation of "intangibles," and it is suggested that these are impossible to remedy. What the critic does not realize is that sophisticated research technicians are well aware of these dangers. But they do not accept them as inevitable; they look for procedures through which survey findings can be safeguarded against pitfalls in the survey procedure, and they work continuously to build these necessary checks and controls into their study designs.[35]

Section 1—INTRINSIC CHECKS IN SURVEY ANALYSIS

Among the pitfalls most frequently discussed by outsiders are five for which Stouffer and his associates provide examples of internal checks. Both the student and the critic should find it useful to see how each of these difficulties is dealt with. Those which we shall consider may be briefly described as follows:

(a) The danger that respondents are incompetent to answer opinion and attitude questions which we ask them;

(b) that respondents are consciously or unconsciously evasive in their answers;

(c) that subjects are unable to describe objective situations accurately;

(d) that the meaning which questions have for respondents can vary greatly with slight modifications in wording;

(e) and, finally, that it is unimportant to study attitudes, because we are interested in what people do rather than in what they feel.

The first three difficulties, when they occur, are introduced by the respondents' inability or unwillingness to provide the kind of material which is wanted. When the last two difficulties arise, it is because of sins of omission or commission on the part of the researcher.

But no matter who is responsible for the various pitfalls, it is the task of the researcher to include appropriate checks and controls in his survey design. These enable him to determine the seriousness of each difficulty, and they may suggest correctives to be applied in the analysis of the material. Our interest here, then, is to outline some of the procedures designed to safeguard against the dangers which we have listed.

[35] Professor Ernest Nagel has provided an interesting parallel from the field of mathematics. Bishop Berkeley wrote a sharp criticism, rejecting the infinitesimal calculus on philosophical grounds. In view of the obvious success of the new instrument, his diatribe had no effect on the development of mathematics. However, the mathematicians themselves, working on concrete problems, developed refinements in their procedures and further clarified the foundations of the calculus. Thus, the intrinsic development of mathematics led to the solution of problems which the outsider held up as basic and unavoidable shortcomings. According to Professor Nagel, progress in empirical sciences is always due to the critical self-analysis of workers in the field (*e.g.*, Poincare, Mach, and Bridgman), and not to the vituperations of men in the gallery.

Inability to give a competent answer

Social researchers have long been aware that, if given an opportunity, many respondents will express an opinion on an issue of
which they are ignorant and therefore incompetent to answer. This
possibility is taken into account in the design of the survey as well
as in the analysis of the results. In planning the study, we see to it
that the schedule includes questions which will later enable us to
classify the respondents according to their competence. In some
instances we may feel that the relevant qualifications are informational ones; we may consider as competent respondents only those
individuals who have a minimum level of information. There are
other situations in which the competence of the respondent depends
on his experiences in certain spheres of activity.[36] In the first case,
then, we would include questions designed to determine how well
informed each of the respondents actually is; in the second case,
the qualifying questions would deal with experiences rather than
with information.

When we came to analyze the results, we take advantage of this
information by comparing the responses of those with varying degrees of competence. This frequently leads to quite different conclusions than would be arrived at were the qualifications of the
respondents not taken into consideration. Thus in studying fear reactions to specific enemy weapons, the analysts recognized that
those who had been in combat longest were best qualified to say
which weapon was most frightening. Questioning of these particularly "qualified" soldiers revealed that enemy artillery was feared
considerably more than enemy air attack: 20 per cent of those who
had been in battle 30 days or more feared air attack most, while
over 50 per cent of those in battle the same length of time were
most afraid of artillery. (II, 236, Chart VIII) This, then, was the
"informed" opinion, supported by the objective evidence of casualty
statistics. But the analysts were not content to let the matter rest
there. They saw the value of comparing this informed opinion with
that prevailing in less well qualified groups. From this comparison
emerged some very interesting results. Among less battlewise soldiers, the picture is completely reversed, with artillery attacks being

[36] The intensity with which an attitude is held can also serve as a criterion
of competence. Because the problems of measuring intensity are dealt with
extensively in the fourth volume of the Research Branch series, we shall not
consider it here.

feared *less* than air attacks. (II, 236, Chart VIII) [37] As the authors point out, this result suggests that:

". . . a learning process operates in combat which has the dual effect of decreasing fear reactions to exaggerated dangers and increasing fear reactions to underestimated dangers. The extinction of fear reactions to pseudo danger cues and the strengthening of these reactions in response to cues of genuine danger would be highly adaptive in an environment which contains a multitude of potential dangers." (II, 240-241.)

This example is interesting in two respects. On the one hand, it shows how the amount of information possessed by the respondent can be introduced as a variable in the survey result. It also shows that the attitudes of uninformed respondents need not be discarded as useless. By comparing informed and uninformed opinion, additional results and leads for remedial action can be found.

Evasiveness of answers

Closely related to the possibility that our subjects are unable to answer questions put to them is the danger that they do not want to respond. In order to meet this danger, social researchers have developed a number of checks to determine the extent to which evasion, conscious or unconscious, has taken place.

Motivations to falsify answers deliberately are probably dealt with most effectively by precautions taken at the time that the data are collected. Emphasis on the anonymity of the respondent and his answers can often do much to reduce desires to withhold "true" attitudes. In Research Branch studies, for example, most questionnaires were self-administered. The soldiers filled out the schedules by themselves, and turned them in unsigned so that their identity would not be disclosed. (Instructions on the cover sheets of the questionnaires generally cautioned the respondents not to sign their names.)

It is also possible to include in the schedule questions which, when cross-tabulated against the crucial item, will permit some

---

[37] One interesting aspect of this analysis is that it is confined, in a sense, only to qualified soldiers. Thus only those who had been exposed to enemy air attacks were asked whether this was the weapon which frightened them most, and so on. The amount of time spent in combat becomes an "additional" qualification in the analysis. See II, IV, fn. to Table 5. For a particularly good case in which the role of information is taken into account, see Leonard S. Cottrell, Jr. and Sylvia Eberhart, *American Opinion on World Affairs* (Princeton, N. J., Princeton University Press, 1948).

estimate of the amount of evasion which has taken place. A striking example in *The American Soldier* concerns desires to avoid service in the Infantry. Research Branch analysts found consistently that, while the Infantry ranked high in prestige, it ranked low in popularity as the branch in which men wanted most to serve. (I, Chap. VII, Tables 2 and 3) One explanation which they offer for this discrepancy is that, while soldiers had respect for the Infantry because of the dangers it faced and the achievements which it made, they were for those very reasons reluctant to serve as Infantrymen. (See I, Chap. VII, 329-337 for a discussion of the role of danger in job satisfaction.) And yet, when a group of men who had said that they wanted to avoid serving in the Infantry were asked why, only 8 per cent said that this was because the Infantry "sees too much combat" or because "Its casualty rate is too high." (I, 331) The great majority indicated such reasons as "I don't think I'm physically qualified for it," "It would not give me a chance to do the kind of work I can do best," and "It would not give me training for a better job after the war." The analysts felt that, in a number of cases at least, such responses were rationalizations of the "true" motive—desire to avoid danger. In an effort to determine the extent of such rationalizations, they studied the relationship between reluctance to serve in the Infantry or in overseas combat units and reported worries about battle injuries. They discovered that there was a marked relationship: the great majority of those who said that they worried often about battle injury—79 per cent to be exact—wanted to avoid both the Infantry and overseas combat service. This is in contrast to 37 per cent of those saying that they never worried. (I, 333, Chart VIII) Frequently a set of interlocking questions of this type permits an intrinsic check on evasions, and their analysis leads to more convincing results.

Where these check questions are not available, careful analysis may still provide some inferential evidence concerning the frequency with which respondents have concealed their attitudes or motives. First of all there is the simple test of noting how frequently the response which we expect will be concealed actually turns up. Somewhat along these lines is the following discussion in *The American Soldier*. The authors note that whenever soldiers were asked questions about their orientation toward the war, approximately 90 per cent said that they felt the United States was "fight-

ing for things they personally felt were worth fighting for." They
then go on to say:

"While it may be objected that any other answer might be considered
treasonable and so would be suppressed, the fact remains that men did
express critical attitudes about officers and various Army policies, for
example, when far swifter and more sure reprisals would probably have
been expected by the men had they ever become identified. If they were
frank about such things, there is little reason to believe that there would
have been conscious misreporting about these more remote questions."
(I, 437, fn. 6)

In other words, because more "treasonable" questions had received
a greater proportion of critical responses, the authors conclude that
few, if any, of their respondents were evasive in their answers to
questions about worthwhileness of the war.

The frequency of "Don't know" responses can also serve as an
index to the amount of evasiveness in answering questions. Research
Branch analysts found, for example, that while the same proportion of Negroes as of whites answered "No" to the question, "As
far as you know, are you now classified by the Army as physically
fit for overseas duty?", considerably more of the Negroes, 32 per
cent as compared with 20 per cent, said that they didn't know how
they were classified. The authors suggest that these "Don't know"
responses may be evasive, indicative of the less favorable attitudes
of Negroes toward service overseas. (I, 540)

Inaccuracy of descriptions

Sometimes it is necessary to have information about the objective
situation in which respondents find themselves. For example, we
might want to determine whether men stationed in isolated camps
are less well adjusted than soldiers stationed in camps which have
easy access to recreational centers. But this raises something of a
problem. To rate the objective isolation of each camp might require sending a team of experts virtually all over the world; [38] the
difficulties which this would entail lead researchers to look for
some kind of shortcut. The one most usually relied on is that the
respondents themselves provide the ratings. In addition to asking
each man questions about his personal adjustment, we ask him
questions to indicate the degree of isolation of his camp. This sub-

[38] See I, 179-181 for an example in which the ratings were supplied by Research Branch analysts.

stitute procedure assumes, however, that respondents are able to appraise objective conditions and that they do not project their more general attitudes onto their evaluations. This is an assumption which requires examination; it is a difficulty which requires appropriate checks and controls. Let us see how the problem was handled in Research Branch studies.

In examining factors affecting job satisfaction in the Army, the analysts wanted to study the relationship of satisfaction to physical comforts. They wanted to find out whether men stationed in camps with adequate food, housing and recreational facilities were more satisfied than men stationed in camps without these amenities. The units were ranked, not according to the observations of experts or the analysis of objective data, but by the subjects themselves: enlisted men in the ground crews of twelve Air Force fighter groups whose job satisfaction was being studied were also asked questions about food, housing and sanitation, and recreation facilities in their various units. The twelve units were then ranked according to the number of complaints received on each count. (I, 356)

The analysts give careful attention to the kind of questions raised earlier. Do these varying numbers of complaints represent true differences in the objective situation? Can we rely on the men to describe their comforts, or lack of them, accurately? Stouffer and his associates attempt to answer these questions through an interesting kind of analysis. To begin with, they note that each of the units had an unusually high proportion of men in the top three non-com grades. For a variety of reasons, it is suggested, their appraisals are most likely to be accurate. They are best qualified to give objective descriptions "if only for the reason that they are less likely to be 'browned off' about the Army than others and their complaints, if they make them, are more likely to have a specific referent." (I, 356) The top non-coms, then, serve as quasi-experts whose opinions provide some kind of standard by which to gauge the objectivity of answers given by others. If the descriptions given by other enlisted men resemble those given by the top three graders in each of the units, then, the analysts argue, there is some basis for concluding that the descriptions are relatively accurate.

Their next step, therefore, is to study the correspondence in the number of complaints given by top non-coms and other enlisted men serving in the same units. For each of the facilities, food, housing, and recreation, Stouffer and his associates constructed a scatter diagram, plotting the number of complainants among the top three graders in each fighter group against the number of complainants among other enlisted men in that same group. (I, 358, Chart XVII) The results indicate very high correlation in each case: with regard to each of the facilities, the number of complaints registered by top non-coms in each of the twelve groups is almost identical with the number of complaints voiced by the other enlisted men in that group. They conclude, therefore, that there were real differences in the physical amenities enjoyed by the various units, and that these differences were expressed in answers provided by the subjects themselves.

Information about a somewhat different kind of objective situation, calling for a different kind of internal check, was required in another Research Branch study. In an analysis of the extent to which soldiers utilized their civilian skills in their Army jobs, each man was asked, "Do you use the civilian training and experience you had before you came into the Army on your present Army job or assignment?" There are a number of grounds, similar to those previously considered, on which one might question the accuracy of such evaluations. In the first place, some of the men may have interpreted "civilian training and experience" in a very broad sense, rather than thinking in terms of specific skills. And, as the authors note, answers to this question might be colored again by general attitudes: soldiers generally hostile to the Army might answer that they never received an opportunity to use their civilian skills where, in fact, they did; other men, perhaps those promoted and therefore more favorably disposed to the Army command, might answer that they did use their civilian skills while actually they did not.

In order to check the soldiers' accuracy, the analysts made use of two items of fact which had been obtained in the survey. The first of these was a description of the last three civilian occupations each man had held; the second was a description of his Army job. On the basis of this information, the total sample was divided into two groups. Those soldiers whose Army jobs, in the opinion of Army occupational experts, made use of their civilian skills were considered "matched" in occupation; the men for whom this was not true were classified as "unmatched." It was thus possible to compare an objective picture of the situation with the soldiers' description of that situation. In general there was a close correspondence between them. Among the soldiers whose Army jobs matched their civilian occupations, less than a fifth said that they "never" had a chance to use their civilian skills, while approximately one-half of the un-matched group gave this evaluation. At the other extreme, exactly the reverse relationship was found: approximately one-half of the matched group said that they used their civilian skills "most of the time," while this response was given by only one-quarter of those in the unmatched group. (I, 327, Chart VII) [39]

Through checks of this kind, we can evaluate the accuracy with which respondents have described objective situations. But it is not always the subjects who introduce inaccuracies into materials. Un-less he makes use of the proper checks, the researcher himself is sometimes responsible for inaccuracies. It is to these situations which we now turn.

Variability of answers

The importance of question wording is a hardy perennial of re-search training and research practice. Stouffer and his associates, aware of the problem, made use of a varied system of checks. They recognized, for example, that there is sometimes a tendency to agree rather than to disagree with statements. Thus if all statements are slanted in a particular way, let us say in an anti-Army direction, the proportions of agreements may overestimate the actual amount of aggressive feelings about the Army. To avoid this distortion, one study carried out by the Research Branch made use of two differ-ent schedules: in the first, some of the items were slanted in a direc-tion favorable to the Army, and others were anti-Army in wording; on the second form the wording of each item was exactly reversed, usually by the insertion or the deletion of "not." (I, 226, Table 8) Two pairs of statements are presented here to indicate the alternate forms:

[39] It may not be immediately obvious why we are concerned with the sol-diers' descriptions if objective information is available. Why do we ask soldiers whether or not they use their civilian skills if this can be determined by a careful comparison of civilian and Army jobs? The answer is that it is very much easier to rely on the soldiers' descriptions. The authors allude briefly to the tremendous amount of work involved in a matching of civilian and Army jobs. (I, 325) We undertake the labor in one study, as a means of checking the descriptions. If they turn out to be reasonably accurate, we rely on them in future studies of comparable populations, and no longer go through the difficult process of actually matching civilian and Army occupations.

"Promotion in the Army is based on *who* you know, not *what* you know." (Used on A form.)
"Promotion in the Army is based on *what* you know, not *who* you know." (Used on B form.)

"The Army places too much importance on spit and polish." (Used on B form.)
"The Army does *not* place too much importance on spit and polish." (Used on A form.)

Twenty pairs were included in the schedule. In seven of them the proportions agreeing with the favorable form were so different from the proportions disagreeing with the unfavorable form that they could not be used. In the remaining 13 pairs, the differences were minor and showed no consistent pattern.

The use of alternate forms, or "split-ballots" as they are called, is one way in which the investigator can safeguard himself against the pitfall of believing that his results are independent of the way in which the questions are worded.

The authors were also aware of the problems of question wording during the analysis phase. Thus, they caution the reader at numerous points (see, for example, I, 45, 168, 220; and II, 612) that it is not the absolute number of men selecting a particular alternative in a check-list which is of interest to the social researcher, but rather the *comparative* numbers in different social groups. They point out that the significant result is not that 76 per cent of the non-commissioned officers in the United States feel that the Army is pretty well or very well run, but that these 76 per cent, in contrast to 63 per cent among non-commissioned officers overseas, express this attitude.

Under certain conditions it is possible to investigate the meaning of questions by reference to the survey results themselves. To do this, however, we must be able to compare the answers of groups whose characteristics and attitudes are known, either from previous sources or from other parts of the survey. The procedure can be exemplified by comparing the responses of veterans and "green" troops to specific questions. It had been established in a variety of studies that veterans were less willing than green troops for combat service. In the present example, this serves as the preliminary information always required in "meaning analysis." The concrete problem was to find out whether the following questions had the same meaning:

"Do you think you have been given enough training and experience so that you could do a good job of taking charge of men on your own in combat?"

"Do you feel that you are now trained and ready for combat, or do you need more training?"

One might expect, after reading those questions, that they would be interchangeable, both directed toward determining soldiers' appraisals of their training. On both, one would anticipate more favorable answers from veterans because of their actual combat experiences. But strangely enough, the replies of veterans and green troops to the two questions were quite different. On the first question, the veterans actually did give more favorable responses—57 per cent as compared with 41 per cent of the inexperienced troops; on the second question, however, it is the green soldiers who are more frequently favorable—35 per cent of them as compared with 24 per cent of the veterans say that they have had enough training. (II, 252. Table 2)

The authors conclude that the questions had very different meaning for the two types of respondents, and they then try to find out in what respects this was the case. One difference between the first and second questions is the emphasis, in the first, on the word "experience." [40] If this word is picked out as being the crucial one, as it evidently was, then it is understandable that the experienced veterans should express more favorable responses than the inexperienced troops. Until one studies the second question more carefully, it is difficult to see why the veterans are less favorable than the green troops. But as the authors state, "An interpretation of this anomalous finding suggests itself from the character of the favorable answer category, 'I'm ready for combat now.' This was an admission which the reluctant veteran might indeed wish to avoid." (II, 251) In other words, the favorable answer carried with it an implication of willingness for further combat as well as an expression of confidence in readiness for combat. [41]

[40] We might also suppose that the suggestion of "taking charge of men in combat" would be a factor in the differential responses of the two groups. However, a third question, "If you were given a group of men and told to take charge of them all by yourself under enemy fire, how well do you think you would do?" showed no differences, the green troops expressing as much self-confidence as the veterans in this particular respect. (See II, 250-251.)

[41] A similar kind of analysis was carried out with a number of other questions. See especially the discussion regarding Table 4 in II, 256.

This kind of analysis might be compared to the chemical identification of metal. By studying its reactions to a variety of acids, the chemist can determine its composition. In the same way the survey analyst submits a question to a variety of groups whose general characteristics he knows. By comparing their answers, he finds out the semantic ingredients of the question, which he might not have obtained from his own reading of the words.

Irrelevance of attitude data

The notion that information about attitudes is useless unless it is predictive of behavior is only partially justified. Whether people are happy or not is an important datum, no matter what they do. One can easily imagine a society in which a periodic census of happiness is taken more seriously than continuous reports of department store sales. As a matter of fact, one of the most interesting contributions of *The American Soldier* is the wealth of data on individuals' feelings, whether in terms of adjustment scores or of psychoneurotic inventories.

Nonetheless, the extent to which attitudes can predict behavior is a problem of paramount importance in social research. Here again the Research Branch analysts report material which, in some cases, is quite unique. Perhaps the most notable result in this connection is the demonstration of a consistent correlation between attitudes ascertained during training in the United States and battle performance in Europe more than a year later. (II, 30-41)[42] In the fall and winter of 1943, sample respondents in a newly activated division, then in training in the United States, were questioned about their confidence in combat skill, their anxieties about battle injuries, and their attitudes of aggressiveness toward the enemy. More than a year later, after they had seen several months of combat, Research Branch psychologists obtained ratings of the battle performances of many of these soldiers. These ratings were then correlated with their original attitudes. It was found that those who had, on the earlier occasion, expressed more favorable attitudes (*i.e.*, more confidence, less anxiety, more aggressive attitudes toward the enemy) performed better in battle. Similar findings emerged from another study referred to earlier in connection with our discussion of panel techniques. In this second study, nine rifle companies and nine heavy weapons companies, in training for the invasion of Europe, were

[42] This is based on the panel study referred to in an earlier section.

classified according to average level of combat willingness and combat confidence on the basis of interviews with sample respondents from each of the companies. (See II, 5-30) Several months later, after the companies had been in combat, the non-combat casualty rate for each was determined. Again consistent correlations were found: those companies which, on the average, expressed more favorable attitudes during their period of training had lower casualty rates in actual combat. It is impossible, in this brief summary of the results, to give an adequate picture of the planning and work which go into these seemingly simple predictions.[43]

A comparable correspondence between verbal statements and actual behavior was found in connection with a test designed for psychiatric screening. In the autumn of 1943, a sample of new Infantry recruits, none of them in the Army for more than a few weeks, were asked to fill out a schedule which included questions about feelings of physical well-being, homesickness, anxieties about battle injury, discipline, and so on. Six months later, in the spring of 1944, it was found that 73 of the original sample had been diagnosed as psychoneurotic by Army medical officers. These 73 were matched in age, education, and marital condition with 730 "normal" trainees in the original sample, and their answers of six months previously compared. Many of the questions were found to discriminate clearly between the two groups. (II, 414, Table 1)

One point often overlooked is that apparent contradictions between attitude and behavior data can themselves be powerful tools of analysis. For example, when the subjective feelings of combat flyers were studied (using the question, "In general, what sort of physical condition would you say you are in at the present time?"), it was found that, with increasing numbers of combat missions, there was a marked deterioration in feelings of well-being. (II, 380, Chart XII) The airmen became more and more concerned with their health as their tours of combat duty progressed. But these concerns were not at all reflected in their behavior. The Research Branch obtained statistics from the Office of the Air Surgeon concerning the relationship between the rate of sick-call and the number of combat missions flown. (The data were obtained for the same time period and from the same theater in which the attitude mate-

---

[43] In Section 3 of II, Chap. I, the authors present the basic data used in the analysis, and indicates some of the different computations which had to be carried out in order to obtain the results.

rial had been collected.) While the verbal answers of the flyers would suggest a positive relationship between number of missions flown and rate of sick-call, *exactly the reverse was found*. With one interesting exception to be noted below, the rate of sick-call *declined* steadily with increasing combat experience. (II, 381, Chart XIII)

It is true that, in this case, the attitude materials were very bad predictors of actual behavior. But that in no way detracts from their value in making clear the motivations and concerns of the flyers. The very lack of correspondence between attitude statements and actual behavior made it possible in this case to understand the importance of a set tour of combat duty. As the authors put it:

"These findings suggest that the behavior of men in heavy bomber crews was strongly oriented toward the goal of completing the number of missions which constituted the tour of combat duty. To some extent sick call was avoided while the 30 missions were in progress, despite the increasing concern about health. Under normal conditions, men with physical complaints had nothing to lose, in general, by bringing their health problems to the attention of medical officers. But for men in heavy bomber crews, temporary or permanent removal from flying status might be the consequence, and this would seriously interfere with achieving the goal of completing the tour of combat duty and being rotated back to the United States." (II, 382)

The validity of this interpretation, that there was a tendency to "save up" physical complaints until the tour of combat had been completed, is given further weight by the fact that, among men who had completed 30 missions, there was a steep rise in the rate of sick calls. Once their tour was finished, and there was no longer any danger that their return to the United States would be delayed, they gave in to their concerns about their health. (See II, 381, Chart XIII.)

In this case, then, the complete story emerged only from the comparison of the two sets of data, the objective and the subjective; the interpretation derived from an effort to explain the discrepancy between them. The attitude materials, if they alone had been available, would have led the analysts to expect quite different behavior. Had they known only what the rate of sick calls was, they would have anticipated a very different kind of attitude. Together, the two sets of materials permitted the analysts to describe a phenomenon which could hardly have been documented in any other way.

Section 2—*INDICES IN SURVEY ANALYSIS*

Because the subject matter of sociology and social psychology often cannot be observed or measured directly, one of the primary objectives in social research is to determine which types of observations or questions can most adequately serve as indicators for less accessible concepts.

The development of indices generally proceeds in three steps. First of all, it is necessary to be clear about the concept for which indicators are sought. Secondly, the specific items—be they observations, types of records or questions in survey schedules—must be selected. Finally, if there is more than one indicator for the same concept, it is generally necessary to decide on some way of combining the several items.

The clarification of complex concepts

Many of the concepts with which we are concerned are labeled with familiar words so that their meaning seems obvious to us. We feel that we know what the phrase "front-line troops," as opposed to "rear echelons," means; it is a concept familiar to us from history books, from journalistic accounts, and from literary works. If pressed for a definition, however, we would very likely find that our conception includes a variety of sometimes conflicting aspects. If we consider as front-line troops those within a specified range of the enemy lines, how do we classify combat air crews who, though based perhaps several hundred miles away from enemy lines, still fly over enemy territory? (See II, 290-91.)

The process of clarifying a concept, then, consists essentially in spelling out the various aspects which must be taken into consideration and then, in the light of our objectives, deciding on a definition—or selecting those aspects—which seem most manageable and most adequate.

There are several sections of *The American Soldier* in which the authors attempt just this sort of clarification. Perhaps the best of these is the section in which they consider what they will mean by personal adjustment. (See especially I, 82-85.) The analysts indicate that this concept might have been defined in a number of ways. For example, they might have defined adjustment as successful adaptation to changing environmental demands, or as conformity to the informal structure of the Army. For a variety of reasons, however, neither of these alternatives was chosen. In Research Branch studies, adjustment was taken to mean adaptation as viewed by the Army command. As we shall see, this definition dictated the kinds of indicators which were selected and the kinds of indices which were constructed.

Similar efforts at clarification were made in other sections of *The American Soldier*. Chapter II in the second volume, for instance, is devoted entirely to a description of the characteristics of ground combat. Variables in the combat situation are outlined (II, 64-69); combat situations in different geographical areas are compared (II, 69-76); types of combat stresses are described (II, 76-95); and so on.

In still another section of the text (I, 432-433), the analysts suggest alternative ways in which a "favorable orientation toward the war" might be defined. For example, such an orientation might involve accepting the defensive necessity of the war, or the denial of cynical or critical motives for our participation in the war.

Once the alternative meanings of a concept have been spelled out, and one of them adopted as a working definition, the next step is the selection of those items which seem to be the best indicators.

The selection of items as indicators

Often the specific items are virtually forced on the researcher by the definition which he has adopted. In the case of "personal adjustment," for example, promotion was taken as one non-verbal indicator, while expressions of good spirits, satisfaction with Army job and status, and generally favorable attitudes toward life in the Army were used as verbal indicators. (I, 82-83)

In another article, one of the co-authors of this paper has outlined some of the more significant contributions of *The American Soldier* to concepts such as the "primary group," "frame of reference," and "position." [44] Rather than repeat that discussion here, we shall turn to other examples in which the ingenuity of the analysts permitted them to find indices for the analysis of complex concepts.

On some occasions a single item in a survey seems sufficient to indicate the existence of a fairly complex set of attitudes. Prior to our active entrance into the war, Research Branch analysts were

[44] Paul F. Lazarsfeld, *"The American Soldier*—An Expository Review," *op. cit.*, pp. 383-395.

interested in determining the extent to which men inducted into the Army through the Selective Service system maintained a feeling of identification with civilian life. The notion of identifying with a group suggests a complicated phenomenon for which one might want numerous and varied indices. Actually, only one question was used in the Research Branch study, but it seems to have accomplished its objective. The question, asked of both regular Army men and the selectees, read as follows: "Which do you prefer to wear on furlough, uniform or civilian clothes?" The difference in the expressed preferences of the two groups was large: 30 per cent of the selectees, as contrasted with 62 per cent of the regulars, said that they preferred to wear their uniforms. (I, 64, Chart III)[45] The choice of what kind of clothes to wear when not on active duty symbolizes so directly one's sense of identification with either the Army or with civilian life that no other index seems needed.

In other instances the index for the concept may be found in the contrasting answers given by one group to a pair of questions. Toward the end of the war, the Research Branch found that 81 per cent of a sample of enlisted men believed that *civilians* would consider a private or a Pfc "not good enough to get a rating," while only 25 per cent felt that *other soldiers* would have this attitude. (I, 231)[46] This simple comparison of the attitudes imputed to civilians and those imputed to other soldiers might be considered an index for "in-group" versus "out-group" experiences. First of all, the finding suggests that soldiers look on other soldiers, co-members of their in-group, with sympathy and understanding; they seem to maintain a kind of solidarity which prevents criticism of those in a low status. Secondly, the fact that these same soldiers attribute very different attitudes to civilians seems to indicate that they do not consider civilians members of the group to which they belong. And, since the attitudes attributed to civilians are critical ones, it appears that soldiers think of individuals on the home front as constituting a "hostile" out-group.

[45] This difference is too large to be accounted for by the educational superiority of the selectees, even though there are educational differences in the preferences expressed.

[46] From the point of view of survey techniques this finding is an important one. It indicates that, contrary to the expectations of many critics of public opinion research, respondents do not answer all questions simply by projecting their own attitudes or opinions. If this were the case, if the answers merely reflected the soldiers' own feelings about promotion and status, there would be no such difference in the proportions agreeing with the statements.

It is not always possible, however, to find quantitative indices for the concepts being considered. It might happen, for example, that the researcher has failed to ask any questions appropriate to the study of in-group attitudes. This is particularly likely to be the case in secondary analyses which make use of data collected primarily for other purposes. But even where there are no quantitative indices, the researcher can sometimes call on *qualitative* evidence for the concepts or relationships in which he is interested. The qualitative material is generally the observation of symbolic acts or incidents. A few characteristic illustrations may help to clarify the nature and use of these indices.

At one point in their analysis, Stouffer and his associates wanted to indicate that certain features of Army life bore a resemblance to the situation one would find in a *caste system*. Had this concern been a major one, the analysts might have proceeded in a number of different ways. First of all, they might have carried out a survey among officers and enlisted men, noting the numbers and kinds of contacts which took place between them. From such a survey, quantitative indices of caste structure might have been developed. Or, a second type of study, an "institutional analysis," might have been undertaken. Here the researchers would have examined all the formal rules and regulations of the Army, studied lines of command, and so on. From such an analysis they would have decided the extent to which the Army exhibited features typical in a caste structure. Neither type of data was immediately available, and since the point was of incidental rather than primary importance, no attempt was made to collect the data in precisely the form we have suggested.

The index which actually was used by the Research Branch was the existence of a ritualistic tradition which would not have been maintained had the Army not had certain elements of a caste system. The authors note that while it was possible for enlisted men to become officers, there was no direct promotion:

"Enlisted men selected for officer candidate school were first discharged from the Army and then readmitted in their new and very different status." (I, 56, fn. 2)

Just as it is impossible to move from one caste to another, in an ethnic caste situation, so an enlisted man about to become an officer must leave the Army system before reentering in his new status.

The index of caste features in the Army was a custom sanctioned and maintained by formal rules of Army procedure. Another custom, this time one which grew up spontaneously among combat personnel in the Air Corps, is cited by Research Branch authors as an index of the importance of a fixed tour of combat. A result from *The American Soldier* referred to earlier in this paper suggested the importance of that tour, and other findings pointing to the same conclusion are reported in other sections of the volumes. But as the authors themselves state:

"The sharp focus among men in the heavy bombers upon completion of the tour of duty would be almost sufficiently documented by a single fact, namely the widespread existence of the 'Lucky Bastard' clubs. By the spring of 1944 it was common for bomber groups to award 'Lucky Bastard' certificates to crew members after the completion of their thirtieth mission. This practice appears to have developed spontaneously among the men themselves and was not explicitly sanctioned by the high command." (II, 383)

In other words, the fact that men who had completed their missions were made members of a special club, and the fact that they were called the "lucky bastards" is a qualitative index of the psychological importance of a stated tour of combat.

Along somewhat similar lines, the Research Branch analysts noted the importance which returnees placed on being allowed to wear the insignia of their overseas units when serving in new units in the United States. (II, 508) This observation was used to indicate the ambivalence experienced by these soldiers.

The combination of items

In survey work, we generally use several items to indicate the particular concept with which we are dealing. We feel more confident that a respondent really is optimistic about the future if he indicates this in answer to a number of questions, rather than in answer to only one. But this requires the construction of an index. The multiple items must be grouped into classes which are both meaningful and easily manageable.

Usually the Research Branch analysts combined their items into the familiar kind of scales, grouping together those respondents who had given specified responses to the same number of questions, without respect to the particular questions thus answered. Through this technique, they developed a number of attitude and behavior scales which are used extensively throughout the two volumes. For example, they worked out a scale of conformity to the Army (I, 265, Chart XI), a scale indicating degree of vindictiveness toward the enemy (II, 163, Table 15), another concerned with job adjustment (II, 502, Table 21), still another dealing with confidence and pride in one's outfit (II, 336, Chart IV), and a score of fear symptoms. (II, 179, Table 20)

The theory and technique of such combinations of items into scales has been greatly advanced by the Research Branch. In the fourth volume of their series, called *Measurement and Prediction*, Stouffer and his staff will themselves report on the basic principles underlying their scale construction. It does not seem necessary, therefore, to discuss the matter any further in the present context; the main purpose of this paper is to codify those operations which are implied, but not explicitly formulated, in *The American Soldier*. There is one aspect permeating many of the examples which deserves special attention. The matter is best introduced by the notion of "level of complexity" according to which indices can be viewed.

The correspondence between personal and unit data

Let us start out with the fact of promotion. First of all, we can ascertain whether a soldier who entered the Army as a private has been promoted. This is typical of the items which might be included in a scale of Army success; other indicators with which it might be combined are the citations and decorations which he received, the way in which his superiors evaluate him, and so on. Secondly, confining our attention to promotion only, we can count how often each soldier was promoted. In that case, the number of promotions, summed over a period of time, would be used as an index of success. We can go still further, and determine how many men in a whole unit have been promoted during a specified time period. This would be an index of the opportunities which a given unit provides. The incidence of a single promotion, the index of success pertaining to a man and the index of opportunity pertaining to a unit differ in their complexity: the second index comes about by summing the first over time; the third comes about by summing the second over the population.

It can be seen quite easily that the notion of complexity is a relative one. We cannot speak of the complexity of a single index, but only of the relative complexity of two indices. If a second index is formed by some procedure of combination in which the first index is an element, then the second index is said to have a higher level of complexity. A detailed discussion of the numerous consequences which derive from this notion of complexity would go beyond the limits of this paper. We shall restrict ourselves to a discussion of the relation between an individual index and a group index of just one higher degree of complexity. We thus exclude cases where combinations are formed over other units than groups, and we also exclude the discussion of more than two complexity levels. Even then, the necessary considerations are rather intricate.

In order to have a uniform and neutral terminology, we shall use the following expressions. A *personal datum* is a fact predicated about a single individual. If several personal data about the same person are combined in some way, we shall talk of a *personal index*. Any kind of aggregate of persons will be called a *unit*. A group of people, for instance, who interact with each other, form a unit; but an aggregate of people who serve in a regiment together or who live in the same census tract will also be called a unit, irrespective of whether or not they are in contact with each other. A *unit datum* is any fact predicated about a unit. If a number of unit data are combined to characterize a single unit we shall talk of a *unit index*. Units as well as persons can form the elements of a statistical analysis. (The statistics in many studies of urban ecology, for instance, have units as elements.)

Our main interest here is directed toward the *logical relationship between personal data and unit data*. In order to be as concrete as possible we start with data taken from Table 18 in II, 450.

TABLE E—ANXIETY SYMPTOMS AND CERTAIN RELATED FACTORS AMONG COMBAT INFANTRYMEN IN FOUR DIVISIONS IN THE SOUTH AND CENTRAL PACIFIC AREAS (MARCH-APRIL 1944)

	DIVISION A S. PACIFIC	DIVISION B S. PACIFIC	DIVISION C CEN. PACIFIC	DIVISION D CEN. PACIFIC
Percentages who have had malaria	66	41	2	2
Percentages receiving critical scores on the Anxiety Symptoms Index	79	63	56	44
Median number of days in combat	55	31	19	3
Number of cases	1,420	1,388	1,298	643

Here four Army divisions, each a unit, are compared in a variety of ways. The first row shows the proportion of malaria cases in the four divisions and the second row the proportion of soldiers exhibiting a pre-established number of neurotic symptoms. A glance at the two rows shows that the greater the incidence of malaria the greater also the incidence of neurotic cases. Let us look at the character of the data in the first row. On an individual level, the only possible distinction is between those who have had malaria and those who have not. But a unit of soldiers (in this case, a division) can be characterized by the proportion of soldiers with malaria. The personal datum, *incidence* of malaria, is an attribute.[47] To it corresponds as a unit datum the malaria *rate* which is a continuous variable. This correspondence will be called that of *Type I*.

Now let us turn to the unit datum in the third row. Each individual soldier was obviously characterized first by a continuous measure— the length of time he had been in combat. The unit is characterized by an average formed over the personal data, in this case the median. If the personal datum is a variable and the corresponding unit datum an average of the same variable we shall talk of correspondences of *Type II*.[48]

On a somewhat impressionistic level, the two types mentioned so far have something in common. The personal datum and the corresponding unit datum have what one might call psychological similarity. We use practically the same terms in talking of the malaria-beset soldier and the malaria-infected division or in talking of the veteran soldier and the veteran division. We shall see presently that the similarity does not need to be as great as the linguistic usage suggests.

If the personal datum is a variable, then there can be still another correspondence. It is entirely possible that two divisions have the

[47] The number of times a soldier has had malaria would be a summation over time, which is excluded from the present discussion.

[48] For the sake of completeness we should also reflect a moment on the index used in the second row. It is based on an index of psychoneurotic symptoms which the Research Branch had developed. This was originally, again, a kind of continuous variable where soldiers could vary over a wide range of scores. But, for a variety of reasons, this variable was reconverted on the individual level into a dichotomous attribute: soldiers were divided according to whether their score was above or below the critical level. Out of this dichotomy, then, on the group level, a continuous rate was formed as in the case of malaria. This double conversion, however, is rare and will not be considered further.

same "median number of days in combat" and still differ in an important respect. One division might be quite homogeneous in that most of its soldiers had the same amount of combat experience. The other division might have received many replacements, so that some of its soldiers have much more than the median amount of combat experience, while others have hardly any. It is quite obvious that this homogeneity of combat experience can only apply to a division; by the logic of the way it is measured, homogeneity can only be a unit datum and never a personal datum. We shall talk of correspondence, *Type III*, when the unit datum is a standard deviation, a measure of skewness or any other parameter of a distribution derived from a personal datum variable.

In the three types discussed so far, the personal data could be attributed to individuals without any reference to the unit. Number of days in combat, number of psychoneurotic symptoms, incidence of malaria are typical examples of this kind. There are, however, certain personal data which imply either a reference to other members of the unit or to the unit as a whole. While not used in *The American Soldier*, the best examples to draw on here are so-called sociometric measures. Whether a person chooses as a friend a man in his own unit or one in another unit; whether a man is chosen as a friend by many people in his unit or by few—these would be typical examples of what one might call relational personal data. They are predicated about individuals but refer to the unit in their definition. The corresponding unit data can be of three kinds, repeating, as it were, the previous three correspondences. The structure of a unit, for instance, could be characterized by the even distribution of sociometric choices over all members of the unit, or by the concentration on a few "leaders." The cohesion of the group might be characterized by the ratio of choices made within and outside the unit. We shall lump together as *Type IV* all those cases where the personal datum is of a relational nature, and the corresponding unit datum is any kind of aggregate of an individual relational datum. In a more systematic discussion this would not be justified, but in the present context Type IV is mentioned only for the sake of completeness. It will not be taken up again because no examples are provided in *The American Soldier*.

There is, finally, one kind of unit datum which is distinguished by the fact that no individual datum can correspond to it. Table E conveys the general impression that the divisions are arranged according to the amount of battle strain they have undergone. Suppose we were to construct a general unit index of strain to characterize a division. We would combine the different pieces of information into a scale, just as in common test practice various items of information pertaining to a single individual are combined into a scale. But if we form a strain index for a division, a new kind of material can be introduced. One item which we might use, for instance, is a measure of the extent to which the mess equipment of the division is worn out. Homogeneity of combat experience can only be predicated about a unit, but the datum is formed on the basis of information collected from each member of the group. The state of mess equipment, however, is something which, even as a datum, pertains only to the unit and never to the individual. In such cases we shall talk of *Type V*.

We thus have five main correspondences between personal and unit data.

NATURE OF THE PERSONAL DATUM	NATURE OF THE CORRESPONDING UNIT DATUM
I. An attribute pertaining to one person only.	I. A rate.
II. A variable pertaining to one person only.	II. An average.
III. As in Type II.	III. A parameter of the distribution of the variable, *e.g.*, standard deviation or measure of skewness.
IV. In characterizing an individual, a reference is needed either to other members of the unit or the unit as a whole.	IV. Any of the statistical aggregates used in the previous types.
V. No information introduced about a single individual.	V. The unit item characterizes the group only, but belongs in a meaningful context with data of the previous type.[49]

A clear distinction of these different types of relationships between personal and unit data is important to many sociological discussions,

[49] It should be helpful for the reader to think of a variety of other areas where these five types would obviously apply. A good example can be taken from ecology. The home of an individual man can be in good or bad repair; the census tract can be characterized by the proportion of houses in good repair. (Type I) The census tract can also be characterized by the average rent paid. (Type II) The census tract can be either homogeneous or heterogeneous in regard to rent. (Type III) The tracts can also be classified according to the proportion of shopping which people do within the tract. (Type IV) Finally, the tract can be characterized by the playground areas to be found there. (Type V) All five items together might be combined into a broader index of "area wealth" of the kind Thorndike has developed for the "goodness of life of cities."

and indispensable for a clear understanding of much of the work reported in *The American Soldier*. This understanding can be increased by considering how unit data are used in the two volumes.

The interchangeability of personal and unit data

The most common use of unit data is as a substitute for personal data which, for one reason or another, are not available. In this case the analysts will always deal either with Type I or II. The classic example of this kind in social research is the use of voting data prior to the development of polls. Because an individual's vote is secret, the only way to find out whether Al Smith received more support from poor than from rich people in Chicago was to relate the proportion of Democratic voters to average rent paid in all of the voting precincts. The kind of statistical analysis carried out in such a case leads to the same problems which were discussed in the first part of this paper: spurious factors, for example, are especially likely to enter into correlations between unit data. The only difference is that the statistical element in an "ecological" analysis is the precinct and not the voter.

The Research Branch had so much information about individual soldiers that they were not forced at any point to rely on correlations between unit data without any reference to the constituent individuals. Suppose this were not the case, however. Suppose that in setting up the table quoted above, the analysts discovered that they lacked information as to how long each man had been in combat. It is still conceivable that there would be general agreement as to how the four divisions, as units, ranged themselves according to combat exposure. Then the third row would most likely be used as evidence that increased exposure to combat makes for an increase in neurotic symptoms. Consciously or unconsciously, everyone would accept the correlation between the two sets of unit data as a substitute for a correlation between two corresponding sets of personal data.

Very frequently, the Research Branch turned to a closely related application: they used both types of data to reinforce specific findings. The most elaborate parallel example can be found in II, Chap. I. This is a chapter dealing with the predictability of combat performance from paper and pencil tests. Section 1 is based on unit data. The average morale score obtained from units in training is related to the rate of battle fatigue cases during the Normandy invasion. It turns out that the average test score permits us to predict fairly well the non-battle casualty rate. In the second section of this chapter, the same relationship is established for two sets of personal data. Here the attitude score of the individual soldier is related to the combat rating he later obtained from his fellow soldiers and his superior officers. In I, Chap. VII, another instructive double check can be studied. Chart II shows that soldiers who chose their own assignments liked their jobs much better than those who did not. Chart I shows that in branches where a large proportion chose their jobs there was also a large proportion of soldiers who liked to be in that branch. On an individual level (Chart II), we only have four-fold tables. On a group level (Chart I), we have a correlation diagram between two variables which permits a more refined analysis.[50]

An important question is *whether a correlation between unit data and one between the corresponding personal data must always give the same result.* Stouffer and his associates are very much aware of the problem and at various points stress that this does not need to be the case. We shall make an effort here to collate the pertinent examples in *The American Soldier,* and to derive from them some general methodological considerations. The following three examples provide the best basis for induction.

(1) In I, 290, Chart II, it is shown that soldiers who chose their own assignments liked their jobs better than those who did not. Chart I shows that units where a large proportion chose their jobs also have a large proportion of soldiers who liked to be in that branch. Here an association of two attributes (personal data) corroborates the result derived from the correlation between two proportions (unit data).[51]

[50] In II, 426, Chart I, a psychoneurotic test is validated against the incidence of actual commitments to psychoneurotic wards. This is done in the following way. A cross-sectional sample of soldiers was divided into 12 groups according to age and education. The same was done for a group of hospital inmates. This then defines 12 abstract age-education groups, each of which serves as a unit in the correlation analysis. The two variables which are related are (a) the relative incidence of psychoneurosis and (b) the proportion in the cross-section receiving critical scores on the psychoneurotic test. A high correlation exists. Here the interesting idea is that the two sets of data characterizing each "unit" are taken from different samples.

[51] A similar example can be found in connection with the study of four divisions considered above. On a unit basis, the table from which we quoted gives a positive correlation between a psychoneurotic rate and average duration in combat. A table on p. 451 of the same chapter (II, Chap. IX) shows a corresponding association between time in combat and psychoneurotic score based on personal data.

(2) Chart IX in I, 252, shows on a personal level that soldiers who were promoted were, as one would expect, considerably more optimistic about general promotion chances in the Army than those who were not promoted. But, in addition, a unit comparison between Military Police and the Air Corps is also presented. We learn that the promotion chances in the Military Police were much poorer than in the Air Corps. And yet the satisfaction with promotion in the Military Police was considerably higher among all subgroups. That is to say, using personal data, promotion is positively related to satisfaction; using unit data, satisfaction is negatively related to promotion chances.[52]

(3) For our third example, we draw on a study already considered in another connection. In I, 357, Table 17, 12 Air Force fighter groups, each of them treated as a statistical unit, are compared. We know what proportion in each group complain about their food, and we also know the proportion satisfied with their Army work. There is no interrelationship between these two sets of unit data; the variation in food supply seems to have little effect on general satisfaction and dissatisfaction. No corresponding personal data are given, but from many similar results in *The American Soldier* and from other studies we can take it for granted that on an individual level there would be an association. Soldiers who complain about food are also more likely to complain about other matters, like the job they have.

Let us first fasten on the difference between the third and the first examples. Variations in the rate of food complaints from one unit to another are likely to reflect actual differences in the objective situation; variations in complaints from one soldier to another are more likely to reflect personality characteristics of the individual soldiers. We are not surprised to find that job satisfaction has one kind of relationship with a personality trait and a different relationship with an external situation. The personal data and the unit data in the third example stand for different factors, despite their formal correspondence. In the first example, the personal information that the soldier has chosen his job and the unit rates of soldiers who report this are likely to reflect objective differences equally well. We are not surprised therefore that, in this case, the two sets of data have the same relation to job satisfaction.

The most interesting example is the second one. Here the personal datum of having been promoted as well as the promotion schedule of the various units are both objective facts. But the one reflects in-

[52] A second comparison is made in Chart X between ground forces, service forces and Air Corps, leading to substantially the same results.

dividual experiences and the other what one might call *experiences of the whole unit*. The authors analyze in considerable detail (I, pp. 250-258) how the experience of the unit might affect the expectations and evaluations of the individual: the promoted man in an advantageous unit enjoys his own promotion less and the non-promoted man resents his setback more. This would explain the positive association between promotion and approval of the promotion system based on personal data, and the negative correlation between promotion chances and approval based on unit rates.[53]

Before a complete codification of this whole problem could be attempted, a much larger array of examples is needed. But the few instances permit us at least to preview the kind of generalizations which might develop. At this point we can state one general expectation: *If individual data are more likely to reflect an attitude and unit data an objective reality, then they will not necessarily have the same relationship to a third set of data.* If the personal data and the unit data are likely to reflect the same objective reality and the same experience, it will be safe to use them interchangeably. This, however, will not be the case if the unit data not only reflect each person's experience but also the experience of other people in the unit, which might have quite different meaning for the people directly and those more indirectly involved.

A *further problem*

The last qualification, so well illustrated by our second example, is really a transition to a quite different relationship between personal data and unit data. So far we have questioned whether the two types of data can be used interchangeably and whether the results necessarily must corroborate each other. In all of our examples we compared corresponding statistics where, on the one side, the elements were individuals characterized by individual data and, on the other side, units characterized by unit data. There is, however, one further connection which, from a sociological point of view, is probably the most interesting one.

There is no reason why unit data cannot be used to characterize individuals in the unit. A man who does not have malaria in a unit

---

[53] At several points of the text (*e.g.*, II, 40 and 249), the whole topic is mentioned in the following way. Variations *between* units may have to be interpreted differently than variations *within* units. It can easily be seen that this and our formulation of the problem are equivalent.

where the incidence of malaria is very low probably feels differently about his state of health than does the man who has no malaria but serves in a unit with high incidence and therefore is surrounded by malaria cases. A man who could not choose his job in a unit where the rate of free choice is very high would feel differently than the one working with people who also were denied a choice. In the same way, a man not promoted in a unit with a tight promotion scheme would feel differently than a soldier with the same experience serving in a unit where every other man was promoted.

In terms of actual analysis the matter can be restated in the following terms: just as we can classify people by demographic variables or by their attitudes, we can also classify them by the kind of environment in which they live. The appropriate variables for such a classification are likely to be unit data. A survey analysis would then cover both personal and unit data simultaneously.[54]

This opens the way to a promising combination of the problems discussed in the first and in this second part of our paper. When the formal structure of statistical elaboration was outlined, we saw that variables had to be ordered if we wanted to get a clear understanding of the different types of analysis. The principle of ordering on which we focused then was time sequence. Now we have discussed a different kind of ordering of variables: the level of complexity of the indices used. It is quite obvious that the same formal elaboration combined with a different ordering of variables would lead to important new results. As a matter of fact, level of complexity is only one of a number of ordering principles which could be introduced. Another would be an ordering by degree of generality, exemplified, for instance, by the relationship between a single test item and the whole test. We can be sure that a full survey of the many insights to be gained by combining the formalism of "elaboration" with a formalism classifying indices according to different sequences would cover a great part of what is known today on the logic of survey analysis. But this is a story which must be told some day from data other than those assembled by the Research Branch.

[54] Again, comparisons with other fields should be helpful. Workers in England are more likely to vote for the Labour Party than white-collar people. But a worker in a white-collar district is less likely to vote Labour than a worker in a workingman's district. In the same way, the crime rate of Negroes in Negro sections of a city seems to be lower than the crime rate of Negroes in mixed areas.

SAMUEL A. STOUFFER

SOME AFTERTHOUGHTS
OF A CONTRIBUTOR
TO "THE AMERICAN SOLDIER"

*A*S one of the authors of *The American Soldier,* I have been invited to make some comments.

We said in Chapter I of *The American Soldier* (I, p. 6): "Science, unlike art or literature, is cumulative, in the sense that a scientific achievement is most successful when it stimulates others to make the concepts and techniques it has used look crude and become obsolete as rapidly as possible. In this spirit the present volumes have been prepared."

While I have seen only a few of the pages which my colleagues have written in the current interpretative handbook, I know that they share the sentiments expressed above. It is a humbling experience for a research worker to encounter, after his work is finished, mounting evidence of his lack of insight and of missed opportunities to exploit his data. But if nobody sought to dig out such evidence, he should be even more disconcerted.

Over a year has passed since the manuscript of Volumes I and II were delivered to the printer. All of us who worked on those volumes have become involved in new research undertakings. For the benefit of a new generation of social scientists, to whom it is suggested my remarks be addressed, can some further reflections be presented? In particular, as the war-time research experience recedes in time, can one speak more clearly and understandingly about what that experience has taught to one of those who shared in it? Perhaps.

My remarks will be in two parts. First, I wish to discuss somewhat generally the relation of theory, empirical operations, and action. Second, I wish to consider some of the specific kinds of further study which are needed if we are to improve our techniques.

THEORY, EMPIRICAL OPERATIONS, AND ACTION

AS we tried to spell out in Chapter 1 of *The American Soldier* (Vol. I), the need to solve quickly a practical problem—or at least to clarify some of the variables involved in it—is often fatal to the kind of reflection which leads to the formulation and testing of a scientific proposition. This time urgency was the source of the greatest frustration to many on our staff who came from academic groves to what seemed to some a Washington madhouse. Pressures for "the practical" were insistent and sometimes almost intolerable.

Yet, I am convinced that such pressures are not necessarily and wholly bad:

1. If social science is to be taken seriously and receive large financial support, its "engineering" applications must visibly pay off. It is an interesting speculation as to how much of the vast financial support of the "pure" research in so-called natural science would be forthcoming except for the spectacular applications in industry, in health, in war. If, for example, social science can help explicitly and visibly to show how a counselling system can be most effective in public schools, the public recognition of the importance of social science would be enhanced.

2. "Applied" research demands many of the same tools of investigation as "pure" research and stimulates the improvement of known tools and the discovery of better ones. Just as the laboratories in physics or chemistry or biology benefit from the use of instruments and techniques developed in engineering or medicine, so social science research benefits from techniques developed by practitioners in applied fields. The first big uses of mental testing were in applied fields, such as the Army in World War I, and it is inconceivable that subsequent studies as in factor analysis could have been carried on without large prior bases of practical past experience in test construction and administration. Public opinion research owes more to the practitioners who were out to make money than it owes to

the academicians. The problems the practitioners encountered in questionnaire design, in sampling, and in interviewing have stimulated much of the methodological interest in improvement of the techniques. If dozens of industrial firms are making panel studies, some of them at least under the direction of imaginative and inventive researchers, it is inconceivable that our knowledge of how to avoid specific technical pitfalls will not be increased. Although it may be still fashionable in some academic circles to speak condescendingly of "mere gadgeteers," it has become increasingly clear to me that research in social science, lacking these gadgets, would be no less sterile than research in medicine lacking microscopes and clinical thermometers.

3. "Applied" research can speed up thinking about the kind of basic theory that is needed. It would be silly to suggest that because one does research on cancer one is thereby necessarily prevented from thinking about the general problem of cell growth. Often the pressure to "explain" or interpret a surprising empirical practical finding may lead to reflection which organizes a good many such findings. In the Research Branch I well remember our puzzlement, which went on for months, over the finding that Northern Negroes in Southern camps, in spite of the fact that they said they wanted to be stationed in the North and that they resented discrimination in Southern buses and by Southern police, showed as favorable or more favorable responses to items reflecting personal adjustment in the Army than did those in Northern camps. Some of our analysts were almost in despair at this discrepancy. They actually held up the report on their study for over a month while they checked and rechecked in the vain hope of finding errors in the data or analysis to explain the paradox. When, eventually, it was suggested that the Northern Negro soldier in the South had very great advantages over Negro civilians in the South and that the advantage over Negro civilians in the North were much less, a clue to the paradox appeared. After a number of such experiences, it became evident that some concept like "relative deprivation" might be useful. Armed with that concept, we would know how to anticipate such discrepancies better and to build into a study a means of checking up directly. I shall speak more on this point later. The history of scientific work is full of examples of how a practical emergency has led to the discovery of scientific principles. Those of us who use statistics with

small samples, for example, owe a debt to the Guinness brewery in London, where "Student" was faced with a practical problem of studying what happened in a very few vats of beer. His work paved the way for that of R. A. Fisher, who, faced with the practical problems of design of agricultural experiments, developed theories of very great generality for handling statistical problems. I remember asking Fisher once how he happened on one of his very general theorems. "The rabbits came in and ate up two degrees of freedom," he said, "and I had to do something about it."

The three points made above have suggested ways in which applied social research can contribute to social science. It is taken for granted that such research, well done, makes contributions to practical policy. It is likely that, in spite of setbacks such as were experienced by the public opinion pollsters in 1948, current reporting in areas of social psychology, political science, economics, and sociology will increase rather than decrease in public importance. And it should also be noted that such reporting can leave a legacy for history. The reception by historians of *The American Soldier* has not yet provided convincing evidence that historians have been trained to use quantitative data as effectively as they have been trained to use personal and official documents. Doubtless, that time will come. But in my present remarks I should like to focus especially on the branches of social science represented in sociology and social psychology, which are concerned with developing theories from which subsidiary propositions can be derived and predictions made with some confidence in new situations.

Having recognized three ways in which the importunities of applied research can help social science, I want to emphasize even more strongly the perils. *The American Soldier* is witness to these perils and I am sure that my colleagues in the present volume will have pointed out chapter and verse by way of documentation. For the very fact that *The American Soldier* has received a certain amount of acclaim may mislead not only students but also their elders, who may be in important positions in universities or foundations, into thinking that the kind of atmosphere in which our work was done is exceptionally favorable for social science.

Most of our time was wasted, irretrievably wasted, in so far as any contribution to social science was concerned. Sometimes a study like whether men preferred Coca-Cola to Pepsi-Cola or whether they preferred nuts in their candy bars may have had a neat technical twist, but ordinarily it did not, or if it had we just did not have time to investigate. As director of the professional staff, I was always facing a dilemma. In order to help the Army, or to help "sell" research to the Army, I had to be concerned first and foremost with what was immediately wanted or purchasable. When I supported longer range studies, I ran the risk of being suspect of trying to exploit our situation for social science and on several occasions was severely censured by superiors. When we coopted our best analysts to direct quick studies which practically and politically seemed of much tactical importance, I faced justifiable resentment from these analysts when they found the studies frustrating. Sometimes nerves were taut on both sides. If we had been successful in finding more officers who could serve as effective middlemen between research and the consumers in the top brass, we could have planned farther in advance and thus had a better chance both to use social science and feed back to social science, at the same time serving the Army even better. I cannot overestimate the importance in applied social research of such middlemen. Some day we may have them, in government and business, as members of a specialized profession.

But the greatest danger of applied social science lies in our reward system. In many respects the most valuable people on our staff were those who could write quick, simple, lucid reports, who could make simple figures "talk" so that a general could understand them. This may be true in industry, too. The rewards are much more likely to go to the man who has the knack of seeing clearly if superficially the practical problem of the consumer and writing a report which appears to smack the problem on the nose, than to the reflective analyst. Sometimes, the skills are combined in one man and there lies the greatest threat. For the salesman in him will be rewarded far above the analyst in him. Yet the very gifts of clarity and lucidity, when combined with technical competence, integrity, and intellectual depth, are precious jewels for social science.

That is why I have said, on several occasions, that the very success of social science in application is also a grave danger. I believe that the universities—and especially the foundations—have a social obligation to counteract the tendency to drain off into applied research so many of our best trained minds.

A reason why this tendency is difficult to counteract is that so much academic research is sterile. This sterility deserves a much more searching inquiry than I can give it here. Basically, I suspect it stems from misconceptions about the relation between theory and empirical research. As long as theory is the monopoly of verbalists who have no interest in formulating propositions precisely enough to permit empirical verification except by the illusory device of "illustration," and as long as research is the monopoly of people with technical equipment but with an interest only in naked fact, the situation is not likely to improve. The bridges are most likely to be built by men who have simultaneously within their own skulls *both* the intellectual curiosity and urge for generality of the theorist and the technical equipment of the empiricist. Such men are not likely to worry about whether theory comes first or observations crying for generalization come first. They will be equipped to shuttle back and forth, because they know how to ask "If this were true, how could I show it?" and because they have the technical tools (*i.e.*, the gadgets which an older generation shrugs off) to answer that question.

Some critics of *The American Soldier* find it lamentably lacking from the theoretical standpoint. Others who feel that there may be certain contributions to social psychology are uncomfortable about what they feel is a lack of contribution to sociology. The authors, who, it happens, are deeply concerned about theory, frankly recognize its inadequacy. "Assuredly," we wrote in Volume I, Chapter 1, "neither the Armed Forces, nor the historians, nor the social psychologists, who may chance to read these books will find in them the quality of incisive formulation of theory, isolation of variables, and rigorous verification which should some day become not only the ideal but the standard practice of social science." The kind of thinking which already has been stimulated by these volumes is most encouraging, however. If the way in which we organized some of our concepts and analyzed and presented our data provides, as it has, the basis for brilliant further thinking of the kind which, I am told, may be represented in some of the chapters of the present book, our work has not been in vain. But some of the older school of theorists may not recognize the kind of organizing which Robert K. Merton, for example, is doing as theory at all. For it is not theory on the grand style. Nor are the sometimes fumbling efforts which many of us made in *The American Soldier* recognizable as theory by some who are not accustomed to ideas and data in juxtaposition.

Our hope is that acquaintance with *The American Soldier* and other publications of recent years will speed up the joining of theory with empirical study and give new vitality to academic research. Thus reinvigorated, such research should be able to attract and hold first-rate minds who otherwise might be tempted by the more immediate rewards in fields of practical application.

One final word in this context. While I believe that an academic environment is the ideal for reflective, theoretically oriented research, I also believe that there are values to be gained, theorywise, in keeping one eye open for the possibilities of practical applications of this same research. We may (I think, usually *should*) work on data which are as trivial as Mendel's wrinkled peas when compared with the wheat crop of the world, but it ordinarily should not hurt us to be aware of possible uses of our findings, *some day*. Thus, if we have to choose between emphases which eventually could have important social implications and those which could not, it obviously would be better to choose the former. Such a comment is hardly needed, since the pressures—notably financial—are mostly on the one side. Just as there is gain in shuttling back and forth between theory and data, so there may be gain in shuttling between the basic and the applied. For example, if one does some sociological research to study some theoretical phase of the subject of vertical mobility, the study may suggest something that schools might do to manipulate the situation. Eventually, if educators in a given school system could be induced to conduct a controlled experiment, a test of some of the findings of the sociological study might ensue and feed back into new ideas for further theoretical study of vertical mobility. One must be on guard, however, lest the applied research becomes the tail that wags the dog.

To summarize, I have sought to point out that applied research contributes to social science (1) by providing the kind of convincing evidence of the usefulness to society which is necessary to continuing support; (2) by utilizing and developing techniques which can also be made to serve so-called basic research; and (3) by providing data and ideas which may speed up the process of generalization. But, as in the case of the work represented in *The American Soldier*, it can be an inherently wasteful and inefficient method of building social science. There is a danger that our best minds will be drawn away from theory making and theory testing by the greater rewards available in applied research. One reason why the rewards are greater is because of the sterility of so much academic research. It is suggested that this sterility is traceable, in part, to the traditional separation of theory and empirical research. A hope of the authors of *The American Soldier* is that a study of these volumes will stimulate a greater shuttling back and forth between ideas and data—a process which requires the theorist to be a master of techniques of research which heretofore have not been thought to be his concern. Similarly, some shuttling back and forth between basic and applied research on a given problem may pay dividends if properly safeguarded.

NEEDED—SOME IMPROVED RESEARCH TOOLS

THE foregoing discussion has indicated my belief that the development of social theory calls for reciprocation between ideas and data and that the theorist needs to be equipped with empirical research techniques.

Just as we hope that the study of *The American Soldier* will stimulate a new and fresh approach by a younger generation to the problem of formulating and testing theoretical propositions, so also we hope that such study will spur the interest in and development of new research tools. While Volumes I and II exhibit a wide variety of uses of the tools at our disposal, I am sure that the previous discussion in the present book will have pointed out their shortcomings as well as their adequacies. We hope, in particular, that serious students will not limit their attention to Volumes I and II, but will go on to Volumes III and IV which seek to fund the principal technical contributions of the Research Branch.

The extensive post-war interest in the use of controlled experiments in social psychology and sociology—as evidenced by large-scale programs at Michigan, Yale, Harvard, and many other universities—is testimony to the scientific coming-of-age of social science. The Research Branch, from its inception, held up the controlled experiment as our ideal. Though seldom realizable in practice, the ideal was physically symbolized in the Experimental Section headed by Carl Hovland, and we constantly tried to measure the inadequacies of mere panel studies, or, worse, mere correlational studies, against the ideal of the controlled experiment. Some fully controlled experiments do appear in *The American Soldier* (see, for example, Volume I, 309-11, 461-468, 473-481; Volume II, 213-20). The major analysis of the experimental program was reserved, however, for Volume III, *Experiments on Mass Communication*. Here a wide variety of technical problems in the design of experiments are analyzed in detail—some of them for the first time in the literature of social psychology. Special attention is directed to the appendices. The titles of the appendix papers suggest something of the generality and importance of the problems considered:

"The Baseline for Measurement of Percentage Change."
" 'Marginal' vs. 'Internal' Effects."
"Comparison of the Before-After and the After-Only Design of Experiments."
" 'Regression' in the Analysis of Effects of Films."

Just as Volume III analyzes the main contributions of the Research Branch to technical problems of experimental design, Volume IV, *Measurement and Prediction*, analyzes the main contributions with respect to scaling and prediction. A few chapters of Volume IV are quite technical and can be read critically only by the student with considerable mathematical competence. But most of the contributions can be understood by any student with ordinary training in statistics. We expect Volume IV to be quite controversial. Here the Guttman and Lazarsfeld scaling techniques are described in detail. Not only does some of this work constitute a challenge to many conventional procedures, but also there are adventures into the future which go well beyond present empirical work in their claims to generality. Guttman's theory of principal components and Lazarsfeld's generalized latent structure theory are models which are quite likely to elicit discussion and further testing for some years to come.

I wish to limit my present remarks to a very few selected types of technical problems to which I think special attention is imperative in the next few years.

1. *Projective Tests.* We need to develop better projective tests and to learn more about the conditions as to when the manifest content of a verbal response can or cannot be trusted.

It was fortunate that most of the questioning reported in *The American Soldier* was done under conditions guaranteeing anonymity. It may be that anonymity was not as important a consideration as we generally thought—at least, we should have made many more studies about this than we did. (See, for example, Volume II, 435-6.) But there are ample grounds for warning against the danger of carrying over blindly into civilian research the direct questioning techniques used in *The American Soldier*. For example, the Neuropsychiatric Screening Adjunct described in Volume II, Chapter 9, and in more detail in Volume IV, Chapters 12 and 13, may have worked as well as it did because a man who was motivated to escape duty stood at least a chance of being rewarded if he displayed psychosomatic symptoms. But if the same items were used to screen applicants for employment in a department store it is likely that the applicant would expect to lose out if he admitted to psychosomatic symptoms.

It happens that most of the creative, imaginative people who have pioneered in the development of projective tests have been clinical psychologists without rigorous statistical training. In consequence, the claims made for the effectiveness of the Rorschach, Thematic Apperception Test, various kinds of sentence completion tests, and others often fall apart when exposed to the white light of a statistical appraisal. On the other hand, psychometricians have tended to be rather wooden and uncreative. Concerted research attacks from several points of view are needed: (a) To clarify (shuttling back and forth between ideas and data) the whole theory of projection. (b) To study and compare existing types of instruments under a variety of control conditions with criterion groups. (c) To build new and better devices; in particular, to explore the application of scale theory, as developed in Volume IV, to projective tests. Logically, for example, the Lazarsfeld latent structure theory seems to be peculiarly well adapted to projective inquiry; whereas, the Guttman procedure by definition is designed for situations in which the manifest response to each question is to be treated as a definition of the variable being studied.

2. *Measurement of Social Norms.* What do we mean by a social value, a role obligation, a social norm? This has been the subject of almost interminable discussion, almost exclusively by theorists whose definitions are so vague, complicated, or self-contradictory that they are not too usable in empirical research. One way of looking at the problem is to define a social norm as a mode, or mean, or median of the responses of a representative sample of individuals to such a question as "What is the right thing to do in this (specified) situation?".

The American Soldier makes some crude beginnings in Volume I, Chapter 9, in the discussion of social control and informal and formal codes. (pp. 410-429) Other efforts are represented by such work as that of Floyd H. Allport in his J-curve hypothesis. Since the War, some of us have begun quite intensive new work on this problem. A study by the present writer[1] describes several different logical types of variability which can be measured empirically and may be important to consider in building theories of normative behavior. There are many intriguing and, from the point of view of the older type of theorist, very earthy technical problems which need study. For example, under what conditions would these three different types of question phrasing yield apparently contradictory results?

"What do you think is the right thing for you to do in this (specified) situation?"
"What do you think others would say or do if you did such and such in this situation?"
"What would you do in this situation?"

Finally, there is the problem of the relation of verbal responses like these to non-verbal behavior, either as role playing on a Moreno psychodramatic stage, as participation in a small group experiment, or as what is observed in a "natural" situation.

It has seemed to some of us, especially as an outgrowth of the studies of the role of non-commissioned officers in the Army, that role conflicts provide a peculiarly strategic setting not only for studying social norms but also for studying the ways in which different individuals tend consistently to choose one or another polar types of solutions of role conflicts. This seems to have important theoretical implications in linking role theory in sociology to personality theory in social psychology. Also, if the insights of an author like Chester I. Barnard, in *The Functions of the Executive,* are right, it may open new avenues for the study of leadership. A stupendous amount of careful detail work lies ahead. After a few years we may begin to have some important light on such problems.

Incidentally, I have been somewhat surprised to see certain of my sociological colleagues dismiss most of our attitude studies in *The American Soldier* as "merely psychology." Could it be that an anthropologist trying to write a grammar of a non-literate people is

[1] "An Analysis of Conflicting Social Norms," *American Sociological Review,* December, 1949.

studying "merely psychology" when his only data are derived from
what individual respondents tell him? I suspect that, although many
of our techniques will look pretty sorry a few years hence even if
they don't now, we were studying not only the American soldier
but also the American Army.

3. *Better Criteria for Holding Factors Constant—for Knowing
When to Control and When Not to Control.* Here is a problem about
which there is practically no guidance in the literature, especially
when some or all of the variables are qualitative. We have been
criticized for not controlling enough variables in *The American Soldier* and again for controlling too many. For example, one reviewer
felt that we had done serious injustice to our data in controlling
education and age in a panel study where we wished to see if attitudes of privates were related to subsequent promotions. His point
is that if the better educated tend more than others to say they are
in good spirits and the better educated also get the most promotions
we cut the heart out of the psychological variable when we hold
education constant in studying the relation between good spirits and
subsequent promotion. This is unfair to the psychological variable
and represents a sociologist's bias, he says. But he cannot eat his
cake and have it too. For younger men were more likely than others
to say they were in good spirits and *less* likely than others to get
promotions. Therefore, control of age magnifies, not diminishes, the
apparent relation of the psychological variable to promotion. Are
we now too generous with the psychology? What we tried to do,
where possible, was to show the whole structure; that is, show how
the attitude was related to age and to education, and how each of
the three variables, holding constant the others, as well as all of them
taken simultaneously, were related to promotion. (See, for example,
Volume I, Chapter 3, 147-154.)

Thinking about such problems has been clearer when quantitative variables are involved throughout than when some or all of the
variables are in the form of attributes.

Part of the difficulty lies in the fact that people are accustomed
to expect only one answer describing a particular relationship,
whereas an adequate report may require two (or more) answers.
For example, the general attitudes toward the Army, of soldiers
taken as a whole, tended to deteriorate the longer they were in the
Army. (See Volume I, Chapter 5, Section III.) But when we hold

rank constant the deterioration appears sharper than when rank is not held constant. This is because (1) the non-coms had better attitudes than privates and (2) the ratio of non-coms to privates increased throughout the war. The point I wish to make is that the reader needs *both* pieces of information—not just the uncontrolled finding or just the controlled finding. Because of space considerations, *The American Soldier* often failed to give both types of data on a particular problem, even when data were available. I think we erred more often in not controlling enough variables (often because data were lacking or the number of cases was too thin) than in controlling too many. But probably no other element contributes so much to making the volumes rather difficult reading for some laymen than the fact that, to a degree still quite unfashionable in social science, we did introduce so many controls—some of our charts involving relationships among as high as six or seven variables.

No text books in statistics or social research deal, except in passing, with problems like this. We not only do not have very systematic logical rules to guide us, but also we do not know how to train students in this area. If the number of cases is small, and we have several variables, when is it safe to discard some? Related to this is the stubborn problem, with qualitative data, of the need to condense several categories of a variable into a dichotomy or trichotomy. How do we decide what to condense? If variable X with 5 categories is much more closely related to Y than other variables, we may no longer be "holding Y constant" if we dichotomize X in the interest of economy. So it goes. Granted that each problem is a case in itself and that the operations in it involve implicit and explicit theory about the way the variables should hang together, one would think that the intuitive procedures now used could be improved if we had better formal rules and better pedagogical methods of teaching students how to play within these rules.

4. *The Index Problem.* The student of *The American Soldier* will have noted the extraordinary difficulties which were encountered in trying to get bases for classifying situations. When troops were stationed in tropical or arctic regions, for example, the location itself served as an index of a variable we were interested in, such as bad climatic environment. We seized upon such opportunities. But when we lacked such ready-made sorting devices, we were often in

trouble. Consider this question: Is poor food associated with low job satisfaction? (Volume I, Chapter 6, 353-61.) We already know enough from Guttman's and Lazarsfeld's work on scaling to distrust a straight correlation of attitudes toward food with attitudes toward job. Both attitudes may mainly contain a common factor of dissatisfaction with the Army. Therefore, it is unsafe to take attitudes toward food as an index of quality food preparation—except, possibly, under conditions where there is much agreement within a group on the subject. If A company has only 15 per cent complaining about food and B company has 90 percent complaining about food, there is a reasonable possibility that food in A company really is better than in B company. This would be strengthened if the non-coms, who are less likely to be chronic gripers, agree with the privates. Under such conditions we have some right to use the attitude data to sort out companies on a food index. But if the range of approval of the men were narrow, say from 40 per cent in the lowest company to 60 per cent in the highest company, this procedure would be quite unsafe.

Some of the most elaborate twisting and squirming in *The American Soldier* occurred in efforts to avoid the halo fallacy in correlating two attitudinal variables. Sometimes our foot slipped and I am afraid there are some bad examples in our volumes, although we usually caution the reader.

Like the problem of when to control variables, the problem of when it is or is not justifiable to use an attitude variable as an index of a situation (or conversely, when it is or is not justifiable to use a "demographic" variable, like education, as an index of an attitudinal variable) needs much more systematic logical study than it has received. If it contributes nothing else, *The American Soldier* offers an abundance of examples, good and bad, for the logician who is hopeful of clarifying this problem. Also, there has been hardly a start in devising systematic ways of teaching students how to cope with such situations.

Among other things, it can be predicted that further developments in scaling will prove especially important in this area.

5. *Experiments and Good Approximations Thereto.* Finally, I think that *The American Soldier* will have a dangerous influence on future research if the survey methods on which it relies for so much of the data are regarded as the ideal. This point we tried to underline in Volume I, Chapter 1, 47-49. It would be particularly in-

structive for a seminar to work through Volume I, Chapter 7 on "Attitudes Toward Leadership and Social Control in the Army" and ask how controlled experiments could be set up to test hypotheses rigorously. I would trade a half dozen Army-wide surveys on attitudes toward officers for one good controlled experiment.

Keeping the model of the controlled experiment as an ideal, it is sometimes possible for one to approximate it—as in our study of attitudes toward Negro soldiers in white companies. (Volume I, Chapter 10, 586-95) Ingenuity in locating ready-made situations is much needed. In any program of future research, I would put far more emphasis on this than ever has been done in the past.

As mentioned earlier, there is an exciting post-war development in experimentation at several universities. Students new to social science will be riding the wave of the future, I think, if they become masters of experimental design early in their careers.

Social science has not been cumulative, mainly because we have not used rigorous methods of testing our theoretical propositions. Our folkways are such that plausibility is rewarded by laymen— and even by many social scientists—almost as highly as proof. By keeping the model of the controlled experiment as our ideal, by devising ingenious approximations to it when it is not fully realizable, and, above all, by stating frankly when and where and how we have fallen short when we do fall short, we may slowly change the folkways of our discipline.

The five subjects I have discussed—projective testing, measurements of social norms, criteria for holding factors constant, the index problem, controlled experiments and approximations thereto—are just a few samples of subjects which are crying for further study. Many others could have been discussed in detail, Methods of Prediction, for instance. And, above all, Methods of Scaling. I hope that the appearance of Volume IV on *Measurement and Prediction* will usher in a new era of concentrated effort which will make that volume obsolete just as fast as possible.

The present book represents a challenge to the new generation of social psychologists and sociologists to be dissatisfied with the past, including that part of the past which is funded in *The American Soldier*, and to master the techniques necessary to make better techniques, better social theory, and more effective social action.

THE AMERICAN SOLDIER AND THE PUBLIC [1]

OF BOOKS AND BATTLES

*P*UBLICATION of a book lays a claim upon the flow of public attention. An important book presents a challenge to the stock responses of its public. If the challenge is *felt* widely, it may even provoke a crisis. A test of its importance, then, is the depth, breadth, and variety of response which a book evokes in the affective life of its public. Importance in this sense lasts just so long as conflicts of interpretation and evaluation are carried on publicly. The critical phase may coincide with the book's appearance, may persist over centuries, or may fluctuate between epochs and locales.

Thus, the books of Aristotle were important from their appearance in the Attica of 4th century B.C. until the closing of Aristotelian schools by Emperor Justinian, according to historical convention, in 525 A.D. Then followed seven centuries during which Aristotle's writings were of no discernible importance, until they were "rediscovered" in the 13th century A.D., when they became a focus of medieval attention and a paradigm for its diverse intellectual efforts: "the Arab Averroes, the Jew Maimonides and the Christian Aquinas strove equally to harmonize their own religious systems with the ideas of Aristotle." (1) With the decline of scholasticism, the importance of Aristotle's writings diminished. Today, they stimulate little public interest and hence, though they appear on every inventory of Hundred Great Books, their importance is limited.

[1] This is a preliminary sketch for a more detailed thematic content analysis of responses to *The Soldier* and other significant books. These studies are designed to reconstruct the public images of social science current among book reviewers and similar spokesmen. This is M-2 of the Hoover Institute series.

Other important books, which have had the good fortune to be more discussed than read, show different patterns of fluctuating impact upon the flow of public attention. The Bible has persisted, and perhaps augmented its status through the centuries, as an important book. Its mere existence today supports a profession more numerous even than those employed in the flourishing Shakespeare industry. A crisis of great magnitude was provoked during the 19th century by the appearance of Darwin's books. While this crisis was subsiding, another was growing up over books by Karl Marx, published about the same time, which announced that a specter was haunting Europe. By gathering wide and varied public attention to this announcement, Marx helped to spread the influence of his spook. In the 20th Century the books of Freud have evoked still other ghosts in public, and have even revived the importance of Sophocles' Oedipus plays, whose eclipse was longer if less total than the works of Aristotle. There can be little doubt that contemporary chills and fevers are largely structured according to categories supplied the public imagination through Freud. One of our brightest young publicists certified, only a few months ago, that "Anxiety is the official emotion of our time." (2)

We shall understand these fluctuations better if we consider the nature of the challenge presented by a book. This varies, naturally, with the character of the book and the composition of the audience whose attention it commands. In general, however, an important book challenges its reader to reconsider his recollections of the past, his identifications in the present, and his expectations for the future. Such a book constitutes the stimulus in a dramatic interpersonal situation. The receptive reader must refigure his position in its universe of discourse, while the rejective reader refigures the rationale by which he can defend more effectively his old position unchanged (or apparently unchanged). In either case, to remain a moment longer on this tautological level, the important book confronts its "significant reader" (*i.e.*, the reader by whom its importance is felt) with a public image against which his self-image must be matched. He is challenged to locate himself with respect to the recollections, identifications, and demands which it advocates. The important book thus operates as stimulus in the affective life of its public in addition to, and sometimes quite apart from, its operation as data in the enlightenment of its public.

The American Soldier appears to be an important book in this sense. Without intending to suggest that any new Aristotle has arrived, we simply note that already it has provoked a variety of affects (not merely effects) in a number of unexpected places. Whether it will provoke a crisis by multiplying the number and variety of public responses it stimulates remains to be seen. One of the admirable results of the present symposium, I presume, may be to help elicit responses both affective and effective, at least among the variety of audiences in America which justify their own activities by the name of social science. The present paper proposes to characterize some of the responses to *The Soldier* stimulus, among these and other audiences, which are already discernible in the flow of public communication.

How does one go about discerning types of response to such a stimulus? In other times and places, the matter was easier. The response to books was made evident by unambiguous and observable action in the public domain. Some books were prevented from reaching the attention of the public through "pre-publication scrutiny" by authorized guardians of the public psyche, a procedure nowadays favored in the Soviet Union. A different method of eliminating undesirable bibliographic stimuli was based on "post-publication scrutiny" by defenders of official doctrine. This has been applied for centuries by the various Indexes of the Roman Church. (3) The Nazis simplified this method by simply burning books already in print, public attention to which was not desired.

Such methods provided unambiguous evidence of response on official levels. Other indicators of unofficial response were available for those books which survived official screening. In England books were considered appropriate subjects and objects of public controversy, as indicated by Swift's famous *Battle Fought between the . . . Books* (1704). In France, such controversy frequently erupted into violence among the interpreters and evaluators of important books. We are told that it was not uncommon on the Left Bank for the respective ateliers of current Maîtres to supplement the flow of oratory with a flurry of fisticuffs.

In contemporary America the response to books, as to so many other cerebral stimuli in the affective life of the nation, has been internalized to a depressing degree. We do not, happily, ban or burn books—but neither do we battle over them. The main vehicle for the public expression of private responses to books is provided by the tepid columns of book reviewing media. Being mainly genial appendages of the best-seller lists, or specialized media of professional readers, these are not particularly devoted to the stimulation of a lively and affective public intellectual life. This conventionalized repression of loves and hates, jealousies and admirations, keeps psychoanalysts busy and complicates the relations between a book and its public.

THE PUBLIC IMAGE OF
THE AMERICAN SOLDIER

SINCE an important book presents a public image with respect to which the reader is challenged to refigure his own self-image, it is useful to consider some specifications of the public image presented by *The American Soldier*. Our study deals only with published commentaries, considered as data on responses to this stimulus. To deal only with the affective features of such materials is not to deny, or minimize, their cerebral content. Some intellectual "positions" found among reviewers are discussed, on strictly intellectual ground, in the other chapters of this volume. Here we confine ourselves to the affective responses of reviewers, on the view that how a man "feels" about a book may influence what he "thinks" about it.

Ideally, in handling such materials, one would desire a large number of responses to the common stimulus from a variety of sources. These could be treated statistically to differentiate in rank order those challenges in the stimulus which were widely felt, *i.e.* frequently responded to. A frequency tabulation of the normal concurrences of precategorized responses would yield a correlation matrix, from which could be reconstructed the specifications of the public image presented by the stimulus. Deviations from this normal correlation in particular reviews would provide some of the clues needed to locate special affects in the response of the particular reviewer—*e.g.*, that he was responding to *The Soldier* stimulus by repression instead of aggression or affection.[2]

Insufficient time has elapsed since publication of *The Soldier* to permit this ideal accumulation of numerous and varied published responses. Our reconstruction of the public image of *The Soldier* therefore is based on data from only a single source: the promotional literature which preceded and accompanied publication of the two volumes. (4) Such a source gives us a public image, not on the basis of stimuli responded to, but on the basis of stimuli especially designed to elicit public response. This will serve our initial purpose of identifying the themes which figure in the public challenge of the book. We may begin with six main thematic categories, differentiated below by the key symbol in each category. These symbols are enclosed in quotes because they are taken directly from the promotional literature:

The Public Stimuli (Thematic Categories)

1. "Unprecedented" ("unique")
    a. "First"
    b. "Largest"
2. "Modern Methods" ("experts," "scientists")
3. "Mine of data"
4. "Implications" ("universal")
5. "Social Engineering"
    a. "Policy decisions"
    b. "Practicality"
6. "Wide influence"

To illustrate the themes into which these symbols were worked, we reproduce below the main paragraphs of the publicity announcement which Princeton University Press released prior to publication of *The Soldier.* The occurrence of each main theme is noted by italicizing the key symbol, which is followed by a parenthetical reference to the number of the appropriate category in the above list:

"Princeton University Press has just announced that it will publish the record of *one* of the *largest* (1 b) social science investigations *ever made* (1).

"The United States Army during World War II did something no

[2] An application of this general procedure is made in a content analysis by Ithiel de Sola Pool entitled "The Symbols of Democracy." (Mimeographed copies obtainable, by request, from The RADIR Project, Hoover Institute and Library, Stanford University.)

army in history had ever done before (1 a). It called in *trained* psychologists, sociologists and other *experts* in opinion *research* (2) to make studies of the morale problems of soldiers *all over the world* (1 b). Using the *most modern scientific methods* (2), *hundreds of studies were made* (1 b, 3). In all, more than a *half million men* were interviewed during the war (1 b), in situations guaranteeing anonymity. At first the Army command was skeptical of the value of such research, but came to lean upon it in making some of its most important *policy decisions* (5 a).

"These volumes deal with American young men at war and are a *unique* (1) *contribution* to American history (3), but their aim is *much broader* (4). They represent one of the *most elaborate* (1 b) applications *ever made* (1 a) of the *new methods* of objective study (2) which are *revolutionizing* social science *research* (2, 6) and taking the study of man out of the realm of *guesswork* and *conjecture* (4). These are *not mere* studies of soldiers (4), but are studies of *men associating* with other men (4), and many of the *findings* (3) have *applications* (5 b) in business, in education, and in *civilian society generally* (4).

Some of the *new methods developed* in the course of these studies (2) are already having an *influence* on social science development (6), since many of the men who directed the studies hold high positions in *American universities* (2), *business* (5 b), and *government* (5 a)."

These themes, largely identical in wording, were repeated in printed brochures distributed to editors, reviewers, booksellers and others. Some interesting variations on these themes appear in the blurb printed on the dust jacket of the book, which re-specified its stimuli for the prospective or actual buyer about to expose himself:

"One of the *largest* (1 b) social science research projects *in History* (1 a) was undertaken by the Army during the war, and the results are reported in these volumes, drawing on a *mine of data* (3) perhaps *unparalleled* in the *whole period* (1) of work in sociology and social psychology. The specific *data* (3) are important to *specialists* (2), but the general *conclusions*—as to learning processes, social institutions, social adjustment—are of *profound significance* (4) to a *wide range* of people in many professions (6), from *educators* (2) to industrial personnel *managers* (5 b). For the *first time* (1 a) on such a *scale* (1 b) an attempt was made to *direct human behavior* (5) on a basis of *scientific evidence* (2), and the results suggest the opening of a *new epoch* (1) in social studies (2) and in social *management* (5)."

Illustrations could be multiplied, but we have perhaps sufficiently indicated the main themes on which the publishers based their claim to the attention of the reading public. Originality, size, cost, findings, methodology, universality, practicality, influence—all these were proclaimed as virtues of a book whose appearance, the impression was created, certified the birth of "the new social science."

This promotional literature was widely disseminated and used. The clipping-books of Princeton University Press contain published notices in 22 different sources, on the appearance of *The Soldier* volumes, which use *verbatim* only the passages just quoted. In addition to the usual scholarly journals (sociology and psychology) and "serious" periodicals (*Nation, Current History*), these include such widely scattered newspapers as the Cleveland (Ohio) *Press* and the Pasadena (Calif.) *Star-News*. Several sources carried these notices several times: e.g., three times each in the New York *Times* and *Herald-Tribune*, and ALA *Booklist;* twice each in *Publisher's Weekly* and *America*. The passages quoted above constituted, with perhaps an additional sentence or two, the *whole* "review" of the book in five other sources: *Christian Century, Journal* of the American Medical Association, *U.S. Quarterly Book List, Shipmate*, and the Minneapolis *Cresset*.

In addition, Princeton University Press ran at least 14 full page advertisements in the major professional journals (5) and in such "special" media as: *American Scholar, Princeton Alumni Weekly*, and *American Scientist*. Approximately half page ads appeared in the Sunday book supplements of the New York *Times* and *Herald-Tribune*, in the Washington *Post*, the *Saturday Review of Literature*, and *The Survey*. Smaller ads appeared in other places. All of these used mainly, or exclusively, sentences from the passages quoted above. Many of the large ads, in fact, dropped some qualifiers and began with the following in bold and italic print:

ANNOUNCING
THE FIRST TWO VOLUMES OF
A Monumental Work on the
Psychology of Americans

All this publicity apparently began to mold the public image of *The Soldier*. (We have said nothing yet, in this paper, of what Stouffer and his associates claimed for the book in the volumes themselves. We have simply described some of the publicity which preceded and accompanied publication of the volumes.) It announced claims to public attention, channeled public expectations, and provided public stimuli around which a pre-scrutiny public

image of the book was constructed. The importance of this image
is clear from the opening passages of one review, by a reviewer who
is often useful for his picturesque assertion of public opinions:

"Too many obvious frauds were at last committed in the name of
sociology . . . So the old and toothless beast was put out to pasture.
In its place has come its more carnivorous son, known in his more modest
mood under some such name as 'social relations,' or, more often, in a tone
of majestic simplicity, as 'social science' . . .
    "Well, the 'social science' machinery has been grinding away for some
years now. Occasionally skeptics approach the devout and say with
proper humility: You have basked in the smile of deans and in the favor
of foundations. You are discovering the secrets of the ages. We wish to
share in the new enlightenment you are bringing us. But what, oh wise
one, should we read? Can you name a single book that would give some
idea of the great revelations that lie in wait? The oracle at that point
used to become muffled. Then one began to hear of *The American Soldier.* This work, one was told, was the real stuff; this would settle the
doubts." (6)

This is the anguished cry of a young historian, unwilling to de-
scend from the mount on which historians through centuries have
disputed pride of place only with poets and philosophers, but
petulant because his epoch finds little use for Wise Men on pin-
nacles. We shall soon look a bit more closely at the attitudes of this
academic Miniver Cheevy. We wish here to note particularly that
in the passage quoted, which spreads over two pages of his review,
this reviewer deals only with the pre-publication publicity, and not
with the contents, of *The Soldier.* A good deal of this hostility may
therefore be traced not to *The Soldier,* but to the general anxiety
of traditional disciplines in the face of the recent prestige-increment
of the younger social sciences. The flame was fanned by the somewhat windy publicity which preceded *The Soldier.* Hence, even
several reviewers who commend the modesty of its authors nevertheless go on to use their reviews of *The Soldier* as an occasion for a
general pronouncement on modern social science. The book stimulates a *profession de foi.*

This illustrates the proposition which we have been discussing in
this section of our paper: that the public image of *The Soldier* has
become identified with the public image of "The New Social Science." It is the latter image, with *The Soldier* serving as its paradigm-
atic model, to which most of our reviewers are responding. The

remainder of our paper is devoted to a classification of the main
type-responses to *The Soldier,* thus conceived, and to a closer analysis of some of the more interesting specimens.

SELF-IMAGES AND RESPONSES: WHICH WAY DO THE BROWS POINT?

THE core challenge of *The Soldier,* as paradigm of the new social
science, is that of "modern method." The idealized characteristics
of this "modern method" may be synopsized as: the rigorous testing of explicit hypotheses on largely quantified data accumulated
by structured observation in empirical situations approximating
(with specified deviations) the model of controlled experiment.
This formidable nomenclatural sentence is not intended to illustrate
the burdens which our generous English syntax has learned to
tolerate, but to provide a convenient checklist of the symbolic stimuli
which draw affective response in our data. (7) The challenge of
"modern method" is contained in any social research which exhibits
(or claims to exhibit) these features.

The responses to this challenge contained in reviews of *The Soldier* are what we wish to classify and analyze. The treatment of such
writings, intended as intellectual criticism, as "merely" response-
data may seem presumptuous and partial. Two points may be
brought to the attention of the reader: first, no evaluation of the
gospel according to *The Soldier* is made or needed here. So long as
the reader finds our criteria sufficiently explicit to enable him to
replicate the observations and to substitute his preferred labels for
those here assigned to the same observed attitudes, the present observer's own affective response to *The Soldier* is of no consequence
(though it would merely be tiresome to pretend that I personally
am neutral rather than friendly). The only presumption involved
here, therefore, is that the remarks made by reviewers, which by
other criteria may be judged either silly or sensible, usually are also
enlightening as response-data revealing personal attitudes. The second point is this: the present sketch *is* partial, in that it deals only

with responses to the methodological pretensions of *The Soldier*. So long as it is understood that we assert only that this is *one* distinctive challenge of the book to the self-images of its public, and not that this exhausts all the possible relations between the book and its readers, we shall have no difficulty with the term "partial." In this sense *all* attitude research is, more or less but nevertheless, "partial."

A brief look at the alternate stimuli may be useful. Another important challenge presented by *The Soldier* is that symbolized in the checklist of themes as "social engineering." A thematic analysis of responses to this challenge would be rewarding. However, only a few of our reviewers respond emphatically to this particular stimulus. Robert S. Lynd, in a review captioned "The Science of Inhuman Relations," organized his critique around this central theme:

"These volumes depict science being used with great skill to sort out and to control men for purposes not of their own willing. It is a significant measure of the impotence of liberal democracy that it must increasingly use its social sciences not directly on democracy's own problems, but tangentially and indirectly; it must pick up the crumbs from private business research on such problems as how to gauge audience reaction so as to put together profitable synthetic radio programs and movies, or, as in the present case, from Army research on how to turn frightened draftees into tough soldiers who will fight a war whose purposes they do not understand. With such socially extraneous purposes controlling the use of social science, each advance in its use tends to make it an instrument of mass control, and thereby a further threat of democracy." (8)

The response to modern method, *qua* method, is not central in this review. While the general method is regarded as a promise, and its applications in *The Soldier* highly praised, the focus of the reviewer's attention is on the potential threat presented by development of the method through use on "Caesar's problems."

The same stimulus elicits the central response of the review by Alfred M. Lee. This sets forth with equal explicitness that the principal challenge of modern method, since its general technical efficacy is clear, is its use for "social engineering" of the kind illustrated by *The Soldier:*

"If managerial problems for industry and the military are to continue to dominate the research of leading social psychologists and sociologists, the value orientation of the managerial technician rather than the value orientation of the social science educator will dominate what evolves and is called social science. The emphasis can thus shift from service to citizens in a democracy to service for those who temporarily control and who wish to continue to control segments of our society." (9)

Doubtless, the challenge of "social engineering" presented by *The Soldier* is important, as are the other themes listed above. The category of "implications" was selected as a principal challenge of *The Soldier* by a few reviewers. Toward this challenge, the friendly response was that the implications of the book are, indeed, universal or at least very general. The hostile response was that *The Soldier* contained few or no implications of wide generality, that it lacked sufficient general theory or even adequate conceptualization of its own "mine of data" to be much use as a guide for future research of social scientists.

To ignore such views, as we do in the remainder of this paper, is not to minimize their importance. In part, they are presented and analyzed in detail, on their intellectual merits, elsewhere in this volume. As samples of affective response to the public image of *The Soldier*—the subject of this paper—they are of limited utility. Few reviewers selected the themes of "social engineering" or "implications" (or even "mine of data" or "wide influence") as principal stimuli of the book. A clear majority took the central challenge of *The Soldier* to be contained in the theme we have categorized as "modern method." To the affective responses of these reviewers we turn our attention.

In analyzing the variety of opinions expressed in our data, we began with two questions on how the reviewer located himself with respect to *The Soldier:* (1) How does the reviewer *stratify* himself— superior, inferior, neutral? (2) How does he *polarize* himself— friendly, hostile, neutral?

Three main strata, relevant to our purposes, emerged from the data. These we designate by the descriptive labels: Highbrow, Middlebrow, Lowbrow. (10) (The descriptive, not deprecatory, intention was tested introspectively by this writer, who assigned himself to the Friendly Middlebrow category in this nomenclature and felt quite comfortable there.) The Highbrow reviewer stratifies himself in a superordinate position vis-à-vis the "modern method" represented by *The Soldier.* This is the distinctive posture of the "humanists"—historians, belle-lettrists, philosophers—and involves a claim (usually implicit) for the superiority of the professional "self" for which the reviewer is spokesman. The Middlebrow posture is adopted mainly by reviewers who speak in the name of social science—sociologists, anthropologists, psychologists—and who identify the method of *The Soldier* as a variant within their image of their own professional self. The Lowbrow stratum is occupied by reviewers whose professional self-image does not include a systematic and explicit methodology, and who therefore feel no need either to identify with social science method in *The Soldier* or to subordinate it to the professional self. Such reviewers—mainly journalists, but also some military men and social workers—discuss *The Soldier* methodology not in relation to a theory of knowledge or a theory of value, but only as a utility: *i.e.,* they judge the method only by the immediate uses they find for the results it produced.

One other stratum of response to *The Soldier* was discernible, which may be characterized in passing. We designate this as the "Nobrow" category of reviewers who exhibit no adjustment of self-image to the challenges presented by the public image of *The Soldier*. This general stratum, which is distinctive for the absence of any important affective response, presents a number of interesting features which might well be made the object of detailed investigation. For further study, one might wish to subcategorize the "Nobrows" into: (a) "Browsers," who exhibit no unified response to *The Soldier*, but who, in wandering through its pages with an aimless amiability (or hostility), occasionally reveal an awareness that the book contains some stimuli; (b) "Browless," who do not show any awareness that the book is a challenge in any sense.

We do not take up these reviews here, since their lack of a unified affective response produces comments which are irrelevant to the central purpose of this paper. We may illustrate this by representative passages from "Nobrow" reviews. The following is the headline and lead paragraph of a newspaper report on *The Soldier:*

"PRAYER HELPED KEEP TROOPS GOING,
VETS REVEAL IN SURVEY
Prayer helped more than anything else to keep American GI's fighting when the going was tough during World War II. . . . Second only to prayer as a source of support in combat was the thought 'that you couldn't let the other men down.' "

This is quoted from the Tulsa (Oklahoma) *World* of June 5. The article was credited to United Press, however, and datelined New York, June 4. The clipping-books indicate that the same story was used in at least seven other provincial papers. This is a typical "Browless" response to *The Soldier*—in which no challenge is perceived and no affect is felt. A typical "Browser" response, in which a variety of stimuli in *The Soldier* are detected but no unified affect is produced, is the review published in the Knoxville (Tennessee) *News-Sentinel* of May 22 under the headline:

"AMERICA'S CITIZEN ARMY IN WORLD WAR II DEEPLY RESENTED PRIVILEGES GIVEN TO OFFICERS ACCORDING TO RECENTLY PUBLISHED BOOK."

Since the author is described as "Science Service Psychology Writer," presumably this review also appeared in other newspapers. An interesting feature of this review is that, in about 500 words, it "deals with" some 14 important researches reported in the two volumes of *The Soldier*. This is the sort of note-taking an impoverished student, loathe to part with $13.50, might do while browsing through the volumes in a bookstore. The review reveals about the same level of awareness of stimuli in the book, but does not demonstrate even the level of affective response contained in the marginal comments frequently penciled into books by highstrung students. The "Browser" may detect some of the challenges but does not indicate how he feels, or whether he cares at all, about them.

The case is quite different with the responses we have designated as Highbrow, Middlebrow, Lowbrow. These reviewers place themselves rather clearly with their brows looking down, straight ahead, or up at *The Soldier*. These stratifications are matched by equally explicit polarizations. There is no difficulty in determining which of these brows is friendly or hostile to this two-volume illustration of modern method. The complication, more often, is in finding out why. To simplify our analysis, the following table was constructed to represent the distinctive characteristics of the friendly and hostile polarities within each of our three strata of response:

	FRIENDLY	HOSTILE
Highbrow	Paternal	Oedipedic
	Benedictory	Imprecatory
Middlebrow	Fraternal	Rivalrous
	Missionary	Diabolic
Lowbrow	Filial	Juvenile
	Pietistic	Delinquent

The first of each pair of words is intended to designate the characteristic role taken by friendly and hostile reviewers in each of our categories. The second word of each pair is used to characterize the attitude found at the extreme among reviewers taking each of these roles. There is no suggestion that all hostile lowbrows are properly classified as juvenile delinquents, or that the only available posture for friendly lowbrows is filiopietism. We select these extreme cases for study because they exhibit, with fewer inhibitions, the characteristic affects of the role and attitude they represent. In an exhaustive analysis, one would wish to study also the typical inhibitions of more restrained spokesmen. For this preliminary sketch, it may be sufficient to identify and characterize the six main types of affective response to *The Soldier*.

(1) *Friendly Highbrows:* The *paternal* role fits comfortably on those whose self-image is sufficiently broad and stable to include vigorous young offspring as a promise rather than a threat. The *benedictory* attitude one would expect to find among maverick historians of high repute, who are not affectively bound to the dominant impressionistic precedures of their profession, and among empirically-oriented philosophers with an approved methodology (*e.g.*, logical analysis) of their own. No such persons appear as reviewers in the material at hand, but the posture can be illustrated by a parody of itself. One historian, who reaches throughout his review for the paternal role but cannot quite make the grade, concludes with a sentence which has the appearance of a benediction. But the pat is ironicized, paradoxically, into a slap. The passage reads:

"The charts and statistical tables are in some cases beyond praise. In others, in their solemn documentation of the obvious, they are beyond belief. They can be highly recommended to historians for both information *and gentle entertainment*." (11)

(2) *Hostile Highbrows:* This posture is found more frequently than the paternal-benedictory among Humanistic reviewers. One regrets the neologism *Oedipedic,* but no familiar word was handy to designate the role of jealous parent grown hostile to an offspring conceived as threatening the once powerful self-image of its elder. (The term was adapted from the vivid terminology of psychoanalysis, which is welcome to this convenient way of plugging one of the holes in Oedipus.) The extreme Oedipedic attitude might be exorcism, verbally expressed by *imprecation.* The characteristic affect is the desire to rid the house of the threatening offspring. This would seem to be the point of the repeated insistence that social science's allowance be cut off. Presumably the recalcitrant child would then have to get out and hustle. We have already noted that one historian's review opens with a petulant complaint that social science has (undeservedly) "basked in the smile of deans and in the favor of foundations." A few pages later this reviewer, A. M. Schlesinger, Jr., elaborates and rationalizes the same theme for his conclusion:

> "*The American Soldier* is an entirely harmless book . . . 'Social science' as a whole is perhaps doing no present harm, *except as it engrosses money and energy which might be put more wisely to other uses.* But it might eventually do great harm in obscuring from ourselves the ancient truths concerning the vanity of human wishes, and the distortions worked by that vanity upon the human performance." (12)

(3) *Friendly Middlebrows:* The *fraternal* role is appropriate to social scientists interested in research with an empirical focus and quantitative technique. The *missionary* attitude is found among members of this group who are affectively so fully committed to such research that they wish to bring the light to others who may not have seen it. The missionary technique, here as elsewhere, depends upon the vigorous exposition of a determined view of life. (The skillful missionary intuits, for his audience, the findings of Carl Hovland and associates on the value of presenting only "one side" as against "both sides" of his argument.) (13) An illustration of the fraternal-missionary reviewer in action is the article by Paul Lazarsfeld entitled, significantly, "*The American Soldier*—An Expository Review." (14) The expository technique involves a decision not to question axioms or postulates; the focus of attention is on the exegesis of content and implications. In our competitive cul-

ture, this technique is possible only for a social scientist whose self-image is very nearly congruent with his other-image of *The Soldier*. Such "self-other" identification commits loyalty and, in moments of high affective experience, evokes religiosity. A moment of this sort occurred, apparently, as Lazarsfeld comes to the last of *The Soldier's* 1200 pages. At first, there is chagrin: "Here was gripping and seemingly inexhaustible reading material which suddenly comes to an end, like a novel of which only the first chapters are available." But there is promise in the final words of *The Soldier*: "What happened afterwards is a story which must be told someday from data other than that assembled by the Research Branch." This laconic remark indicates that missionary work, beginning with prayer, is needed. And Lazarsfeld concludes with:

"Where, O Lord, will they [the data] be coming from?"

(4) *Hostile Middlebrows:* The *rivalrous* role is enacted by social scientists whose interest in empirical research, quantitatively reported, is low. Since no reviewer has taken the view that better research *of this type* is available or in sight, the rivalrous posture involves a preference (stated or implied) for research of *a different type*. When this preference is merely implied, and no alternative specified, the result is a vigorous negativism which leads to the extreme attitude we have designated as *diabolic*. Such a posture was exhibited by Herbert Blumer's critique of *The Soldier* in the panel devoted to this book at the 1949 convention of the American Sociological Association. Only one reviewer has approximated this extreme view in print—Nathan Glazer, who is a young man at the periphery of the profession, and hence perhaps less heedful of its imperatives toward discretion. Glazer's review, which we shall look at later, exhibits the distinctive characteristic of the diabolic attitude, *i.e.*, that social science of *The Soldier* variety is not possible (not merely expensive, or obvious, or antidemocratic, but impossible). The title of the review raises the question "Can Sociology Fulfill its Ambitions?"; and the text gives in reply a round, firm, and fully packed "No!"

(5) *Friendly Lowbrows:* The *pietistic* attitude expressed by several reviewers seems to be a transfer to *The Soldier*, mainly on account of its heavy preoccupation with statistical tables and the occasional mathematical equations in its footnotes, of a posture

regarded as appropriate for the Altar of Science. I would suspect that it is among this group of reviewers that the Princeton Press's heavy emphasis on Science ("modern method") in its pre-publication promotional literature paid off. Just as this publicity irritated many Highbrows, and was ignored or selectively treated by most Middlebrows, so it appears to have certified the sanctity of *The Soldier* for friendly Lowbrows with predispositions to pious affects. The *filial* role seems appropriate because the book deals with familiar subject matter, whose importance to us all has long been recognized. It is easy to be pietistic, but hard to be filial, about a mathematical treatise on, say, the behavior of plutonium under fission in experimental situations—hard to be filial, that is, until this subject becomes familiar under the title of Atom Bomb. The filiopietistic posture toward *The Soldier* may be characterized by the meditation, from kneeling position, "What wonders Science worketh before our eyes that looketh but seeth not." (This may be contrasted with R. S. Lynd's free association, in reviewing *The Soldier* studies on control of fear in combat, to the blindness of the Gadarene swine.) An illustration is provided by a reviewer in the *Infantry Journal*, apparently carried away by the first volume, who was moved to assert:

"This book and *those to follow* show that there is *only one scientific way* of discovering the *true* morale of troops." (15)

One wonders how this reviewer learned this lesson from "those to follow" the first volume, in which the present writer detected no such moral.

(6) *Hostile Lowbrows:* The *juvenile* role is not uncommon among journalistic book critics. It is, characteristically, the pretension of ignorance to knowledge. The *delinquent* attitude found in extreme cases is simply this pretension pushed beyond the limits of plausibility: *e.g.*, that the reviewer knows more (or understands better) about the subject of the book under review than its author. When such a claim is made regarding such a book as *The Soldier* by a reviewer whose lack of qualifications is patent, the review itself is *prima facie* evidence that the claim can be thrown out of court. The usual tactic of the "hep" juvenile delinquent among reviewers is to claim, not that he knows better, but that some other authority knows better. This tactic serves two purposes: (a) It eliminates the need for a specific critique of the contents of the book under review; (b) It affiliates the

reviewer with the higher authority whom he has invoked. Such a tactic is obviously useful for maintaining the self-image in the face of a challenge one wishes to, but does not know how to (since rationality is supposedly required in book reviewing), reject.

An illustration of this posture is provided in the review by R. Ernest Dupuy. He begins by implying his own superior knowledge and understanding of the American soldier:

"The field soldier with two wars under his belt [Colonel Dupuy was Public Relations Officer for the War Department, and later for SHAEF in Paris, during World War II], stumbling through these ponderous tomes, feels kinship with the little woman of Mother Goose fame: 'Oh, deary me, deary me, this is none of I.' This just isn't his army; the men whose minds are dissected here are not the men he was privileged to command." (16)

Then follows an explicit claim for the superior wisdom of another authority:

"Actually, nothing in this work has not been set forth *in one fashion or another* [the Hostile Lowbrow, we recall, cares nothing for 'modern method' except as a utility] by Col. Ardant du Picq, French Army, prior to the Franco-Prussian War of 1870–71 in his *Battle Studies*, the first and—in the opinion of this reviewer—still the best attempt to psychoanalyze the soldier. Better yet, du Picq draws constructive conclusions in his 'attempt to direct human behavior,' conclusions sadly lacking here."

Comes then the identification of self with superior other:

"And *Battle Studies* was a text at our Command and General Staff School when this reviewer was a student."

This sets the stage for dismissal of *The Soldier* in the name of the professional self. Dupuy concludes:

"Perhaps the psychoanalyst may find something of constructive interest in this volume. The soldier will not; he must go back to du Picq."

It is interesting to compare the remarks quoted above with the following passage from a review by Lt. Col. J. D. Hittle of the Marine Corps:

"Ever since Col. Ardant du Picq wrote his classic *Battle Studies* military writers have been increasingly aware of the vast amount of study and exploration yet to be accomplished in the field of Combat psychology . . . These two books of *The American Soldier* series carry the study of the mind of the soldier far beyond Col. du Picq's initial exploration of the subject. In fact, these two recent additions to U.S. military literature comprise what is probably the most comprehensive, scientific, and valuable study of the thoughts of combat personnel yet to appear in print." (17)

THE SOLDIERS ON *THE SOLDIER*

THESE two contrary evaluations of Colonel du Picq, leading to conflicting evaluations of *The Soldier,* occur in reviews which reveal other interesting influences of self-identification on the judgments military writers pass upon new intellectual stimuli presented to them.

Among the professional self-identifications reflected in critiques of *The Soldier* by military reviewers, two seem particularly vivid: service and rank. Lt. Col. Hittle's unqualified receptivity to *The Soldier* surely was not unaffected by his affiliation with the Marine Corps. This is indicated by his choice, for special admiration, of the fact that "these two volumes show no disinclination to expose matters that are unfavorable to the Army." It is noteworthy, too, that his *only* direct quotation from the book is the following sentence by Stouffer: "In the early days of the war, there can be little doubt that the Infantry was the dumping ground for men who could pass physical standards, but who need not pass any other test." The influence of Hittle's service-affiliation upon his affective cordiality to *The Soldier* is made quite clear in the final sentence of his review:

"Aside from the thoroughness and objectivity that characterizes the analysis of this and other problems, Naval readers and marines in particular will derive no little satisfaction from the willingness of the authors to recognize that the Marine Corps was not confronted with the type of morale problem that plagued the Infantry."

Equally clear is the reflection of Colonel Dupuy's Army-affiliation in his considerably less cordial reception of *The Soldier.* After some name-calling (*i.e.,* implicative references to Mother Goose and Alice in Wonderland) and a mis-statement of the book's central purpose (*i.e.,* "the basic objective of all this probing—discovery of the components of the will to win—appears to have been lost in a welter of academic minutiae"), the review gets down to showing that *The Soldier* misrepresents the Army. The *real* explanation of soldier dissatisfactions, he tells us, simply are not given in this book, *e.g.*:

"Actually, both the army and the country in World War II were feeling the effects of pacifistic influences. Lacking universal military service, the army was foreign to the drafted recruit; ergo, he didn't like it. But you won't gather that from this book."

This used to be good top-brass Public Relations doctrine: the only *real* trouble with Army militarism is civilian pacifism. UMT will fix that. The particularistic corollary was that justified complaints in the Army are always personal (not institutional), limited, and local; and Dupuy supplies this view too: "A few individuals in high places, somewhat drunk with power, made matters worse by stupid discriminations."

The item which Dupuy selects to conclude his list of major omissions in *The Soldier* is our most interesting illustration of rank-identification in the affective response of officers to the gripes of soldiers (a topic on which Stouffer and associates present much data) and their reporting in *The Soldier*. Colonel Dupuy asserts:

"For every gripe of the enlisted man set forth here, officers *below the rank of general* could point to *equally obnoxious* discriminations—such, for instance, as 'Yankee Doodle Rooms' for general officers only, and the ability of the bestarred to purchase liquors, cigars, and cigarettes in unlimited quantities. *But you won't find that here.*"

In registering this complaint of the be-chickened against the be-starred, there can be no doubt that the Colonel speaks for his peers.

Several military reviewers invoked a larger self-image in expressing their responses to *The Soldier*. This was the image of the "Armed Services" or the "National Military Establishment"—*i.e.*, all those professionally responsible for the military security of the nation. It is interesting to note that such reviewers were uniformly friendly to *The Soldier*. Spokesmen for this larger self-image, whether affiliated with Army or Navy or Air Force, tended to take a more impersonal and responsible view of *The Soldier*. Their general standpoint is indicated in the sentences which open and conclude the review by Major General James A. Gavin in The New York *Times*:

"One of the most difficult command requirements in a democracy's army is that of reconciling the hardships of war with the personal needs of the citizens under arms. The soldier's attitude toward the machines and methods of war is in itself a weapon. It is, in fact, the major component of military strength.

"It is to be hoped that our national military establishment will continue to undertake studies and evaluations of this kind . . . They are a monumental contribution to the science of making citizens of a free country win its wars." (18)

Several interesting responses are frequently associated with this general attitude among military reviewers. One is their emphasis on the utility of such social science methods not only for *efficient* military management, but for *democratic* military management. This view, stressed in the above quotations of General Gavin, is stated even more pointedly by Colonel W. S. Nye in the *Field Artillery Journal:*

"On the other [credit] side of the ledger is a deep and sincere desire to practice, in the Army, the best principles of democratic human relationship in managing the affairs of both officers and enlisted persons. Attitude surveys, if made with skill and objectivity and used with understanding, can contribute to such a program. Hence, the value to the Armed Forces of a work such as that under review here." (19)

Another response typically associated with the larger self-image among military reviewers is candid concern, rather than obscurantist defensiveness, about Army failures and inadequacies discussed in *The Soldier*. Colonel Nye makes this response to the troubled GI-officer relations revealed both by *The Soldier* and the Doolittle Report:

"Although it is too early to say whether the remedial measures which have been undertaken will effect desired improvements, one can at least repeat the cliché that in knowledge lies power. Anything which can contribute to better leadership is worth exploring."

General Gavin reveals the same readiness to face Army inadequacies candidly in his response to *The Soldier* chapter on Negro troops:

"It is one that every civilian should, and certainly every military man must, read. Unfortunately, though it is more than 100 pages long and liberally illustrated with graphs and statistics, it is still too sketchy for the important subject with which it deals. The problem of the Negro soldier was one of the most difficult of all problems confronting the Army during the war . . . The problem is still with us and must be solved. It will be solved when all citizens understood its many aspects and each contributes what he can toward its solution. The Army tried, and in a measure succeeded, but much more might have been done had the data made available by this study been available earlier."

The distinction between the responsible and self-involved military reviewers is made very clear by comparison of Colonel Dupuy's comments on the GI-officer relationship—that the few justified GI complaints reflected merely local and personal ineptitudes, and that colonels faced "equally obnoxious discriminations" as GI's—with those of General Gavin:

"That there should have been some mistakes and abuses of privilege was inevitable. There were, however, *many more such instances* than one might reasonably expect. And the authors make it clear that if the Army is to be an effective popular instrument, then future commanders, and in particular officer-candidate schools, must place increased emphasis on an officer's first and greatest responsibility—the care and welfare of those in his command."

An important response which distinguishes spokesmen of a National Military Establishment from those who respond in terms of self-identification with a particular service or rank is that toward "modern method." Two stimuli usually draw affective responses on this subject: style and statistics. Generally hostile and defensive reviews contain the usual references to "social science jargon," "belaboring the obvious," and "gobbledygook," *etc.* The friendly group of military reviewers we are discussing here also note the difficulty of reading such a text as *The Soldier,* but this is done without aggressive depreciation of the book or its authors. Instead, there is an almost unanimously expressed wish that these volumes be rewritten in simpler fashion, by competent persons, to make their values more widely accessible. One such reviewer, apparently a tank officer, whose cordiality to *The Soldier* is not unqualified, writes in *Armed Force:*

"It is to be hoped that some experienced, practical field soldier, blessed with time and intelligence, will condense the wealth of information in these volumes into a brief presentation . . . of the lessons that they contain for the duty-with-troops officers." (20)

Another reviewer, in the *Infantry Journal,* presents a more detailed plan to activate the same desire. He proposes that a competent military man collaborate with a trained social psychologist (preferably one of the authors of *The Soldier*) to produce "a less technical version." This reviewer wishes to go beyond the mere translation of data from statistical to prose form, to education of military leadership in modern method:

"The war taught the Armed Services the great usefulness of scientific method, though many leaders of rank are not yet convinced of the value of the sciences that deal with the human mind. No book could be more convincing than a readable transfer into layman's language of the material this book (and the one to follow it) contains." (21)

He regards this as an "immediately practical recommendation" for familiarizing the Armed Services with "modern method" as illustrated in *The Soldier*. His more general interest in social science method is indicated as follows:

"An argument of some substance can be put forward that all professional men today might well be trained in the elements of statistics—that we shall more and more be needing this background for a clear understanding of the important military data that will undoubtedly be gathered from more and more sources."

This, in a leading military journal, is an important affective response to the stimulus provided by so difficult a book as *The Soldier*.

Perhaps the most cogent summation of the responsible soldier's attitude is that by General George C. Marshall, in a letter to Frederick Osborn:

"The volumes of 'The American Soldier' give a unique picture of what the American soldier was thinking and feeling, at home and abroad, before, during, and after combat.

"These are, so far as I know, the first quantitative studies of the impact of war on the mental and emotional life of the soldier. They add enormously to our knowledge of the factors which affect soldier morale. Every serious student of military leadership will find in these volumes important criteria by which to judge the validity of previously established theories of morale and the circumstances which modify such theories . . .

"In the recent war the Research Branch of the Information and Education Division made available, for the first time in any army, a current picture of what was in the soldier's mind. Through special monthly reports, this knowledge provided an important supplement to the information which formed the basis for many staff decisions."

THE INTELLECTUALS AND *THE SOLDIER*

WE turn from the soldiers to the intellectuals, regretfully aware that some important voices are missing from the choir of response. For example, one wishes for material setting forth the attitudes of Negro reviewers toward the book. (22) Of great interest, too, would be a large variety of responses to *The Soldier* by former GI's. Unfortunately, no such material is at hand. Our reviews are the product of white men and officers.

To deplore the absence of others, however, is not to deprecate the presence of intellectuals. This familiar breed is as interesting in the act of responding to *The Soldier* as in most of its varied activities in American life. Their responses showed a greater variety of refined affects than the reviews of other groups, but the polarization of gross response clearly came between Humanists and Social Scientists. With only a few exceptions on either side, the general picture is this: spokesmen for (*i.e.*, reviewers self-imaged in,) Humanism are hostile; spokesmen for Social Science are friendly.

The professional social science journals, in fact, set off their big guns to salute the launching of *The Soldier*. We noted earlier the enthusiastic essay by Paul F. Lazarsfeld, whose response to *The Soldier* is well known: "The results of both [volumes] are without parallel in the history of the social sciences." (23) It is relevant here to notice also the way this essay was handled by *Public Opinion Quarterly*. This exposition, possibly the longest book review ever to appear in *P.O.Q.*, was published as the leading article in the Fall issue (1949). The editorial headpiece stated:

"Publication of *The American Soldier* constitutes an event of first importance in the world of social research. [Sentences paraphrasing Princeton Press publicity in all six thematic categories.] At the request of the *Quarterly*, Professor Lazarsfeld has provided a brief guide to the first two of these four encyclopedic volumes, and has highlighted the significance of many of the findings reported therein. . . ."

The same treatment was given *The Soldier* in many of the professional journals: a prominent reviewer, an enthusiastic review, a leading position, lots of space. A few illustrations will serve. (It should be stressed that we have deliberately selected the most enthusiastic general comments out of contexts which often contain discerning criticism. This is done because our purpose is to illustrate affective response rather than analytic skill among reviewers.)

The *American Sociological Review*, for example, had each volume reviewed separately by a prominent social scientist. Of the first volume, John W. Riley, Jr. wrote:

"This present volume [is] undoubtedly one of the most significant publications in the social sciences during the last twenty years . . . as impressive a piece of scientific reporting as we are likely to see in a long time."

The second volume was reviewed by George P. Murdock, who subsumed his special role as anthropologist under the general role of social scientist (Dec. 1949):

"In view of the epoch-making significance of *The American Soldier* it would be ungenerous to point to its occasional imperfections. It may not be amiss, however, to express the utopian wish that the data gathered and assessed had been as rich in other subjects of social science concern as in those pertinent specifically to social psychology. . . . We are grateful, nevertheless, that social science has been advanced substantially on one front. In addition, Stouffer and his associates have contributed as much in actuality to the morale of their professional colleagues as they have potentially to that of their country's armed forces."

The journal *Social Forces* (Oct. 1949) provided N. J. Demerath with more than twice the usual space for a review of *The Soldier*. His general response illustrates Murdock's point concerning its uplifting effect on the morale of social scientists:

"Here is a book! Not since Thomas and Znaniecki's *Polish Peasant* has there been a socio-psychological work of such scope, imaginativeness, technical rigor, and important results. The first two volumes by themselves mark a great achievement in social scientific development. Combined with the forthcoming volume[s], all kinds of superlatives will no doubt be justified. 'Studies in the Social Psychology of World War II' is a fine tribute to contemporary social science . . . Social science *is* coming of age."

Psychologists exhibited more reserve in their reviews than other social scientists. The general response, however, is friendly. Even Allen L. Edwards, whose review in the *Journal of Applied Psychology* (Dec. 1949) is the most matter-of-fact item in our collection, follows his indication of disappointment with the elementary level of statistical reporting (*i.e.*, emphasis on percentages instead of correlation coefficients and chi-squares) by the following conclusion:

"This is not intended as a criticism. The reader should keep in mind that the work of the Research Branch was primarily directed toward the collection of information about attitudes which would be useful to the army planners of information, orientation, and educational programs. Their job was, as one of the authors calls it, a 'practical engineering' job.

From the evidence reported in these two volumes, it was a job well done."

The psychiatrist who appears in our collection of reviews, Dr. Roy R. Grinker, records a more vivid affect. The self-identification in psychiatry is made more comfortably congruent with the public image of *The Soldier* as "new social science." Grinker, himself co-author of an important book on World War II soldiers, reports the following response in a lead review in *The Survey* (Aug. 1949) captioned "The Soldier—by Science, not by Flags":

"The first scientific attempt to study the attitudes of the American soldier in quantity is now at hand in two volumes of a projected four-volume series . . . Though it raises many unanswered questions, this gigantic work is a milestone in social science research."

The picture looks quite different in the camp of Humanist reviewers. The philosophers and poets have been conspicuously silent; historians are the chief spokesmen in our collection of reviews. Since historians are primarily trained in reportage of the past, their general chilliness toward *The Soldier* is expressed in a variety of styles. Some favor irony: *e.g.*, the reviewer quoted earlier who recommended the book to historians for the "gentle amusement" it would provide them. (24) Others are straightforward: "Occasionally they [the volumes] suggest an optimism as to what may be possible with improved techniques in social science which a skeptical historian may not share." (25) Still others are strident: *e.g.*, Mr. Schlesinger.

Whatever the tone of their affective response, certain hostile themes are common. These may be indicated by quoting the key symbols which recur in reviews by historians:

Hostile Themes (*The Humanist Warhorses*)
(1) "Documentation of the obvious"
(2) "Social Science jargon"
(3) "Pretentiousness"
(4) "Statistical vacuum"
(5) "Lack of insight"
(6) "Committee thinking."

The central theme is the first: the obviousness of social science. Every historian-reviewer in our collection uses the phrase "documentation of the obvious" (or some variant like "belaboring the obvious") to express a hostile response to *The Soldier* and social science. The word "knowledge" figures here as an ambiguous referent in a theory of knowledge which makes no distinction between intuitive beliefs (based on direct personal experience of the environment) and certified information (based on explicit criteria of evidence). The social scientist usually reserves the term "knowledge" to designate only the latter. Lazarsfeld expresses the view of social scientists in these terms:

"Since every kind of human reaction is *conceivable,* it is of great importance to know which reactions *actually* occur most frequently and under what conditions; only then will a more advanced social science develop." (26)

We are not concerned here with the validity of either view. We stress only that the argument of "obviousness" is central to the hostile Humanistic response. It is by reference to this argument that our present group of reviewers justify the remaining themes symbolized above: that the claim of social science to more certain knowledge (than that afforded by intuition) is merely "pretentious"; that its involved nomenclatural apparatus is mere "jargon"; that its complex techniques produce merely a "statistical vacuum"; that its methodological emphasis is merely a cause of (or excuse for) the "lack of insight"; that all of this leads away from the initiative and originality of the individual scholar to a dependence, for mutual support, upon "committee thinking."

These common themes provide the basis for a coalition between Hostile Highbrows and Middlebrows, and lead extreme spokesmen for the traditional "humanities" to attitudes we have labeled "Diabolic" and "Oedipedic." The prototypical Diabolic attitude was delivered orally by Herbert Blumer. It took a less experienced diabolist to set such views down in print. This was Nathan Glazer, apparently a former apprentice to social science who has since been alienated into humanistic affairs. Glazer's main effort is to show that science and wisdom are incompatible, which is just one of those assertions that leaves things pretty much as they were. It may sound plausible or silly, depending on the prose garb it wears, but either way nothing has been changed. Glazer's prose is smooth, so his statement becomes an elegant justification of a private preference for ratiocination over investigation. Such a preference is quite plausible for a person gifted with dialectical skills, who enjoys formulating problems in a forensic arena where his gifts show to best advantage. The thing one regrets is that Glazer finds it necessary to justify his private preferences by resort to the intellectual vulgarity of dichotomizing empty categories. Science and Wisdom, as he sets them up, are classes with no significant members, *i.e.*, fictions for fables.

The interest of Glazer's assertion is not its transparent logical fallacy (*i.e.*, it is either tautological and trivial, or referential and unverifiable), but the psychological affect it exhibits. This affect seems increasingly current among Highbrow Intellectuals who have been over-exposed to the "eclipse of reason" style of talking. The new wrinkle is that Science itself, formerly a pillar of Reason, now is non-rational or even anti-rational. We can pass up this point, since Eddington has distinguished between "symbolic" and "intimate" knowledge more clearly, and drawn the logical consequences by a straightforward "defence of mysticism." (27)

Applying this to *The Soldier*, Glazer announces that, not only is Science not Rational, but social science is not even Science. Moreover, it can never hope to be. This is due, we are told, to the material with which social science deals, *viz.*:

". . . *for various reasons having to do with its subject-matter,* and not with its techniques, no true social science is possible."

It seems pretty cavalier to put such a large remark in a subordinate clause, particularly when this is the central claim of his essay. Although this is precisely the statement that requires demonstration, Glazer does not even return to it until the very end, in an aside:

". . . whatever the reason why human affairs are so peculiarly resistant to the [scientific] type of organization that has been successful in so many other spheres, it *is* so."

The underscoring of "it *is* so" seems intended to establish by emphasis—*e.g.*, raising the voice with each repetition—what one cannot demonstrate by evidence. The casual begging of the central question, in the phrase "whatever the reason," eliminates the basic issue between Glazer and social science. What is left, mainly, is a tone of voice.

The diabolic urge exhausts itself with the destruction of the disturber. This can be done with malignant dignity, even with mournful grace. The Oedipedic attitude, however, is a sustained shriek to get the little devil out of the house. The technique required is exorcism and the style is that of the witch-hunt. This is a difficult posture for the urbane. An extraordinary Oedipedic display of Highbrow vulgarity is provided by A. M. Schlesinger Jr.'s response to "The Statistical Soldier" (*Partisan Review,* Aug. 1949). Here we find each Humanist Warhorse listed above: obvious, jargon, pretentious, statistical, insightless, committee thinking. In the following convenient passage, we can watch them all trot by:

"Indeed, the more basic questions are raised, not by the relatively innocuous practice of 'social science,' but by its mystique—its pretensions to new knowledge and new certitude (3). . . . Most of *The American Soldier* is a ponderous demonstration in *Newspeak* (2) of such facts as these (1) [four examples cited]. Indeed, one can find little in the 1200 pages of text and the innumerable surveys which is not described more vividly and compactly (2), and with far greater psychological insight (5), in a small book entitled *Up Front* by Bill Mauldin (1). What Mauldin may have missed will turn up in the pages of Ernie Pyle (1). . . . The individual human experience is supposed to vanish away in the whirl of punch cards and IBM machines (4). . . . One comes to feel, indeed, that the American existed, neither in life nor in history, but in some dreary statistical vacuum (4)."

Schlesinger deals separately with item (6) on our list: "The idea of research by committee, six men always being accounted better than one and the responsibility being distributed like the credit lists in a Hollywood film." He also produces a battery of vivid epithets on the other items which, since we are not directly concerned with the dimension of vulgarity, we shall not take space to quote. To give one illustration, the language habits of social scientists (Item 2) are variously characterized as "remorseless jargon," as "barbarous patois," and as "the mark of the beast."

Perhaps the most interesting feature of Schlesinger's review is his recurrence to "the main chance." He gingerly, but frequently, reverts to a preoccupation with the question: who shall get the money? The following passage in Schlesinger's review illustrates the point at issue:

"Bursting onto university campuses after the war, overflowing with portentous if vague hints of mighty wartime achievements (not, alas, to be disclosed because of security), fanatical in their zeal and shameless in their claims, they [the social scientists] persuaded or panicked many university administrations into giving their studies top priorities. Needless to say, they scored an even more brilliant success with the foundations. Certain foundation directors even decided that virtually all their funds for research in the social sciences should be expended on projects of the 'social science' variety; the individual scholar, so far as they were concerned, was through."

The review returns to this theme four times, and reaches a high fever in capping a characterization of the idiocies of social science as follows:

"the whole [is] happily subsidized by the foundations, carrying to triumphant completion their ancient hope of achieving the bureaucratization of American intellectual life."

It is in this connection that we are reminded of Edwin Arlington Robinson's delightful lines about Miniver Cheevy (who also "mourned Romance, now on the town, and Art, a vagrant"):

> "Miniver scorned the gold he sought,
> But sore annoyed was he without it;
> Miniver thought, and thought, and thought,
> And thought about it." (28)

CONCLUDING COMMENTS [3]

BY the test of response, *The Soldier* surely is an important book. The challenge it presents to the stock attitudes of readers is clear from the depth of the affects exhibited by its reviewers: the responsive postures range from piety to diabolism. Whatever their direction, the tone of responses tends to be extreme. The shrill voice indicates that the interpersonal situation stimulated by *The Soldier* is dramatically affective.

Another index of *The Soldier's* importance is the frequency with which it stimulates reviewers to produce a *profession de foi* concerning the nature and destiny of social science. This may be attributed partly to the pre-publication publicity which, as we saw earlier, made the symbols of science ring dominant in the social acoustics, as Lazarsfeld calls it, of the book. Mainly, however, the stimulus was provided by the volumes themselves: their size, their statistical tables, their mode of framing questions and reporting answers, their specialized

[3] I wish to thank R. K. Merton for many valuable suggestions which have been incorporated in this paper, and particularly in the concluding section.

vocabulary. All these are marks of the "scientific look"—generally expected in books dealing with the behavior of colloids under high temperature, but quite a New Look in such matters as the behavior of
soldiers under high temperature.

One's whole stock of responses is called into play by such a stimulus. Adequate adjustment to a distinctively new challenge of this
sort requires a good deal of refiguring in the respondent. But detailed
scrutiny of an interpersonal situation involving so complicated a
stimulus as *The Soldier*—and so complicated a response as one's self-
positioning with respect to it—requires a good deal of time, skill and
inclination. Only Lazarsfeld among our reviewers seems to have had
all three in adequate measure to take his readers on a guided tour
through the corridors of the book and his own reactions to their details. Few others gave chapter and verse from the text to illustrate
their sermons. This is particularly striking in the two reviews next
longest to Lazarsfeld's. Glazer pitched his essay on the high level of
Philosophy of Science, which would only seem vulgarized by "particularistic" references to a finding here or a conclusion there. Schlesinger, who may possibly have read the book, need not have done so
to write his review. There is but one specific reference to the text;
however, comparison of what actually appears on Page 29 of Volume
II with what Schlesinger says is there suggests that he may have a
unique copy.

The lack of time, skill, or inclination to refigure one's position in
The Soldier's universe of discourse meant that most reviewers had to
draw upon their already available stock of attitudes. This leads to
"spontaneous" self-positioning, which accounts for both the regularity
of alignments by occupation (*i.e.*, prior commitments as to scientific
research in human affairs) and the readiness to displace affective responses from the concrete object *The Soldier* to the general symbol
Social Science. To N. J. Demerath, the appropriate conclusion is: "Social science *is* coming of age." To Glazer, the relevant comment is:
"No true Social Science is possible." Neither considers it odd that he
has said little about the specific book under review.

This is what one expects in responses to an important book—that
in raising the affective level of reaction it raises also the level of generality (*i.e.*, importance) of discussion. The Bible has maintained its
influence through the centuries less through scholarly disputes over
specific textual problems than through the persistent general prob-

lem: should we believe it? Were we to arrive at a general consensus
that the Bible need not be "believed," it seems likely that its command over public attention would sink to the level of, say, *Beowulf*.

Such questions of belief and the *professions de foi* they evoke, because they move rapidly into the arena of high doctrinal symbols, tend
to proceed by stereotype and cliché. This is particularly marked in
the hostile responses, where the self-image is being defended against
an aggressive, highly active stimulus (*i.e.*, Science). The stratification
of stereotypical response is of some interest. Hostile Lowbrows tend
to cluster their defenses around the "obvious-jargon-statistical-
insightless" sequence of clichés. The usual way of putting this is:
Bill Mauldin or Ernie Pyle says in one page, with more insight and
more grace, what these fellows fail to say in 1200 pages of statistics.
This responsive technique is itself so obvious that Stouffer had fore-
cast its occurrence in *The Soldier*. (See I, 40.)

This technique of selective invocation—of defending one's Self by
allying it with a prestigeful Other—can be very instructive, however.
For the names invoked to bolster the self reveal the level of information and aspiration of the defendant. The hostile journalist, for example, does not question the impressiveness of Mauldin and Pyle as
sticks to beat back Stouffer and Co. The hostile soldier, however, does
not regard these names as adequate in power and prestige for the de-
fense of *his* professional self: he invokes Col. Ardant du Picq. As one
moves along the ladder of self-stratification, the names selected correspond to the criteria of prestige operative in the defendant's milieu.
Glazer, for example, writing in a Humanist journal, invokes Goethe.
The really agile defendant like Schlesinger, who shuttles between
Highbrow presumptions and Lowbrow vulgarities, mixes in the fast
pitches with the slow ones. He calls on Mauldin and Pyle, of course,
to show the common touch. Lindsay Rogers and Harry S. Truman
serve him as expert witnesses on the Middlebrow level. For the intelligentsia among his readers (*Partisan Review* is, after all, a journal
for the literate), Schlesinger invokes the depth psychologists. He even
selects Dr. Roy Grinker, by name, as a whip against the statisticians—
unfortunately having neglected to notice that Grinker himself, in the
review we quoted earlier, gives *The Soldier* a large round of applause
on precisely this point.

Stereotypical behavior of this type is facile: the most varied objects
are made to look alike. Since all interviews look alike, an allusion to

Lindsay Rogers on Gallup helps Schlesinger settle the hash of Stouffer. Since all numerical tables look alike, one need not know much about statistics to know what one likes. This is the typical Lowbrow mode, which we earlier characterized as the pretension of ignorance to knowledge—and its extreme form is intellectual Juvenile Delinquency, where the pretension is pushed beyond reasonable limits of plausibility. (One wonders, for example, whether Schlesinger can tell the difference between a standard deviation and a typical delinquency.) Precisely because it is Lowbrow, stereotyped discourse is important: stereotypes are the common coin of public communication in mass societies, where the content of public communication becomes an influential shaping force in public life generally. Hence it is well to consider the consequences, for social science, of some stereotypes which occur frequently in the reviews we have examined.

Before turning to this matter, it is interesting to note how some of the points mentioned above come out on a preliminary statistical analysis. It seems clear that the final analysis, when a sufficient body of response data has accumulated, will reveal an extremely high correlation between the degree of identification with social science and the degree of cordiality to *The Soldier*. A preliminary scatter diagram, based on the indices and data discussed in this paper, indicates that the regression lines will sharply distinguish the correlation of Social Science-Friendly Response from the correlation of Humanist-Hostile Response. In addition, a number of interesting sidelights are indicated by this diagram. Many military and journalistic reviewers, not ordinarily regarded as social scientists by the professionals, fit nicely into the Social Science-Friendly Response pattern. It is not that these reviewers pretend to be social scientists, but that their professional self-image as soldiers or journalists coexists comfortably with the public image of "modern method" presented by *The Soldier*.

On the other hand, several professional social scientists do not seem to fit into the pattern. We have already quoted the reviews by R. M. Lynd and A. M. Lee, who praise the "modern method" of *The Soldier* but produce reviews with a heavy admixture of hostility to this feature as the *central* image of social science. The interesting thing to observe is that the level of self-identification with social science in these reviews, though high on a symbol analysis (*i.e.*, the frequency with which the words "social science" occur), is low on a thematic analysis (*e.g.*, social science as "social engineering"). The professional self-image here is not congruent with the public image of *The Soldier*. However, the reviewers wish to retain the words social science in their self-image without undue hostility to the other-image represented by *The Soldier*. Consequently, they focus their reviews upon the incongruous dimensions of the two images—*i.e.*, the social policy of social science. A glance back at the passages already quoted from these reviews will illustrate the point. Interesting, too, is that the reviews of Lynd and Lee appeared, not in the professional journals, but in *New Republic* and *The Annals*, respectively lay and academic media for the discussion of social policy rather than social science.

The point stressed by Lynd and Lee—*i.e.*, the policy orientation of social science—is a matter of great concern to many social scientists. Stouffer and his associates gave careful thought to this problem; the social function of social research is a frequent topic in the professional journals. Few accept the Lundberg-Dodd conception of "social engineering," which in principle can serve any master, as a useful model for American social scientists. Most seem agreed that the profession has a job to do *for* democratic thought and practice. Yet there is no consensus on *how* to do the job. Here is a point where social science is vulnerable and could well profit from discerning criticism by outsiders (including journalists and historians). And yet, it is on precisely this point that our reviewers are conspicuously silent.

The one serious proposal was made by several Friendly soldiers—*i.e.*, that a concise and simplified edition should be prepared by collaboration of a soldier and scientist, for the use of Army men who have neither the time nor training to read the original edition. Their reason is of the greatest interest: that such a handbook of soldier attitudes would help the Army to operate, not only more efficiently, but *more democratically*. Nothing so useful comes out of our philosophers of science and historians of democracy. Their reviews are too busy fashioning straw men and producing platitudes to lay hands on a genuine problem.

To lay the stereotypic ghosts which haunt some of these threatened and defensive reviewers is partly a job for social scientists. The problem of fear, here as elsewhere, is often the problem of ignorance: only a man who has never worked with a correlation coefficient could believe that a prose assertion that two things "often go together" is better *in principle*. The language of size and quantity seems strange and frightening to those habituated exclusively to the language of sort and quality.

Possibly the most important spook which lurks in the windy interstices of our reviews is the "mechanization of man" theme. This fearful notion our academic Humanists share with a wide general public. The Lowbrows express their resentment at such an imputed aim with such phrases as "people are not statistics" and "you can't put people into charts." The Highbrows, naturally, use more elegant terms of opprobrium, like the "dehumanization of society," the "final depersonalization of man," and the "destruction of the rich, full, and varied integrity of the individual human personality." Schlesinger, of course, expressed the commonplace most picturesquely: "The individual human experience is supposed to vanish away in the whirl of punch cards and IBM machines."

We call this a spook because it is essentially a more general reflection of the anthropomorphic view of language mentioned above. No social scientist claims that statistics are people, or that you put into charts anything more than numbers. But the scientist's positivistic use of language is unfamiliar to the humanist and lay public. The language of size and quantity presents them with large aggregates of numbers—whose manipulation and interpretation requires a special training which they do not have. Ignorance breeds fear, and it is an easy step, in self-defense, from the cry that statistics cannot replace brains (which is true, but irrelevant) to the snarl that statistics is evil (which is dubious, but important).

It is obviously fallacious to impute greater wisdom or morality to a fact-form statement that "most people favor democracy" than to the statement that "in this sample 92 per cent approved secret balloting, 71 per cent approved scaled income-taxation, and 57 per cent approved judicial review in principle." It is only the greater facility of the former statement which recommends it. But facility does not save man's soul, nor does exactness damn him. It is not the act of counting rather than guessing, of computing on an IBM machine rather than in one's head, that threatens the individual human experience or the rich human personality. The experience itself, which counting and computation are designed to help us understand and control, will decide man's fate.

This leads to a final problem that emerges from the response to *The Soldier*. To the extent that social science does, in fact, help us understand and control our experience, it becomes one of the influences shaping human destiny. In this, not the counting and computation will be decisive—for these are techniques of knowledge, not of social change. One does not change an experience by enumerating its components and correlatives; one only changes (by increasing) our knowledge about that experience. The use to which this knowledge is put, in changing future experience, depends upon the policy goals of social scientists and their fellows. The judicious use of human skills would require that one clarify goals in advance, so that energy can be devoted to increasing *relevant* knowledge. This returns us to the problem which Lynd and Lee stated explicitly, and which most of the other reviewers sensed without discerning: *i.e.,* the social policy of social science. The question is: what purpose shall be served by controlled observation, statistical computation, rigorous interpretation of human phenomena?

The choice of social goals involves scientists with the rest of their human environment. Our society is not a fellowship of social scientists; indeed, social scientists are but a small community in a society which is highly sensitized to stereotypes and responsive to mass communication. If social scientists wish to claim a share in the shaping of human aspirations and social goals, then the burden of proof is upon us. No one man or book can do this job, but Stouffer and his associates have rendered great service. They have largely won the support of their original audience—the soldiers; not, perhaps, the stereotypical Reactionary Brass Hats, but responsible officers who express gratitude that such studies of soldiers under high temperature help make the Army both more efficient and *more democratic.* Another accomplishment of *The Soldier,* perhaps more important for the long run, has been its electric effect upon the community of social scientists—which Murdock mentions and which the present volume illustrates. In the process of integrating scientific inquiry with social purpose, much depends on the alertness of the scientists. To this purpose *The Soldier* stimulus has indeed made a contribution of great importance.

NOTES

(1) Ernest Barker, "Aristotle," *Encyclopedia of the Social Sciences,* I, 192. See, for high relief to the contemporary scene, H. L. Pinner, *The World of Books in Classical Antiquity* (Leiden: A. W. Sÿthoff, 1948).

(2) A. M. Schlesinger, Jr., *The Vital Center* (Boston: Houghton Mifflin, 1949), p. 52.

(3) G. H. Putnam, *The Censorship of the Church of Rome,* 2 v. (New York: Putnam's, 1906).

(4) The author is grateful to the officers of Princeton University Press, who made available to him their clipping collection, which contains all the texts of promotional and critical materials used in this study.

(5) References to "the professional journals" throughout this paper usually include: *American Sociological Review, American Journal of Sociology, Sociology and Social Research, The Social Studies, American Journal of Economics and Sociology, Journal of Applied Psychology, Psychological Abstracts, Public Opinion Quarterly, American Political Science Review, Political Science Quarterly.*

(6) A. M. Schlesinger, Jr., "The Statistical Soldier," *Partisan Review* (August 1949).

(7) Gayer variations of this symbol list are provided in: A. Cleveland and J. Anderson, *Everything Correlates* (Poughkeepsie, N. Y.: Vassar Cooperative Bookshop, 1946).

(8) *New Republic* (27 August 1949).

(9) *The Annals* (September 1949). (Emphasis supplied here and in all quotations which follow).

(10) This ingenious nomenclature is borrowed from Mrs. Q. D. Leavis, who used it to quite another purpose in *Fiction and the Reading Public* (London: Chatto and Windus, 1932).

(11) Theodore Ropp, in *The South Atlantic Quarterly* (January 1950), p. 108.

(12) Schlesinger, *loc. cit.* (note 6).

(13) See C. I. Hovland *et al, Experiments in Mass Communication* (Princeton University Press, 1949), Chapter 8.

(14) P. F. Lazarsfeld, in *Public Opinion Quarterly* (Fall 1949), p. 377.

(15) G. V., "What the Soldier Thought," *Infantry Journal* (June 1949), p. 54.

(16) R. E. Dupuy, "Study of the American Soldier," *Christian Science Monitor* (2 June 1949).

(17) J. D. Hittle, in *U.S. Naval Institute Proceedings* (January 1950), p. 95.

(18) J. A. Gavin, "A Monumental Study of the Citizen-Soldier in War," N. Y. *Times* (29 May 1949).

(19) W. S. Nye, "Analysis of Our Citizen-Soldier," *Field Artillery Journal* (July 1949).

(20) Unsigned review, *Armed Force* (18 June 1949).

(21) G. V., *loc. cit.* (note 15).

(22) The only relevant item in our collection is a professional review by R. D. Reid in *Journal of Negro History* (July 1949).

(23) P. F. Lazarsfeld, *loc. cit.* (note 14).

(24) See note (11).

(25) R. A. Newhall, in *Mississippi Valley Historical Review* (September 1949), p. 339.

(26) See note (14).

(27) See chapter 15, entitled "Science and Mysticism," in *The Nature of the Physical World* (New York: Macmillan, 1933).

(28) Burke put the Schlesinger-Cheevy nostalgia, with equal poignancy, two centuries ago: "The Age of Chivalry is gone. That of sophists, economists, and *calculators* has succeeded, and the glory of Europe is extinguished for ever. . . ."

APPENDIX

Book Review of *The American Soldier*, in Krasnaya zvezda (*Red Star*), March 18, March 20; Summary in "The Current Digest of the Soviet Press," May 6, 1950.

"American military authorities are attempting to study the behavior of soldiers drafted during the last war in order to make use of the findings for future ideological training in the interests of American reaction. In this connection, there has recently been published *The American Soldier*, a four-volume study carried on during and after the war under army direction by 134 bourgeois psychologists, statisticians and sociologists. Although the authors claim they are engaged in the 'science of human relations,' even the bourgeois press recognized that their goal was quite different. Robert Lynd, writing in the New Republic of August, 1949, noted ironically that their 'science' teaches 'the conversion of frightened recruits into hardened soldiers destined to wage a war with no understanding of its purposes.'

"Although, by careful juggling of figures, the army tried to 'prove' results in accord with its masters' orders, some information on the American soldier in wartime is given in this study. Only for this reason does the book merit analysis. Of course, the authors do not mention the class stratification of the U.S. Army. For them the concept of 'class' does not exist. But it is evident in the words of the common soldier, as cited in the study: 'We are fighting for democracy and freedom, but there is too much class distinction in the army.'

"The American draftee became convinced that in the U.S.A. only representatives of the exploiter classes have access to officer rank, and that Army leadership fears most of all the democratization of the officer corps. Mobilized American soldiers—workers and farmers—were at least suspicious and very often hostile toward the alien officer class.

"The army bears not only the stamp of the class distinction which rives American society, but also the brand of racial discrimination. Segregation of Negroes in the army is in accordance with official provisions and rules. The authors try to excuse this policy by noting that the failure to solve the race problem in the army 'reflects the impossibility of achieving in one part of society, such as the army, what has not yet been achieved in society as a whole.' A remarkable admission! It confirms exactly what the authors avoid saying: the incurable, spreading poisons and contradictions of capitalist society cannot but tell on the armed forces of capitalist countries.

"The army is entrusted by the ruling classes with the systematic stupefaction of the soldier. Persons suspected of progressive views are removed from the armed forces; ignorance is cultivated; morals are corrupted; sadism, hatred and contempt for other peoples are developed.

"The justice or injustice of the war is irrelevant. The authors stress instead the so-called 'direct stimuli' of war—or, simply, pillage, profit and violence against peaceful populations. They frankly admit that during the second world war some troops 'literally raced to arrive first at an objective promising rich loot—a jewelry store, a camera factory, a liquor warehouse—or pleasant encounters with the female sex.' The authors do not condemn such conduct; they even tacitly recommend that the prospect of unpunished looting become one of the chief stimuli for the soldier. Thus, military 'training' becomes the training of war criminals.

"It was to be expected that many soldiers, asked about the goals of the war, said they were fighting for democracy, against fascism. The authors, clearly opposed to such answers, listed them under 'idealistic conceptions.' It is indicative, however, that such answers as 'we were fighting for the sake of the economic interests of big U.S. capital' began to appear as the war went on. The ruling circles were unsuccessful in concealing from the masses of soldiers the true purposes for which they were fighting the war.

"To a question on the peacetime role of the U.S.A., a great majority answered that they advocated participation in an international organization to avert war. The American soldier not only expressed his wish for peace: he indicated no desire to fight against the Soviet Union. A very high appraisal of the war efforts of the U.S.S.R. was given by 99% of those questioned. Most of them believed in August, 1945, that the United States would have normal and even very good postwar relations with the U.S.S.R.

"The American imperialists, of course, are not at all pleased by this expression of friendship and respect for the Soviet Union. Hence the increasingly severe attacks by American reaction, the struggle against so-called 'dangerous thoughts' being waged not only in the barracks but throughout the country. The American imperialists are frightening the people with the threat, actually non-existent, of an attack on the U.S.A. They slander the Soviet Union and persecute those who raise their voices against reaction. They are thus trying in advance to indoctrinate future soldiers for their military adventures. Yet, despite all their efforts, the movement for peace and democracy grows in the United States. Neither the editors of *The American Soldier* nor their masters can block this movement."

INDEX

ALLPORT, F. H., 206
ALLPORT, G. W., 73-74, 95
Assimilation, 29-31, 37, 101, 104: of group values, 74-77, 79; and heterosexual adjustment, 35-36; rate of, and exposure to combat, 37; group contexts of, 80

BARNARD, C. I., 207
BLUMER, H., 227, 238
"bucking," 85, 94
BUTTERFIELD, H., 105

Caste system, 185-186
Class, social: cross-class identification, 92-93, 103-104; and ideological outlook, 121; and "perspectivistic thinking," *see* Sociology of knowledge
Coercion, expectations of, 19-20
Combat: and confidence in leaders, 34-35; and differential privileges among enlisted men and officers, 33-34; effect of, on formation of primary groups, 32-34, 37; and hatred of enemy, 23; motivation, 24, 27; readiness for, 23, 73-75, 115
Commitment, to war objectives, 116-120, 134, 172-173
COMTE, A., 111
Concepts: clarification of, 80; generalization of, 41, 81; re-formulation of, 73-74
Conformity: function of, 74; scale of, 187; and subsequent promotion, 84-95, 144
COOLEY, C. H., 16, 74, 101, 102

COTTRELL, JR., L. S., 171

DEMERATH, N. J., 236, 242
Deviant case analysis, 167
DU BOIS, W. E. B., 100
DU PICQ, A., 229-230, 243
DUPUY, R. E., 229, 231
DURKHEIM, E., 73, 82

EDDINGTON, A. S., 239
EDWARDS, A. L., 236-237
Elaboration, in survey analysis: 147-167
Experiment, controlled, 86, 203, 204, 210-211, 220: approximations of survey results to, 136ff.
Explanation, in survey analysis, 157-158, 165

FERGUSON, A., 112
FISHER, R. A., 200
FRAZIER, E. F., 100
FREUD, S., 213
Functional sociology: 40-41, 84, 101

GAVIN, J. A., 231-232, 233
"GI culture," function of, 36
GLAZER, N., 46, 68, 227, 238-239, 242, 243
Goals: achievement of, 25; corporate, 20, 34; and motivation, 22-23; and primary group relations, 33; of social scientists, 247
GRINKER, R. R., 237, 243
Group: alienation, 92-93; contexts, influence upon attitudes, 71-81
Groups: intimate, and social categories,